The Tyndale New Testament Commentaries

*General Editor:*
THE REV. CANON LEON MORRIS, M.Sc., M.Th., Ph.D.

# THE LETTER TO THE HEBREWS

# THE LETTER TO THE HEBREWS

## AN INTRODUCTION AND COMMENTARY

by

## DONALD GUTHRIE, B.D., M.Th., Ph.D.

*formerly Vice-Principal and Lecturer in New Testament, London Bible College*

**Inter-Varsity Press,**
**Leicester, England**

**William B. Eerdmans Publishing Company**
**Grand Rapids, Michigan**

**Inter-Varsity Press**
*38 De Montfort Street, Leicester LE1 7GP, England*
**Wm. B. Eerdmans Publishing Company**
*255 Jefferson S.E., Grand Rapids, MI 49503*

© Donald Guthrie 1983
*First published 1983*

*Reprinted, May 1989*

Unless otherwise stated, quotations from the Bible are from the Revised Standard Version, copyrighted 1946, 1952, © 1971, 1973, by the Division of Christian Education, National Council of the Churches of Christ in the USA, and used by permission.

Published and sold only in the USA and Canada by
Wm. B. Eerdmans Publishing Co.

**British Library Cataloguing in Publication Data**

Guthrie, Donald
  The letter to the Hebrews.—(Tyndale New Testament
  commentaries).
  1. Bible. N.T. Hebrews — Commentaries
  I. Title   II. Series
  227'.8707          BS2775.3

IVP PAPERBACK EDITION 0 85111 884 4

**Library of Congress Cataloging in Publication Data**

Guthrie, Donald, 1916-
  The Letter to the Hebrews.

  (The Tyndale New Testament commentaries)
  1. Bible. N.T. Hebrews. — Commentaries.
  I. Title.   II. Series.
  BS2775.3.G86   1983       227'.8707'7       83-298

EERDMANS EDITION 0-8028-1427-1

Set in Palatino
Typeset in Great Britain by Input Typesetting Ltd.,
London
Printed in U.S.A. by Eerdmans Printing Company,
Grand Rapids, Michigan

*Inter-Varsity Press is the publishing division of the Universities and Colleges Christian Fellowship (formerly the Inter-Varsity Fellowship), a student movement linking Christian Unions in universities and colleges throughout the British Isles, and a member movement of the International Fellowship of Evangelical Students. For information about local and national activities in Great Britain write to UCCF, 38 De Montfort Street, Leicester LE1 7GP.*

# GENERAL PREFACE

The original *Tyndale Commentaries* aimed to provide help for the general reader in his study of the Bible. They concentrated on the meaning of the text without going into scholarly technicalities. They aimed at a mean between being too short to be useful and being too extensive for the present reader. Most who have used the books agree that there has been a fair measure of success in reaching that aim.

Times, however, change. The first *Tyndale Commentaries* appeared over twenty-five years ago and it is felt that some volumes do not meet the changed needs. New knowledge has come to light in some areas. The discussion of critical questions has moved on. Bible-reading habits have changed. In an earlier day most people read the Authorized Version and comments could be based on that. This situation no longer obtains and indeed the last commentary in the original series was based on the Revised Standard Version. In all the circumstances it is felt that the needs of students will best be served by replacing some of the original volumes. This is not meant as an expression of dissatisfaction with them. They served the needs well, but in these days some new needs will be better served by new books.

The original aims remain. The new commentaries are neither minuscule nor unduly long. They are exegetical rather than homiletic. They do not aim to solve all the critical questions, but none is written without an awareness of the critical questions that engage the attention of New Testament scholars. Serious consideration is normally given to such questions in the Introduction, sometimes in Additional Notes. But the main thrust of these commentaries is not critical. These books are written to help the non-technical reader to understand his Bible better. They do not presuppose a knowledge of Greek, and all Greek terms discussed are transliterated; but the authors have the Greek text before them and the commentaries are written in the light of the originals. The English text used is normally the Revised Standard Version, though it is borne in mind that these days readers use a variety of translations.

The original series owed an immense debt to Professor Tasker. He edited the whole, and wrote four of the commentaries himself. It is fitting to place on record this acknowledgment of our debt. I can therefore conclude in no better way than by echoing what Professor Tasker said of the original series. It is the hope of all concerned with these replacement volumes that God will graciously use them to help readers understand as fully and clearly as possible the meaning of the New Testament.

LEON MORRIS

# CONTENTS

# AUTHOR'S PREFACE

There are some books in the New Testament which hold a certain fascination, not because they have an instant appeal, but because they are more than usually difficult. The epistle to the Hebrews falls into the latter category for me. That in itself might have provided a suitable reason for not writing a commentary on it. Yet its difficulties provide a challenge which cannot be lightly pushed aside. If my first aim has been to clarify my own understanding, this should provide an encouragement to the reader. I am in fact inviting you to join with me in exploring a book which contains many treasures of spiritual wisdom and theological insight.

My hope is that the quest will lead to as much spiritual enrichment for the reader as it has done for the writer. This is not to promise that all the problems have been solved, nor that this commentary can make any claims to fresh explorations. Writing a commentary is something like a personal testament. Although I have been deeply indebted to so many others who have preceded me in the task, my own contribution can claim uniqueness only on the grounds that it is the result of an encounter between the text and my own personal experience of New Testament study and Christian life.

DONALD GUTHRIE

# ABBREVIATIONS

| | |
|---|---|
| *ATR* | *Anglican Theological Review.* |
| *BJRL* | *Bulletin of the John Rylands Library.* |
| *CBQ* | *Catholic Biblical Quarterly.* |
| CDC | Damascus document. |
| *Comm.* | Commentary on the letter to the Hebrews, as listed in the select bibliography. |
| *EQ* | *Evangelical Quarterly.* |
| *ExT* | *Expository Times.* |
| *ICC* | *International Critical Commentary.* |
| *Idem* | The same author. |
| *JBL* | *Journal of Biblical Literature.* |
| *JTS* | *Journal of Theological Studies.* |
| LXX | The Septuagint (pre-Christian Greek version of the Old Testament). |
| MM | Moulton and Milligan's *Vocabulary of the Greek New Testament* (London, 1952). |
| NIV | New International Version. |
| *NTS* | *New Testament Studies.* |
| Qp Hab | Qumran Habakkuk Commentary. |
| *RB* | *Revue Biblique.* |
| RSV | Revised Standard Version. |
| *TB* | *Tyndale Bulletin.* |
| *TDNT* | *Theological Dictionary of the New Testament.* |
| *ThR* | *Theologische Rundschau.* |
| *ThZ* | *Theologische Zeitschrift.* |
| *WC* | *Westminster Commentary.* |
| WH | Westcott and Hort text. |
| *ZNTW* | *Zeitschrift für die Neutestamentliche Wissenschaft.* |

# SELECT BIBLIOGRAPHY

*Commentaries*

Brown, J., *An Exposition of Hebrews* (Edinburgh, 1862, r.p. London, 1961).

Bruce, A. B., *The Epistle to the Hebrews, the first apology for Christianity* (Edinburgh, 1899).

Bruce, F. F., *Commentary on the Epistle to the Hebrews (New London Commentary*, London, 1965).

Buchanan, G. W., *To the Hebrews* (New York, 1972).

Calvin, J., *The Epistle of Paul the Apostle to the Hebrews* (new Eng. trans. Edinburgh, 1963, from first edition, Geneva, 1549).

Davidson, A. B., *The Epistle to the Hebrews* (Edinburgh, 1882).

Davies, J. H., *A Letter to the Hebrews (Cambridge Bible Commentary*, Cambridge, 1967).

Delitzsch, F., *Commentary on the Epistle to the Hebrews* (Eng. trans. 2 vols., Edinburgh, 1872).

Ebrard, J. H. A., *Biblical Commentary on the Epistle to the Hebrews* (Eng. trans. Edinburgh, 1863).

Héring, J., *L'Épître aux Hébreux (Commentaire du Nouveau Testament*, Paris and Neuchâtel, 1955).

Hewitt, T., *The Epistle to the Hebrews (Tyndale New Testament Commentaries*, London, 1960).

Hughes, P. E., *A Commentary on the Epistle to the Hebrews* (Grand Rapids, 1977).

Lang, G. H., *The Epistle to the Hebrews* (London, 1951).

Michel, O., *Der Brief an die Hebräer* (Göttingen, 1949).

Moffatt, J., *The Epistle to the Hebrews (ICC*, Edinburgh, 1924).

Montefiore, H. W., *The Epistle to the Hebrews (Black's New Testament Commentaries*, London, 1964).

Nairne, A., *The Epistle to the Hebrews* (*Cambridge Greek Testament*, Cambridge, 1917).

Narborough, F. D. V., *The Epistle to the Hebrews* (*Clarendon Bible*, Oxford, 1930).

Neil, W., *The Epistle to the Hebrews* (*Torch Commentaries*, London, 1955).

Owen, J., *Exposition of Hebrews*, 4 vols. (London, 1668–74).

Peake, A. S., *The Epistle to the Hebrews* (*Century Bible*, Edinburgh, 1914).

Pink, A. W., *An Exposition of Hebrews* (Grand Rapids, 1954).

Rendall, F., *The Epistle to the Hebrews* (London, 1883).

Riggenbach, E., *Der Brief an die Hebräer* (Leipzig, 1913).

Robinson, T. H., *The Epistle to the Hebrews* (*Moffatt New Testament Commentary*, London, 1933).

Schlatter, A., *Der Brief an die Hebräer*, Vol. 9 in *Erläuterungen zum Neuen Testament* (Stuttgart, r.p. 1964).

Schneider, J., *The Letter to the Hebrews* (Eng. trans. Grand Rapids, 1957).

Snell, A., *New and Living Way* (London, 1959).

Spicq, C., *L'Épître aux Hébreux* (*Études Bibliques*, 2 vols. Paris, 1952).

Strathmann, H., *Der Brief an die Hebräer* (*Das Neue Testament Deutsch*, Göttingen, 1937).

Vaughan, C. J., *The Epistle to the Hebrews* (London, 1890).

Westcott, B. F., *The Epistle to the Hebrews* (London, ²1892).

Wickham, E. C., *The Epistle to the Hebrews* (*Westminster Commentaries*, London, ²1922).

Windisch, H., *Der Hebräerbrief* (*Handbuch zum Neuen Testament*, Tübingen, ²1931).

*Other works*

Barrett, C. K., 'The Eschatology of the Epistle to the Hebrews', in *The Background of the NT and its Eschatology* (ed. W. D. Davies and D. Daube, Cambridge, 1956).

Burch, V., *The Epistle to the Hebrews: Its Sources and Message* (London, 1936).

Demarest, B., *A History of Interpretation of Hebrews 7:1–10 from the Reformation to the Present* (Tübingen, 1976).

Du Bose, W. P., *High Priesthood and Sacrifice* (New York, 1908).

Edwards, T. C., *The Epistle to the Hebrews* (*Expositor's Bible*, London, ²1888).

Filson, F. V., *'Yesterday'. A Study of Hebrews in the Light of Chapter 13* (London, 1967).

Horton, F. L., Jr., *The Melchizedek Tradition* (Cambridge, 1976).

Hughes, G., *Hebrews and Hermeneutics* (Cambridge, 1979).

Käsemann, E., *Das wandernde Gottesvolk* (Göttingen, 1939).

Kistemaker, S., *The Psalm Citations in the Epistle to the Hebrews* (Amsterdam, 1961).

Kosmala, H., *Hebräer-Essener-Christen* (Leiden, 1959).

Manson, T. W., 'The Problem of the Epistle to the Hebrews', in *Studies in the Gospels and Epistles* (Manchester, 1962).

Manson, W., *The Epistle to the Hebrews. An historical and theological Reconsideration* (London, 1951).

Ménégoz, E., *La Théologie de l'Épître aux Hébreux* (Paris, 1894).

Milligan, G., *The Theology of the Epistle to the Hebrews* (Edinburgh, 1899).

Milligan, W., *The Ascension and Heavenly Priesthood of our Lord* (London, ²1894).

Murray, A., *The Holiest of All* (London, 1895).

Nairne, A., *The Epistle of Priesthood. Studies in the Epistle to the Hebrews* (Edinburgh, ²1913).

Scott, E. F., *The Epistle to the Hebrews: Its Doctrine and Significance* (Edinburgh, 1922).

Synge, F. C., *Hebrews and the Scriptures* (London, 1959).

Tasker, R. V. G., *The Gospel in the Epistle to the Hebrews* (London, 1950).

Theissen, G., *Untersuchungen zum Hebräerbrief* (Gütersloh, 1969).

Thomas, W. H. G., *Let us go on* (London, 1923).

Vanhoye, A., *La structure littéraire de l'Épître aux Hébreux* (Paris, 1963).

Vos, G., *The Teaching of the Epistle to the Hebrews* (Grand Rapids, 1956).

Williamson, R., *Philo and the Epistle to the Hebrews* (Leiden, 1970).

Wrede, W., *Das literarische Rätsel des Hebräerbriefes* (Göttingen, 1906).

Zimmermann, H., *Das Bekenntnis der Hoffnung* (Köln, 1977).

# INTRODUCTION

## I. THE ENIGMA OF THE LETTER

For various reasons this book poses more problems than any other New Testament book. So many of the questions which the investigator is bound to ask cannot be satisfactorily resolved. Who wrote it? Who were the original readers? What was the precise historical occasion on which it was written? What was the date of writing? What was the dominant influence behind the presentation? These are some of the questions to which no conclusive answers can be given, although some are not quite as elusive as others. What is most important for the commentator to discover is the present message and relevance of the letter, but he can do this only when he has investigated the historical setting. Some attempt must therefore be made to answer the questions posed, if only to provide some framework against which to set about the task of understanding the message.

There is no denying that the general drift of the argument within the letter strikes the reader as difficult. This is mainly because the train of thought is clothed in language and allusions drawn from the cultic background of the Old Testament. The priesthood of Christ is directly linked to the old Levitical order, but is clearly intended to supersede it. More than most New Testament books, Hebrews requires detailed explanation of the significance of the background allusions. This is the main task of the commentator. In reply to the question, 'Why is such a difficult book included in the New Testament?, the answer is that it deals with what must be regarded as the most important question which constantly faces man, *i.e.* how can we approach

God? It is because of the significant contribution of Hebrews to this ever-present problem that it repays the necessary effort to unravel its message and to express it in contemporary terms.

## II. THE LETTER IN THE ANCIENT CHURCH

We begin by looking at the way the early Christians regarded this letter because this will enable us to trace the steps by which it became a part of the New Testament. It will also show that even the early church was not without its difficulties over it.

In the earliest of the patristic writings which has been preserved, *i.e.* Clement of Rome's letter to the Corinthian church (*c.* AD 95), there is one remarkable parallel (1 Clem. 36:1f.; *cf.* Heb. 1:3ff.), together with a few other parallels. The following extract from 1 Clement 36 will illustrate this. He writes of Christ, 'who, being the brightness of his majesty, is by so much greater than angels, as he has inherited a more excellent name [*cf.* Heb. 1:3f.]. For it is written thus, "Who maketh his angels spirits and his ministers a flame of fire" [*cf.* Heb. 1:7]. But of his Son the Master said thus, "Thou art my Son; to-day have I begotten thee" [*cf.* Heb. 1:5]. . . . And again he saith to him, "Sit thou on my right hand, until I make thine enemies a footstool of thy feet" [*cf.* Heb. 1:13].'[1] It would seem a reasonable deduction that Clement was acquainted with Hebrews, although this has not gone unchallenged. The alternative view that Hebrews has cited 1 Clement raises too many difficulties to be seriously considered. The proposed *via media* that both have used the same source can claim little further support, for no evidence can be produced for such a hypothetical source and in the absence of such evidence it must be regarded as an unsatisfactory theory. The conclusion that Clement must have known Hebrews has important consequences for the assessment of the date of the epistle and for a recognition of its early authority. It must be noted also that in what are virtually quotations from the letter, Clement does not mention the author. In itself this would not be particularly significant since Clement cites other New Testament books (*e.g.* Pauline epistles) without acknowledgment.

---

[1] English translation in K. Lake, *The Apostolic Fathers* 1 (Heinemann, 1952), p. 71.

It is likely that our epistle would particularly have appealed to Clement, who describes the Christian ministry in terms of the Aaronic priesthood,[1] although he adopts a quite different approach from the writer of this letter. This early dependence of Clement on our epistle is all the more remarkable because of the subsequent period when it seems to have been neglected by the churches in the West. It is not until the end of the fourth century that it came into its own among those churches.

Hebrews was not included among the books authorized by Marcion, whose collection purported to represent the teaching of the *Apostolikon, i.e.* the apostle Paul. Marcion, however, would almost certainly have rejected Hebrews because of its strong dependence on the Old Testament which he categorically rejected.

The Muratorian Canon, which contains a list of books thought to represent the canon of the church in Rome towards the end of the second century, contains no reference to Hebrews, although it includes all the letters of Paul by name. It is possible that the text of the list is corrupt and that some part of it has dropped out. Nevertheless it is strange that no specific support for the epistle has been preserved during this early period.

With the turn of the second century more evidence for the use of Hebrews is found in the eastern church, although there was difference of opinion regarding its origin. Clement of Alexandria cites his teacher 'the blessed presbyter' (Pantaenus) as maintaining the Pauline authorship of this letter. He explained the absence of a personal name in the text of the letter on the grounds that Jesus himself was the apostle of the Almighty to the Hebrews, and that therefore, out of humility, Paul would not have written to the Hebrews in the same vein as he did to Gentiles. Clement continued the tradition of Pauline origin and often cited Hebrews as by Paul or 'the Apostle'. His successor Origen, however, raised doubts about the Pauline authorship, although not about its canonicity. He considered the thoughts to be Paul's, but not the style. He reported the view of others (the elders) that Luke or Clement of Rome had been the author, and although he speaks favourably of the suggestion that Luke

---

[1] T. W. Manson, *The Church's Ministry* (London, 1948), pp. 13ff., calls Clement's appeal to the ceremonial oτ laws a 'retrogression'.

wrote down Paul's thoughts in Greek, he himself concluded that God alone knows the author.

Subsequent to Origen's time, his successors did not heed his open decision, and soon it became the undisputed conviction of the eastern church that Paul was the author. It should be noted that Origen included Hebrews among the Pauline letters, sometimes even citing it as 'Paul says'; it is not altogether surprising, therefore, that his pupils followed this pattern. Origen's great influence in the eastern church was sufficient to ensure the continued acceptance of the letter as apostolic. There is no doubt, however, that it was belief in its Pauline origin which secured its universal acceptance. In the Chester Beatty Papyrus of the Pauline letters, Hebrews was included and was placed after Romans.

In the western church, acceptance was more delayed. Subsequent to Clement of Rome's citation of the letter, the evidence is sparse until the time of Jerome and Augustine. Tertullian, at the close of the second century, regarded Barnabas as the author, but mentions this point in one place only. He clearly did not regard this epistle as on a level with the Pauline letters. Eusebius, who was diligent in collecting the opinions of the various churches about the New Testament books, reported that the church at Rome did not accept Hebrews as Pauline, and he recognized that this was causing others to have doubts. Cyprian, who may be regarded as a fair representative of the western church in the mid-third century, did not accept the epistle.

The first patristic writer in the West to accept this letter was Hilary, followed soon after by Jerome and Augustine. The latter's opinion turned out to be decisive, although it raises an interesting point, for Augustine in his earliest works cites Hebrews as Pauline, and in his latest works as anonymous, with a period of vacillation in between. His original acceptance of the epistle was probably on the grounds of Pauline authorship; but he came to estimate the worth of the epistle on the basis of its own authority, and his approach clearly implied a distinction between Pauline authorship and canonicity. This distinction, however, was not maintained by his successors.

This survey of the somewhat chequered history of this epistle has thrown up certain factors which must affect our approach to its exegesis. It has shown that it was generally believed that Hebrews reflects an apostolic authority, even although no specific name can be attached to it. Where there was reluctance to receive it, it was in all probability because apostolic authority was too closely linked with apostolic authorship. It is also understandable that the style and content of the letter would appeal less to the more matter-of-fact westerners than to the more eclectic easterners. Its ultimate acceptance in spite of serious doubts testifies to the intrinsic power of the epistle itself.

A footnote to this early survey may be added from the Reformation period. During this period the epistle again came under attack over its Pauline authorship. This was especially true of Martin Luther, who suggested that Apollos would make a more probable author. In reaction to his opinions, the Council of Trent declared emphatically that the epistle was written by the apostle Paul, thus using the stamp of ecclesiastical authority in an attempt to settle the question.

## III. AUTHORSHIP

In view of the confusion in the ancient church regarding the origin of this letter it is not surprising that modern scholarship has produced a welter of different suggestions. Since most of them are purely conjectural it is not profitable to devote much space to their discussion. Our aim will be to show briefly why Pauline authorship is almost universally regarded as unacceptable and to give some indication of alternative propositions.[1]

The ancient view of Pauline authorship is not supported by any reference to Paul in the text of the letter. It is, however, included in the superscription, which is clearly a reflection of the traditional view and carries therefore little importance. The anonymity of the text is an immediate difficulty for Pauline authorship, since nowhere is there any suggestion that Paul would have written anonymously. An apostle who meticulously claims authority in the introduction to the existing epistles attributed to his name is not likely to have sent a letter without

[1] A more recent major work which argues for Pauline authorship is that of W. Leonard, *The Authorship of the Epistle to the Hebrews* (London, 1939).

reference to that special authority vested in him. Moreover, there is no suggestion in the way that the author of Hebrews writes that he has known the same dramatic experience as Paul underwent at his conversion, which is never far from the surface in his letters.

As early as Origen's time the difference between the Greek of Paul's epistles and that of Hebrews was noted. Origen considered that Hebrews 'lacked the apostle's rudeness of expression' and that it 'is more idiomatically Greek in the composition of its diction' (*cf.* Eusebius, *Hist. Eccl.*, vi.25.11f.). Most scholars would agree with Origen's judgment. The language is a good literary style in koinē Greek and it certainly contains fewer irregularities of syntax than Paul's epistles.[1] The writer knows moreover precisely where his argument is going. If he pauses to exhort the readers, he resumes his train of thought. He does not, as Paul sometimes does, go off at a tangent. To return to Origen's opinion, it may be noted that he considered that the thoughts were the apostle's. Many modern scholars, however, would not agree. They would claim that so many of the characteristic Pauline themes are missing and so much of what is present is unparalleled in Paul (*e.g.* the high priest theme), that it is most reasonable to suppose that Paul was not the author. Two other factors point in the same direction: the method of Old Testament citations, which is different from Paul's; and the statement in 2:3, which presupposes that the writer had had no personal revelation from God, but had received a 'great salvation' attested by those who heard the Lord. Whereas this statement in 2:3 could possibly be interpreted to include the apostle Paul, it is not the most natural understanding of it. Paul would never have admitted having received the core of his gospel second hand, as this author appears to do.

What then are the alternatives? Ancient testimony mentions only three other possibilities beside Paul – Luke, Clement and Barnabas. While there are some affinities between Luke's writings and Hebrews,[2] they do not in themselves support common

---

[1] M. E. Thrall, *Greek Particles in the New Testament* (Leiden, 1962), p. 9, considers that Hebrews may be more typical of cultured Greek than any other documents in the NT.

[2] A. R. Eager examines their stylistic similarities, 'The Authorship of the Epistle to the Hebrews', *The Expositor* 10 (1904), pp. 74–80, 110–123. *Cf.* F. D. V. Narborough, *Comm.*, p. 11. W. Manson, p. 36, also makes much of these parallels.

authorship. Clement may be ruled out on the grounds that there are wide differences in theological content between his writing and Hebrews, and on the almost certain assumption that he has cited directly from Hebrews.[1] The sole claim of Barnabas for consideration is his background as a Levite who came from a Hellenistic environment (Cyprus). But our author is interested in the biblical cultus rather than the Temple cultus.[2]

Of more modern guesses, Apollos has had the most supporters, mainly on the supposition that as an Alexandrian he would have been familiar with the ways of thought of his fellow Alexandrian, Philo, which are supposed to be reflected in the epistle. This view, which was first proposed by Martin Luther, has been strongly supported by those wishing to retain some Pauline connection with the epistle.[3] Other proposals are Priscilla,[4] Philip, Peter, Silvanus (Silas), Aristion and Jude.[5]

If we cannot be sure of the identity of the author we can note his main characteristics which will be invaluable for our understanding of his letter.[6] He is a man who has pondered long on the Christian approach to the Old Testament. What he writes has been well thought out. He knows where his line of argument is going. When he pauses to exhort his readers he does so with fine sensitivity and tact. He prefers to think the best of them, although he issues strong precautionary warnings. In

---

[1] Calvin, *Comm.*, on Heb. 13:23, was prepared to consider favourably Luke or Clement. He definitely rejected the Pauline authorship (cf. *idem.*, p. 1). Cf. also C. Spicq, *Comm.* 1, p. 198.

[2] Both F. F. Bruce, *Comm.*, p. xxxvii, n. 62 and Spicq, *Comm.* 1, p. 199, n. 8, list many advocates of Barnabas as author. Spicq's list is particularly impressive. Among the most recent are H. Strathmann (Göttingen, ²1937), pp. 64f.; F. J. Badcock, *The Pauline Epistles and the Epistle to the Hebrews in their Historical Setting* (London, 1937); A. Snell, *New and Living Way* (London, 1959), pp. 17ff. Badcock held that the voice was Barnabas' and the hand Luke's (*op. cit.*, p. 198). Spicq, however, (*Comm.* 1, pp. 200–202) gives no less than ten reasons for doubting the probability of Barnabas as author.

[3] Cf. Spicq, *Comm.*1, p. 210, n. 2, for a detailed list. Among twentieth-century advocates the most notable have been T. Zahn, *Einleitung in das Neue Testament* (Leipzig, ³1907), pp. 7ff.; J. V. Bartlet, 'The Epistle to the Hebrews once more', *ExT* 34 (1922–23), pp. 58–61; T. W. Manson, 'The Problem of the Epistle to the Hebrews', *BJRL* 32 (1949), pp. 1–17; *Studies in the Gospels and Epistles* (1962), pp. 254ff.; W. F. Howard, *Interpretation* 5 (1951), pp. 8off.; C. Spicq, *Comm.* 1, pp. 207ff. W. Manson criticizes this view on the basis that the Alexandrian church never referred to Apollos as author of this epistle (pp. 171f.).

[4] So A. Harnack, *ZNTW* 1 (1900), pp. 16ff.

[5] For a detailed survey of these other suggestions, cf. C. Spicq, *Comm.* 1, pp. 202ff.

[6] A. Nairne, *Comm.*, p. lvii, considered that the precision of a name would not add much to our understanding of the background.

spite of his anonymity he is a force to be reckoned with in early Christian theology. He gives us the clearest discussion of the Christian approach to the Old Testament of any of the New Testament writers.

## IV. THE READERS

The title attached to this letter in the earliest extant manuscript is 'To the Hebrews'.[1] There are no manuscripts of the letter, in fact, which do not bear this title. As early as Clement of Alexandria and Tertullian the epistle was known by this title. Nevertheless, no specific indication is given in the text of the letter itself that the readers were Hebrews and it is possible therefore that the title was not original. In that case it may have been based on good tradition or it may have been a guess. There have been divergent opinions on this matter, but the fact remains that no patristic evidence gives any reason to doubt the tradition. We must, however, consider the various problems which arise as a result of this tradition.

The first point to note is the definition of the word 'Hebrews'. It could be used specifically of Jews who spoke Hebrew (or rather Aramaic), in which case it would distinguish them from Greek-speaking Jews. This suggestion has some other New Testament support (*cf.* Acts 6:1; 2 Cor. 11:22; Phil. 3:5), but there is no means of knowing whether the traditional title to this epistle was intended in this sense. It may have meant no more than Jews (*i.e.* Christian Jews), whether Aramaic or Greek speaking. This more general use is to be preferred. Some, however, have suggested that the title should be wholly disregarded and that the epistle should be understood as addressed to Gentiles. Clearly the only means of deciding the issue is by a careful examination of the internal evidence.

---

[1] H. M. Schenke, *ThZ* 84 (1959), pp. 6–11, points out two passages in the apocryphal Gospel of Philip, in which the term 'Hebrews' is used, which appear to draw a distinction between 'Hebrews' and 'Christians'. But this Gnostic work is no sure guide to orthodox usage.

*Evidence of a specific group*

In view of the very general nature of the traditional title, it is significant that certain indications are given that a particular community was in mind. Certainly the author knows something of their history and background. He knows they have been abused for their faith and that they have reacted well to the plundering of their property (10:33, 34). He is aware of his readers' generosity (6:10) and knows about their present state of mind (5:11ff.; 6:9ff.). Certain practical problems such as their attitude to their leaders (13:17) and matters of money and marriage (13:4, 5) are mentioned. It seems most reasonable to suppose that the writer has personal knowledge of the specific people he has in mind throughout the epistle (*cf.* 13:18, 19, 23). If this is true, the vague character of the title is clearly misleading. One further feature which confirms this is the specific mention of Timothy in 13:23, for Timothy also must have been known to the readers.

Still further indication of the nature of the group may be deduced from such references as 5:12 and 10:25. The former is addressed to those who ought by now to be teachers and this has given rise to the suggestion that the readers were a small part of a larger group of Christians. The most favoured suggestion is that they formed a house group which had broken away from the main church. The exhortation in 10:25 would support this view. There the writer urges the readers not to forsake the assembling of themselves together. It seems reasonably conclusive that the whole of a church would not have been thought of as potential teachers, and it is highly probable that a separatist group might have considered themselves superior to the rest, especially if they were endowed with greater gifts. The closely argued theme in this epistle is in line with the suggestion that a group of people of a more intellectual calibre is in mind.

Some support has been claimed for the view that the group consisted of former Jewish priests who had become Christians. From the book of Acts it is clear that considerable numbers of priests were among the people converted in the early days. As a matter of conjecture it may be supposed that these would naturally form groups for the study of their new approach to the old cultus. Their special interest in the Levitical order would then be highly intelligible. But there is no evidence of any churches comprised of priests and some caution must be exercised over this view. Moreover, we shall need to discuss whether the general drift of argument is favourable to this view.

An extension of the same idea is to see in the group of readers former members of the Essene community at Qumran who had been converted to Christianity.[1] At first sight this seems an attractive proposition, particularly because the epistle to the Hebrews shows some corrective to the Qumran tendencies (*e.g.* their separation). The Qumran Covenanters had quarrelled with the main Jewish parties over the current Temple procedures and this would fit in with the concentration in this letter on the tabernacle ritual rather than the Temple. But the evidence is capable of wider application than this restricted view of the readers would allow. The theory begins with the initial disadvantage that no mention is made anywhere in the New Testament of Essenes. Nevertheless, the Qumran community has supplied some useful background information which has thrown some light on the epistle (but see further discussion on pp. 40f.).

*In support of Gentile readers*
The wide appeal to the Old Testament in this letter does not necessarily demand a Jewish group of readers, in view of the fact that the Old Testament was universally the Scriptures of the early church, whether Jewish or Gentile. Indeed, some parts of the New Testament which are addressed to predominantly Gentile readers (*e.g.* Romans, Galatians) still allude extensively to the Old Testament. It would not have taken long for Gentile converts to become sufficiently acquainted with the Old Testament to raise questions about the meaning and relevance for them of the Levitical cultus. It is not impossible that such questionings may have prompted the author's exposition of the high priest theme. Another line followed by some advocates of a

[1] Y. Yadin, 'The Dead Sea Scrolls and the Epistle to the Hebrews', *Scripta Hierosolymitana* 4 (1958), pp. 36–53 (cited by E. Grässer, *ThR* 30 (1964), p. 172), suggests the recipients of Hebrews were former Qumranites who had not completely given up their Qumran practices. H. Kosmala, *Hebräer-Essener-Christen* (Leiden, 1959), goes further and argues that the readers had never fully embraced Christianity. But against this type of theory, *cf.* Bruce, ' "To the Hebrews" or "To the Essenes"?', *NTS* 9 (1962–63), pp. 217–232.

Gentile destination is to argue that the absence of the allusion to the Jewish controversy favours that theory, but this point would seem to be neutral if it has any validity at all. Of more weight is the contention that the readers were in danger of apostatizing 'from the living God' (3:12), which would be inappropriate as a reference to Jews thinking of forsaking Christianity to return to Judaism. But again this is not conclusive if the author thinks of all forms of apostasy, whether from Jewish or Gentile Christians, as a 'falling away from the living God'. The writer further mentions 'dead works' (6:1; 9:14) and the elementary principles of the faith (6:1), which are thought to be inappropriate for Jewish readers. It could reasonably be maintained that Gentiles would fit the context here better than Jews, but it can hardly be claimed that the words could never be applicable to Jews. On the whole, in view of the intricacy of the style of argument, demanding as it does a wide understanding of the Old Testament (cf., for instance, the style of discussion in Heb. 7:11ff.), it seems that the traditional view is more likely to be correct. This will become more evident when the purpose of the epistle is discussed below.

## V. THE DESTINATION

In view of the lack of specific information about the author or the readers, any suggestions about where the readers lived are bound to be fraught with uncertainties. The best we can do is to mention the most feasible. We begin with the idea that the Jerusalem church was in mind.[1] This is claimed to be supported by the title and by the emphasis on the Levitical ritual. In addition, the reference to persecution (10:32; 12:4) in 'former days' would well fit the sufferings endured by the Jewish Christian community in Jerusalem. Some have seen allusions to a coming disaster in 3:13; 10:25; 12:27, but the wording is much too general to have any significance. Others have argued that because no church claimed the letter to the Hebrews, the recipients may well have been a church in a place that was sub-

[1] Jerusalem has been suggested by W. Leonard, *The Authorship of the Epistle to the Hebrews* (London, 1939), p. 43, and A. Ehrhardt, *The Framework of the New Testament Stories* (Manchester, 1964), p. 109. The latter dates the epistle after the fall of Jerusalem.

sequently destroyed, as Jerusalem was in AD 70. But we may discount the argument; indeed, there is no evidence that every New Testament book, whose definite destination is known, was specifically claimed by the church(es) addressed. If it could be established that the author has the Temple in mind, even though he speaks in terms of the tabernacle, there would be some support for a Jerusalem destination since the writer uses the present tense as if the ritual were still being observed. A question of dating also enters here, for if the epistle was written after AD 70 (as some maintain), the Jerusalem destination would be more difficult to maintain.

Yet there are some serious objections to the idea of Jerusalem as the destination. The statement in 2:3 that neither the writer nor the readers had heard the Lord personally is clearly difficult if the Jerusalem church is in mind, for it is hard to imagine that there were any communities, like house churches, in Jerusalem, where not one of the members had heard Jesus. Another diffi-culty is the predominance of Hellenistic ideas, which are more difficult to imagine at Jerusalem than elsewhere; this line of thought, however, must not be overweighted in view of the Qumran evidence for an infiltration of Hellenistic ideas into an otherwise Jewish milieu by the shores of the Dead Sea, not far distant from Jerusalem. The consistent use of the LXX is a further difficulty if Jerusalem Christians are in mind, for it is hardly likely that the Judaean church used this version. On the other hand it could be pointed out that since Jerusalem boasted sev-eral Hellenistic synagogues (Acts 6:9), it is not impossible that these may have used the Septuagint. But taking the essentially Greek character of the epistle into account, it must be conceded that a destination other than Jerusalem is more probable. One concluding point may be mentioned, *i.e.* the probable reference to the generosity of the readers in 6:10 does not fit too well a church whose poverty is mentioned elsewhere in the New Tes-tament in connection with the collection by Gentile churches for its assistance.

It is natural that Alexandria has been proposed in modern times as the destination in view of the parallels which have been claimed between this letter and the writings of Philo of Alexandria. It has been noted already that the Alexandrian church was never mentioned in antiquity as the possible recipient of the epistle. But an even greater difficulty is the fact that at Alexandria it was assumed at an early date to be a letter sent by Paul to the Hebrews.

The suggestion which is supported by most internal and external evidence is Rome. It was at Rome that the epistle was first known and quoted, and since this was during the last decade of the first century, it shows that the epistle must have reached there at a very early stage in its transmission. Some connection may be seen between a Roman destination and the greetings from 'those who come from Italy' (13:24). The most natural way to understand this expression is of people whose home is in Italy, but who are living elsewhere and are desirous of sending greetings home. The vagueness of the expression would have no point unless the writer thought it worth while to draw attention to the readers' compatriots who were with him. It would have more point, therefore, if addressed to a destination somewhere in Italy rather than anywhere else. It is not, however, conclusive since the wording of 13:24 could be understood in terms of the author's location or equally in terms of the readers' origin.

There is no need to go into details at all regarding other suggestions. We will merely note them in passing – Colossae (T. W. Manson), Samaria (J. W. Bowman), Ephesus (W. F. Howard), Galatia (A. M. Dubarle), Cyprus (A. Snell), Corinth (F. Lo Bue, H. Montefiore), Syria (F. Rendall), Antioch (V. Burch), Berea (Klostermann), Caesarea (C. Spicq).[1] The list is sufficiently varied to show that the scanty evidence can be made to do service to support any number of possibilities. It should at least put anyone on his guard against being too dogmatic over the destination of the epistle.

We would conclude that the most likely destination is Rome, while leaving the options open for other possibilities.

[1] T. W. Manson, *BJRL* 32 (1949), pp. 1–17; J. W. Bowman, *Hebrews, 1 & 2 Peter* (London, 1962), pp. 13–16; W. F. Howard, 'The Epistle to the Hebrews', *Interpretation* 5 (1951), pp. 8off.; A. M. Dubarle, *RB* 48 (1939), pp. 506–529; A. Snell, *New and Living Way* (London, 1959), p. 19; F. Lo Bue, *JBL* 75 (1956), pp. 52–57; H. Montefiore, *Comm.*, pp. 9ff.; F. Rendall, *Comm.*, pp. xvii, xviii; V. Burch, *The Epistle to the Hebrews* (1936), pp. 137ff.; A. Klostermann, *Zur Theorie der biblischen Weissagung und zur Charackteristik des Hebräersbriefes* (1889), p. 55, cited by O. Michel, *Comm.*, p. 12; C. Spicq, *Comm.* 1, pp. 247ff.

## VI. DATE

Our previous discussions will not have left us too sanguine about the possibility of fixing a date for this letter with any precision. All we can hope to do is to suggest limits within which the letter was probably written. We may, at least, conclude that it was written before the letter of Clement of Rome (AD 95), unless of course it be maintained that Hebrews used Clement[1] or that both used a common source. But since there is good reason to suppose that Clement borrowed from Hebrews, this fixes a terminus for Hebrews, before which it must have been written.

An internal consideration is the relation of the letter to the fall of Jerusalem. Since the writer shows no awareness of this event and suggests on the contrary that the ritual is still continuing, it would need to be dated before AD 70. As already pointed out, however, the author appeals to the tabernacle rather than to the Temple, and this could as legitimately be claimed as evidence that the Temple no longer stands. But the present tenses, used for instance in 9:6–9 (cf. also 7:8; 13:10) would have more point if the Temple ritual was still being observed.[2] The distinction between tabernacle and Temple may not have been as sharp to the original readers as appears to the modern reader. On the whole this line of evidence is more in favour of a date before rather than after AD 70, especially if weight is given to the strange omission of any mention of the catastrophe if it had already happened. It would have been a valuable historic confirmation of the major thesis of the epistle – the passing of the old to make way for the new.

If, on the other hand, the doom of the city was imminent it would give a strong edge to the exhortation to the readers to come out of the camp (13:13). Again the mention of Timothy in 13:23, if he is the same man as Paul's companion, must require a date within his probable lifespan, but our problem here is that

---

[1] G. Theissen, *Untersuchungen zum Hebräerbrief* (Gütersloh, 1969), pp. 34ff., discusses the relationship between Hebrews and 1 Clement and concludes that a literary dependence of the latter on the former is unlikely.

[2] On the use of present tenses it should be noted that 1 Clem. 61 also uses present tenses in describing the Temple, clearly in his case a literary device and not a historical usage. *Cf.* the comment on these tenses by E. C. Wickham, *Comm.*, p. xviii.

no independent knowledge exists of his death. All that could safely be concluded is that a second-century date is wholly out of the question. Certainly the state of the church which can be detected in this epistle is fairly primitive, for there is no mention of officials by name, only the somewhat vague expression 'your leaders' (13:7, 17). Moreover, the strong Jewish flavour of the theology favours an early date.

Another suggestion is that the reference in 3:7ff. to the Israelites' forty years in the wilderness (citing Ps. 95:7ff.) may be more pointed if this epistle was written forty years after the death of Jesus. But the connection of thought is far from obvious and can make no contribution to our discussion. Of more point is the reference in 12:4 to the fact that 'you have not yet resisted to the point of shedding your blood'. This may be understood metaphorically, in which case it is no help in dating, but if it means that there had been no martyrs among them, it would require a date before widespread persecution had taken place. If the readers were in Rome this would seem to require a date before Nero's persecutions. Nevertheless, if this was a small house-church separated from the rest it may have escaped the intensity of persecution which the main body of Christians had suffered. Another consideration is the reference to 'former days' (10:32) when the Christians were subjected to persecution. Again, if these days refer to Nero's persecution the epistle would have to be dated after the fall of Jerusalem. But the same problem arises that there is no suggestion that any had died[1] and it is difficult therefore to appeal to Nero's persecution as an explanation of the 'former days'. It would be safer to assume that there was not so much an officially organized attack as the sort of constant harassment to which both the Acts and the epistles testify.[2] Indeed the 'former days' could conceivably refer to the period following the edict of Claudius exiling Jews from Rome, since Jewish Christians would presumably have been implicated (cf. Aquila and Priscilla, Acts 18:2). Between this event and Nero's persecution a period of fifteen years had

---

[1] E. Riggenbach, Comm., pp. 332f., rejects strongly the idea that 10:32–34 implies any martyr deaths.

[2] J. Moffatt, Introduction to the Literature of the New Testament, p. 453, suggests it may have been mob violence.

elapsed, which would set the limits within which the epistle must have been written. There is no means of knowing whether it was written before Paul's death, although it has been inferred from Hebrews 13 that Paul was probably no longer alive, based rather precariously on the solitary reference to Timothy.

Those who date the epistle before the fall of Jerusalem are generally influenced by their view of the occasion in deciding a more precise dating. For instance Montefiore suggests a dating similar to 1 Corinthians[1] and T. W. Manson a date similar to Colossians,[2] because of their respective views of the situation addressed in the epistle. Most, however, do not date before the sixties, and prefer a date just prior to or during the Neronic persecutions if the epistle was sent from Rome,[3] or just prior to the fall of Jerusalem if sent from somewhere else.

Those who consider that the evidence does not require a date before the fall of Jerusalem usually suggest a time about AD 80–85.[4] There are two main considerations. The first is the use of the epistle by Clement of Rome. It must obviously be dated before that epistle, but how long before? According to Goodspeed's theory, Clement wrote in response to Hebrews 5:12, in which case no great interval could have elapsed between them. But this theory is tenuous. If, on the other hand, Clement did not use our Hebrews, there would then be no need to limit Hebrews to a time before Clement's letter. However, the primitive character of the community structure in Hebrews demands an earlier provenance than Clement's epistle. The other consideration is the opinion held by some that Hebrews shows dependence on the Pauline epistles. As usual with arguments from literary affinities, dependence is difficult to prove. The Pauline affinities are sufficiently explained by the supposition that the author was an associate of the apostle. The evidence is certainly not sufficient to show that Hebrews could not have

[1] H. Montefiore, *Comm.*, pp. 9f. *Cf.* also J. M. Ford, *CBQ* 28 (1966), pp. 402–416.

[2] T. W. Manson, *BJRL* 32 (1949), pp. 1–17.

[3] J. A. T. Robinson, *Redating the New Testament* (1976), pp. 200–220, prefers a Roman destination and a date *c.* 67 just prior to Nero's death.

[4] *E.g.* E. F. Scott, *The Literature of the New Testament* (Colombia UP, 1932), p. 199; A. H. McNeile, C. S. C. Williams, *Introduction to the New Testament* (Oxford, ²1953), p. 235. D. W. Riddle, *JBL* 63 (1924), pp. 329–348, thought that only a short interval could have separated Hebrews and 1 Clement. H. Windisch, *Comm.*, p. 126, guessed a period of at least 10 years.

been written before the collection of the Pauline letters. The cumulative effect of these arguments for a late first-century date are not convincing.[1]

## VII. THE PURPOSE OF THE LETTER

The writer makes only one specific statement about his purpose and that is in 13:22 where he simply says, 'bear with my word of exhortation, for I have written to you briefly'. If 'word of exhortation'[2] means here, as in Acts 13:15, a homily, it would suggest that the structure of the letter owes its origin to a sermon given on a special occasion and later adapted into letter form by the addition of personal comments at the end. This suggestion has much to commend it and would account particularly for the frequent asides which contain direct appeals to the hearers. If the word 'exhortation' is given its literal force, those passages which contain such direct appeals must be regarded as the crucial points in the author's argument, even although they are asides, and they must be taken into account in deciding the author's purpose.[3] There is, however, much difference of opinion over what the author was warning his readers to refrain from. The various suggestions may conveniently be classified according to whether they suppose a Jewish or Gentile destination.

*Suggestions which assume that the readers were Jewish*
Since the traditional view was that the readers were Hebrews, we will begin with the traditional explanation of purpose.[4] This begins from the warning passages (mainly chs 6 and 10) and

---

[1] It is surprising how many NT scholars adopt a late date for this epistle without giving detailed attention to the possibility of an early date. *Cf.* Wikenhauser, Kümmel, Marxsen, Fuller, Klijn and Perrin in their Introductions. Yet many commentators have adopted an earlier dating: *e.g.* W. Manson, C. Spicq, H. Montefiore, F. F. Bruce, J. Héring, G. W. Buchanan, A. Strobel.

[2] *Cf.* F. Filson, *Yesterday* (1967), pp. 27ff., for a discussion on this word of exhortation.

[3] It has been suggested that if 13:22 is taken as the cue the essentially practical aim of the author would not be lost sight of in considering his discussions of the high priest theme. Th. Haering, 'Gedankengang und Grundgedanken des Hebräerbriefs', *ZNTW* 18 (1917–18), pp. 145–164, compared the structure of Hebrews to ancient admonition discourses. *Cf.* also G. Schille, 'Die Basis der Hebräerbriefes, *ZNTW* 47 (1957), pp. 270–280.

[4] *Cf. e.g.* A. Nairne, *Comm.*, pp. lxxi ff.

proceeds to interpret the whole epistle in terms of these. The passages themselves certainly contain warnings expressed in the strongest possible way. The danger of 'crucifying the Son of God' afresh (6:6) and of 'spurning the Son of God' and 'outraging the Spirit of grace' (10:29) are set squarely before the readers. Such critical possibilities are said to threaten those who commit apostasy (6:6). In attempting to understand the nature of the apostasy, appeal is made to the statement in 2:3 which speaks of the disaster of neglecting the great salvation which has been provided. If the 'camp' in 13:13 is ancient Judaism, a reasonable suggestion would be that these people were converted Jews who had nevertheless retained their allegiance to Judaism and were in danger of falling between two stools, or even of leaving the Christian church and returning to their former Jewish faith.

To appreciate the strong pull of Judaism on Christians who were formerly Jews, it must be remembered that Christianity could offer no parallel to the ritual trappings to which they had been accustomed. In place of the Temple to which all Jews looked as the centre of worship, Christians met in different homes without even a central meeting-place. They had no altar, no priests, no sacrifices. The Christian faith seemed denuded of any evidences of the usual kind of religious observances. It is hardly to be wondered at that there were Jewish converts who explored the possibility of holding on to both, particularly as both Jews and Christians appealed to the same Scriptures. If they retained the old while secretly professing the new, they would possess a status which was denied to those who made a clean transference to Christianity. The attraction of apostasy in the sense of returning to an outward allegiance to Judaism would have been strong for those who found it hard to face the determined opposition of their Jewish compatriots (*cf.* 10:32), although they had been prepared to do so at first.

If the situation just outlined is correct, it is possible to see what the writer of the epistle had in mind in setting out his argument. He was concerned to reassure his readers that the loss of ritual glories was more than compensated by the superiority of Christianity. His line of approach was that everything in fact was better – a better sanctuary, a better priesthood, a better sacrifice, a better covenant. Indeed, he aims to show that there is a theological reason for the absence of the old ritual, glorious as it may have seemed to Jews. The Christian faith pronounced a complete fulfilment of all that the old order strove to do. The very absence of the ritual was the greatest glory of the new faith, proclaiming as it did its superiority over the old order. Moreover, the writer goes beyond this and main- tains that Christ was a priest of a different kind from the Aaronic line, typified in Melchizedek. The warning passages would then set out the serious consequences for any who deliberately turned their backs on this superior way. It would be tantamount to asserting the superiority of the old and identifying with those who were responsible for crucifying the Son of God. This un- derstanding of the apostasy would be sufficiently serious to warrant the strong terms used in the warning passages. It would also account for the impossibility of restoration for those who so blatantly turned their backs on the 'better' terms of the Christian faith. Uppermost in the author's mind was not so much the question of a return to Judaism as that of the rejection of Christianity which such a return would involve.

Although in general this understanding of the apostasy pro- vides a reasonable understanding of the purpose of the epistle, some caution is needed. It must be admitted that the warning passages say nothing about apostasy *to* Judaism, but only apos- tasy *away from* Christianity. The interpretation outlined above rests on an inference drawn from the general drift of the epistle. It is, of course, possible to interpret the warning passages in a different way, although no other suggestion seems to be in such close agreement with the general context.

An interesting development from this traditional view is the suggestion that former Jewish priests were in mind, a sugges- tion which has already been noted in the discussion on destination.[1] What light would it throw on the author's purpose? Converted priests would at once forfeit the dignity of their office. They would, in fact, become nonentities, after having

---

[1] *Cf.* K. Bornhauser, *Empfänger und Verfasser des Hebräerbriefes* (Gütersloh, 1933); M. E. Clarkson, *ATR* xxix (1947), pp. 89–95; C. Sandegren, 'The Addressees of the Epistle to the Hebrews', *EQ* 27 (1955), pp. 221ff. The latter suggests the title may originally have been 'To the Priests' which in Greek would bear some similarity to 'To the Hebrews'.

been respected for their official position. Many of them must have been faced with the temptation to forgo their new faith in order to retain their old status. They would be even more lost without the cultus than the rank and file adherents of Judaism. They may have expected a superior position in the Christian church by virtue of their former professional status in Judaism. For such people the theme of Christ's high-priesthood and the spiritual interpretation of the cultus would be highly relevant. Of all people these would need to be reminded in the strongest possible terms of the consequences of a return to Judaism. The warning passages would, therefore, be of the greatest relevance. If the readers were tempted to think that a religion without priests was unthinkable, it would amount to a denigration of Christianity to the extent of pronouncing it to be ineffective. Their threatened apostasy would then amount to a deliberate turning of their backs on a priestless faith. But the writer's challenge is that in spite of the absence of a line of priests Christianity is not, in fact, priestless since it has a perfect high priest in Christ, who is infinitely superior to the very best of the Aaronic priests.

Yet another variation in the understanding of the purpose of the letter, if it was addressed to Jews, is the view that the epistle was directed to former members of the Qumran sect.[1] A main purpose would then be to present a true method of exegesis of the Old Testament. The Qumran Covenanters were keen students of the Old Testament Scriptures and many of their commentaries have been preserved among the Qumran finds. But they had their own style of exegesis which concentrated on relating the restoration of the old covenant in terms of their own community.[2] By means of the method known as *pesher*, they contrived to bring out the contemporary relevance of the Old Testament text, often with little regard to the original context. The letter to the Hebrews does not use this method, for the author shows the modern relevance without ignoring the

---

[1] Cf. C. Spicq, *Revue de Qumran* i (1958–59), p. 390. Cf. also J. Daniélou, *Qumran und der Ursprung des Christentums* (1958), pp. 148ff.; H. Braun, *ThR* 30 (1964), pp. 1–38; Y. Yadin, 'The Dead Sea Scrolls and the Epistle to the Hebrews', *Scripta Hierosolymitana* 4 (1958), pp. 36–53; F. M. Braun, *RB* 62 (1955), pp. 5ff.

[2] Cf. F. F. Bruce, *Biblical Exegesis in the Qumran Texts* (London, 1960), pp. 7ff.

historical context. If ex-Qumran Christians are in mind they may well have needed a truer exposition of the Old Testament based on the new covenant in Christ. Since the Qumran community was essentially a priestly community the predominance of the high-priestly theme in this epistle would also be intelligible, as would the reference to ablutions in 6:2, since ritual washings are thought to have formed an important part of the Qumran procedures. Nevertheless there are problems over this hypothesis. In addition to the absence of any corroborating evidence for the existence of a group of ex-Qumran Christians (although such a group is not impossible), the parallels between Hebrews and the Qumran literature are not impressive. The absence of any discussion about the Law in the former is a major difficulty since it was prominent among the Qumran Covenanters.

On the whole the view that posits the threat of an apostasy to Judaism among certain Jewish Christians, whether former priests or not, has generally more to commend it than alternative views.[1] But one other suggestion which still envisages a Jewish destination, but which does not see the warning passages as requiring apostasy to Judaism, must be considered. It is the view that a group of Jewish Christians were failing to embrace the world mission of Christianity. According to this theory the readers were thinking in terms of Christianity being essentially Jewish and were attaching no importance to its universal scope. It is suggested that this group had a similar outlook to that of the more restricted members of the Jerusalem church. Perhaps they wanted to retain contact with Judaism for security reasons, since Judaism was a *religio licita*. To cut loose from the security of this anchorage and to enlarge the borders to include Gentiles would introduce an acute embarrassment.

The dilemma was undoubtedly real. It would be much simpler to insist that all Christians should come under the umbrella of Judaism, just as the Judaizers at Galatia did. But here, it is suggested, the vision of the extent of the Christian mission was too restricted. It is further claimed that it was this too narrow view that Stephen had to combat. There are certainly some

[1] William Manson, *The Epistle to the Hebrews* (London, 1951). *Cf.* also W. Neil, *Comm.* F. F. Bruce, *Comm.*, p. xxiv, n. 8, expresses great sympathy for Manson's view.

similarities between Stephen's speech in Acts 7 and our epistle, particularly in the approach of both to the cultus. This view has brought some interesting insights to the understanding of the epistle, but it cannot adequately account for the strong warning passages. It is difficult to see how anyone would describe a failure to broaden the mind to embrace the world mission as a re-crucifying of the Son of God or as apostasy. It may have been part of the writer's purpose to urge adoption of the world mission, but he was contending with a problem more radical than this.

*Suggestions which assume that the readers were Gentiles*
The theory of Gentile readers has been prompted by the belief that Hellenistic thought forms the major background to this letter. Some, however, also postulate Gnostic influence.[1]

We may quickly dispense with the view that the writer is combating speculative Judaism which was affecting his Gentile readers. Surrounded by many religious ideas, they would want to know that Christianity was unique in offering the only acceptable way to God. To answer this need, the writer appeals to the Old Testament to prove the absolute character of Christianity, which is itself superior not only to Judaism but to all other religious faiths. But the problem with this theory is that the epistle gives no inkling of any knowledge of speculative or of pagan rites. Indeed, the author's considerable interest in the details of the cultus are difficult to square with a Gentile audience which had had no previous contact with Judaism. The most acceptable form of such a theory would be to suppose that the 'Hebrews' were Hellenistic Jews.

The view that Gnostic ideas permeate the letter and that in effect the author is combating incipient Gnosticism has had some persuasive advocates.[2] One view is that the readers be-

---

[1] So J. Moffatt, *Introduction to the Literature of the New Testament*, pp. 44ff.; *idem.*, *Comm.*, pp. xxiv ff. E. F. Scott, *Comm.*, was a staunch advocate of Gentile readers. He maintained that the author misunderstood Judaism (p. 200). *Cf.* also R. H. Strachan, *The Historic Jesus in the New Testament* (London, 1931), pp. 74ff. Moffatt's view gains partial support from A. C. Purdy, 'The Purpose of the Epistle to the Hebrews in the light of Recent Studies in Judaism', *Amicitiae Corolla* (ed. H. G. Wood, 1953), pp. 253–264, who nevertheless concludes that the problems behind Hebrews were normative in Judaism in the first century.
[2] *Cf.* for instance F. D. V. Narborough, *Comm.*, pp. 20–27.

longed to a sect of Jewish Gnostics who were corrupting the pure Christian faith by the infiltration of Gnostic ideas. Some of the ideas which are appealed to may be briefly summarized as follows: the emphasis on angels which was detracting from the uniqueness of the mediatorial work of Christ; the idea of salvation through selected food (*cf.* 13:9), mixed with strange teachings; the reference to lustrations; deliberate wrongdoing (to which the warning passages are said to relate, and which reflected the blurring of moral values in some types of Gnosticism, *cf.* 12:16). Although some of these parallels may be valid, it is extraordinary that the author goes to such lengths to expound on the Jewish culture if his main target was Gnosticism.

A similar criticism may be made of the view that chapters three and four are the real key to an understanding of the letter, and that these chapters must be understood against a Gnostic background.[1] Hence the readers are seen as the wandering people of God and their journey is understood in terms of the Gnostic redeemer myth. The quest for 'rest' (*katapausis*) is the main aim of salvation. The view of Jesus as high priest is said to be influenced by the Gnostic redeemer myth in which the redeemer must himself be redeemed before he is entitled to act as redeemer and in a similar way the high priest must be perfected.[2] There is no question that this reads much more into the epistle than is justified. In the author's mind the perfection of the high priest relates to his perfect obedience to the Father's will. It is essentially moral not mystical. Even if the Gnostic emphasis is overplayed in this theory, the bringing into relief of the importance of chapters three and four and the 'rest' motif is a valuable insight, which should not be overlooked.

Another view is that some deviation of a similar kind to that

[1] The main exponent of this view is E. Käsemann, *Das wandernde Gottesvolk* (Göttingen, 1939). Käsemann has been criticized because he gives insufficient weight to the chronology of his sources. Another point is that the theme of the wandering people of God occurs only in ch. 3 & 4 and can hardly be claimed to be central. Käsemann claims a pre-Christian Gnosis, but not all would agree with this. R. M. Wilson, *The Gnostic Problem* (1958), distinguishes between Gnosis and Gnosticism, a valid distinction which insists that it is confusing to speak of first-century Gnosticism.

[2] For a different view of the perfection theme in Hebrews, *cf.* A. Wikgren, 'Patterns of Perfection in the Epistle to the Hebrews', *NTS* 6 (1960), pp. 159–167, who considers that by means of symbolic patterns of perfection the author is presenting a philosophy of history.

which Paul combats at Colossae is in mind.[1] This was probably connected with some form of Gnosis, although not with developed Gnosticism. There are two features of the Colossian deviation which are paralleled in this letter. One is the excessive esteem given to angels and the need to correct this (*cf.* Col. 2:18 with Heb. 1 and 2). The first section of the letter aims to show Christ's superiority to angels. The other feature is an over-emphasis on the ceremonial law, which might be contrasted with the spiritual interpretation of the cultus in Hebrews 5 – 10. These features have prompted the suggestion that Apollos sent this epistle to the Colossian church before Paul wrote his letter to the Colossians with full knowledge of what Apollos had written. While support for this suggestion of a Colossian destination is slight, the theory has some value in drawing attention to common features which were probably widespread in early Christian experience.

In conclusion, we shall lean towards the view that some kind of apostasy to Judaism is implied, but it will be borne in mind that there were other streams of influence which cannot be ignored in rightly interpreting the thought. If the author seems obsessed with Old Testament interpretation, he has more than an antiquarian interest in it. He is helping perplexed Christians to discover its true meaning, a meaning which for him is focused in Christ. But it is probable that he is also concerned to show its relevance in a world influenced by Greek ideas.

## VIII. THE BACKGROUND

Any writing becomes illuminated when it is set against its background, and it is necessary to indicate briefly the milieu of this epistle. It has already been pointed out that the readers were almost certainly Jewish Christians. It is logical therefore to note first the features which particularly align with a Jewish background.

---

[1] Advocated by T. W. Manson, *BJRL* 32 (1949), pp. 1–17.

*Old Testament*

The most obvious of these is the strong influence of the Old Testament upon the author.[1] It goes without saying that his mind was steeped in Old Testament thought, but it is clear that he was most interested in the testimony of the Pentateuch. His treatment of the cultus bears witness to this, for he does not base his observations, as we might have expected, on the contemporary Temple procedures, but on the Levitical details. He is clearly wanting to establish a Christian approach to the Old Testament cultus and he finds his key in the thought of the superiority of Christ both as a priest and as a sacrifice. Even when citing the heroes of faith, he draws most of his examples from the Pentateuch.

Nevertheless, the writer's mind is also steeped in other parts of the Old Testament, particularly the Psalms.[2] Indeed, it may be said that Psalm 110 plays a key role in the development of his argument, supplying him particularly with his Melchizedek theme. Another important passage for him is the new covenant section in Jeremiah 31, which he quotes extensively in chapter 8. The manner of his citations is also significant, for he undoubtedly regarded the Old Testament text as authoritative. He assumes that what the text says God says, which comes out strikingly in chapter 1. Even so vague a formula as 'it has been testified somewhere' to introduce a quotation from Psalm 8 (2:6ff.) is in itself an evidence that the author wished to back up his discussion of the humanity of Jesus with scriptural support, although he does not specify the original context. The fact that the text is regarded in this authoritative way is of vital importance for a right understanding of the argument and purpose of the epistle. If as seems probable one of the writer's aims is to clear up difficulties which the readers were having in deciding on a satisfactory approach to the Old Testament, the epistle itself becomes a useful guide, not only for its original readers, but also for the modern reader. Much of what might on the surface appear irrelevant falls into place when the more

---

[1] For a careful treatment of the use of the OT in Hebrews, *cf.* J. van der Ploeg, *RB* 54 (1947), pp. 187–228. K. J. Thomas, *NTS* 11 (1965), pp. 303–325, has discussed the type of text cited in Hebrews and concludes that two different editions of the LXX have been used.

[2] *Cf.* S. Kistemaker, *The Psalm Citations in the Epistle to the Hebrews* (Amsterdam, 1961).

general question of the Christian approach to the Old Testament comes into focus.

One question which arises is whether the writer always does justice to the Old Testament context. Some have suggested that for him the context held no significance, but this would be an exaggeration.[1] He certainly applies the Old Testament text at times in a new way, as when he applies to the Son words originally spoken of God (1:8), but it is questionable whether it can be maintained that the author has ignored the context. The same applies to the development of the rest theme from Psalm 95 in chapters 3 and 4. It would be more correct to say that our author brings out the latent and extended meaning of the original text. Such a principle permits him to apply his Melchizedek theme in a way which looks on the surface as if he is basing his argument on the silence of Scripture, rather than on its statements (cf. 7:3).

*Qumran*

Our next consideration must be to discover whether the kind of development seen in the Jewish sect at Qumran has any relevance as background to this epistle. Certain features suggest a connection, such as the dominance of the priestly caste at Qumran and the evidence that some interest existed among the sectarians on the Melchizedek theme.[2] The Qumran community had some interest in angels and this might suggest a connection with the readers of this epistle. But interest in angels was widespread among the Jews of the intertestamental period. Moreover, it appears as part of the so-called Colossian heresy (Col. 2:18).[3] Another feature is the extensive interest among the sectarians in biblical exegesis[4] and there is certainly some parallel with the writer of this epistle. As the exegetes of Qumran were more concerned with the application of the text to their own day than to its historical context, so our author tends to stress

[1] Cf. F. C. Synge, *Hebrews and the Scriptures* (London, 1959), pp. 53, 54.
[2] Cf. J. A. Fitzmyer, *JBL* 86 (1967), pp. 25–41, who thinks the Melchizedek theme at Qumran may account for its use in the epistle to the Hebrews. Cf. also M. de Jonge and A. S. van der Woude, '11 Q Melchizedek and the NT', *NTS* 12 (1966), pp. 301–326.
[3] Cf. T. W. Manson, *BJRL* 32 (1949), pp. 1–17, who proposed the theory that the writer to the Hebrews was answering a Colossian-type heresy.
[4] Cf. F. F. Bruce, *Biblical Exegesis in the Qumran Texts* (London, 1960).

the present relevance while not, however, ignoring the context. There may be some parallels between the Qumran Teacher of Righteousness and Jesus Christ, but the writer of this epistle has no doubts that Jesus is superior to all others and is in any case the final revelation of God to man.[1]

One feature which may have some bearing on our discussion is the conjunction of the priestly and kingly aspects of Messiah in the Qumran community although not apparently linked in the same person. The priestly Messiah of Aaron was distinguished from the Messiah of Israel.[2] By way of contrast the presentation of Jesus in Hebrews is of a priest-king after the order of Melchizedek.

The Qumran community observed certain rites particularly of a purificatory nature. This purificatory theme occurs in Hebrews, but is not tied to outward rites. In fact the readers are told to move on from elementary doctrines like ablutions (6:2). Nevertheless the idea of purification is present, but applied in a spiritual manner, as the statement in 10:22 about hearts being sprinkled clean from an evil conscience shows. There is some suggestion that the purificatory rites at Qumran might have developed as a substitute for the cessation of sacrifice. One of the reasons for the location of the community in the Judaean desert was because the sectarians had become dissatisfied with the arrangements for the Temple sacrifices in Jerusalem. It is not without significance that the epistle to the Hebrews concentrates on the 'better' sacrifice of Christ.

In view of all this there is justification for the view that the Qumran literature and cultic practices throw some light on the milieu to which the readers of this epistle belong, although it is questionable whether any direct contacts can be assumed.

---

[1] H. Kosmala, *Hebräer-Essener-Christen* (Leiden, 1959), has adopted the view that the people addressed in the epistle to the Hebrews were former members of the Qumran community. But *cf*. F. F. Bruce's discussion of the connection in ' "To the Hebrews" or "To the Essenes"?', *NTS* 9 (1962), pp. 217–232, who concludes that the readers were not Essenes.

[2] *Cf*. the discussion on the Messianic hope at Qumran in F. F. Bruce's *Second Thoughts on the Dead Sea Scrolls* (Exeter, 1956), pp. 70–84. In the Damascus document the royal and priestly appear to be combined (*cf*. CDC 19:11; 12:23; 13:1; 14:19; 20:1).

## Philo of Alexandria

It has long been maintained by interpreters of this epistle that a strong strand in the background is Hellenism,[1] particularly the variety of Hellenism seen in the writings of Philo of Alexandria.[2] Much has been written on the relation between our epistle and Philo's writings and it will be possible to give here only a brief summary of the salient points. Philo as an exegete is notorious for his use of allegorization in an attempt to make the Old Testament text relevant for his contemporaries. His aim in this was to trace the main concepts of his Greek environment back to Jewish sources. To accomplish this apologetic aim he paid little regard to the historical context. Yet it will at once be seen that although the writer of this epistle may at times border on an allegorical tendency, he differs radically from Philo in that he treats seriously the historical context. The whole of his argument would fall to the ground if the historical basis were denied. When discussing the Israelites' quest for 'rest', he never suggests that the wilderness wanderings were not historically significant, and indeed he builds upon the fact that the Israelites actually disobeyed God and were excluded from entering the promised land through unbelief.

Both Philo and our author, in spite of their differing methods of exegesis, share in common a high regard for Scripture. They both use extensively the Septuagint version and introduce the text with similar formulae of citation. Moreover, there are many significant words and phrases which appear in both Philo's writings and this epistle. A few common ideas may be mentioned to illustrate this point. The significance of names is clear from Hebrews 7:2 and this is a kind of deduction familiar to Philo. Both writers abound in antitheses like the contrast between the earthly and the heavenly (*cf.* Heb. 8:1ff.; 9:23f.), between the created and the uncreated (9:11) and the passing and the abiding (7:3, 24; 10:34; 12:27; 13:14).

---

[1] A strong advocate for Hellenistic influence in this epistle was E. Ménégoz, *La Théologie de l'Épître aux Hébreux* (Paris, 1894). *Cf.* the discussion on this theme by A. M. Fairhurst, *TB* 7–8 (1961), pp. 17–27.

[2] The most thorough recent work on the relation of Philo to the epistle to the Hebrews is R. Williamson, *A Critical Re-examination of the Relationship between Philo and the Epistle to the Hebrews* (Leiden, 1967). *Cf.* also S. G. Sowers, *The Hermeneutics of Philo and Hebrews* (Richmond, 1965). C. Spicq has a section on the same theme in his *Comm.* 1, pp. 39–87.

This fondness for antitheses has raised the question whether our author, like Philo, was indebted to the Platonic theory of ideas. There has been a difference of opinion over the answer to this question. Some have maintained that this theory so dominates the epistle that the author must be regarded as an Alexandrian Jew who has learned his approach from contact with Philo's teaching. There may superficially seem to be some parallels with the Platonic theory which regards what is seen as unreal, but as a shadow of the reality behind it. Certainly much of the epistle is taken up with the concept that the ceremonial is but a shadow of which Christ is the superior reality to which it points. But it is questionable whether this idea is indebted to the Platonic theory. It is better explained by the author's conviction that in many points Christ is better than the old order – a better priesthood, a better sacrifice, a better sanctuary and a better covenant. This author's approach is more biblical than Philo's because he is working with a different key.

This is not to deny the author's Hellenistic background, but rather to affirm that he did not arrive at his interpretation through the application of Hellenistic ideas. Nevertheless, his background equipped him to express in Hellenistic forms what he had already deduced from the Christian conviction that Jesus Christ was the key to the understanding of the Old Testament.

*Pauline thought*
Still within our discussion of background we need to apply ourselves to the problem of the relation between this epistle and Pauline thought. We have already seen reason to reject the view that Paul was the author, but that does not mean that it is of no consequence to discuss whether the author has been exposed at all to Paul's theology, and whether his approach may be considered to be a development from Paul's position.

It is valuable to note first the many features of Paul's theology which are shared by the letter to the Hebrews.[1] Certainly the Christology is very similar. The pre-existence of Christ and his part in creation, which is a major feature in the Christological passage in Colossians 1:15–17, is stressed in the introductory passage in Hebrews 1. As Paul sees Christ as the illuminator of

[1] *Cf.* H. Windisch, *Comm.*, pp. 128f.

the believer, so Hebrews sees him as reflecting the glory of God (*cf*. 2 Cor. 4:4 and Heb. 1:3).

Alongside this high Christology we also find a stress on the humiliation of Christ (Phil. 2:7; Heb. 2:14–17). This remarkable combination of exaltation and condescension shows that Paul and our writer have come to the same understanding of Christology. Our writer does not seek, any more than Paul does, to explain the paradox; but there is no doubt that, for both, the godward and manward side of the nature of Christ was a basic conviction. Whereas our letter expounds an aspect of Christ's person and work which does not occur in Paul, his Christology is essentially the same. Linked with the self-humbling of Christ is the idea of his obedience (Rom. 5:19; Phil. 2:8; Heb. 5:8), which for both writers is set over against the disobedience of other men.

Although Paul does not deal with Christ as high priest, he portrays his work in the figure of sacrifice and this provides an important link between the two authors (*cf*. 1 Cor. 5:7; Eph. 5:2; Heb. 9:28). Since sacrifice plays such an important part in the argument in Hebrews, it is important to note that it is certainly not a unique idea, but was shared by the early church as one way of explaining the death of Christ.

Another common feature between Paul and Hebrews is the importance attached to the new covenant (*cf*. 2 Cor. 3:9ff.; Heb. 8:6ff.) Both show this new covenant to be better than the old. Paul speaks of the greater splendour of the new, although he does not deny that the old had a splendour of its own. Hebrews, however, is rather more blunt in declaring that the old is obsolete (Heb. 8:13). There is no fundamental difference between them over the significance of a covenant mediated by Christ himself.

In his catalogue of heroes of faith, the writer gives pride of place to Abraham. He has already mentioned him earlier in the epistle in reference to his descendants (2:16); in reference to the promise of God to him (6:13); and in reference to his relation to Melchizedek (7:1–10). A similar high regard for Abraham is found in Paul's epistles (Rom. 4:1ff.; 9:7; 11:1; 2 Cor. 11:22; Gal. 3:6ff.; 4:22). In this connection we might note that Hebrews sometimes cites Old Testament passages which Paul also cites, *e.g.* both cite Psalm 8 (Heb. 2:6–9; 1 Cor. 15:27); Deuteronomy 32:35 (Heb. 10:30; Rom. 12:19); and Habakkuk 2:4 (Heb. 10:38; Rom. 1:17; Gal. 3:11).

The above evidence is sufficient to show that the letter to the Hebrews, while not written by Paul, is very much in the same theological mould. It will not do to drive a wedge between them or to suppose that Hebrews is a later development from Paulinism. It is truer to say that although both are distinctive developments, they are not totally divorced from the mainstream of early Christian opinion.

### Other New Testament parallels

It remains only to enquire whether there are points of contact between Hebrews and other books of the New Testament. Some have seen parallels with Johannine literature, especially with the idea of Jesus Christ as the intercessor for his people.[1] Most would agree that John 17 presents Jesus in such a role praying for his people in a manner which would well link up with the idea of Jesus the high priest interceding for his people in Hebrews 7:25. There is strength in this comparison, which adds weight to the contention that Hebrews has links with the various streams of early Christian tradition. It cannot be affirmed for certain that the author of Hebrews knew of John's Gospel, but it is not outside the bounds of possibility that he was acquainted with a tradition which preserved at least the fact, if not the content, of Christ's prayer for his disciples. The intercessory theme occurs also in 1 John 2:1f., where the idea of Christ as our advocate appears.

Apart from the Johannine literature, we may also note that there are some similarities between Hebrews and Stephen's speech in Acts.[2] These have led some to conclude that Luke was the author of both works. Nevertheless, questions of authorship apart, it is significant that both stress Abraham's call and both attach importance to a temple not made with hands. There is some agreement between Hebrews and Acts 7 in the approach to and assessment of Old Testament history.

There can be little doubt in view of the above discussion that

[1] *Cf.* C. Spicq, *Comm.* 1, pp. 109–138.
[2] W. Manson, *The Epistle to the Hebrews* (London, 1951), pp. 184f.

Hebrews cannot be divorced from the mainstream of New Testament literature. There is nothing to suggest that the general readers of the early Christian literature would have had difficulty with the drift of argument in this letter, nor may we suppose that they would have seen no relevance in it.

## IX. THE THEOLOGY OF THE LETTER

There is no difficulty in locating the major themes of this letter, but it is not easy to see how they all fit together. This is the main task of the theologian. It is based on the reasonable assumption that the author has not thrown together a mass of unrelated themes, an assumption which is supported by the orderly nature of the arrangement. It is clear that he has planned his work with care. Whenever diversions occur in his train of thought they are not permitted to interfere with the main development of his argument. We shall first seek to discover whether there is one key idea, which would explain why prominence is given to such themes as the Son, the high priesthood, the sacrificial system and the new covenant. What binds these together into a unity?

We note at once from the introduction to the epistle (1:1–3) that the writer is insisting on *the finality of the Christian revelation*. Whatever God has made known before is now superseded by his revelation through his Son. The fact that the writer at once introduces the uniqueness of the Son suggests that he is not certain that his readers are convinced of this. But it is not at once apparent why the Son is introduced at this point, and why it is not until 2:9 that he is identified as Jesus. This cannot be accidental and the reason for it must supply some clue to the drift of his thought. There is no doubt that the status of Jesus Christ as Son plays a leading role in the epistle as a whole, even in those parts which concentrate on Jesus as high priest. We may perhaps see the early introduction of Jesus as Son as an indication that it is through him that a new era in God's dealings with men has been inaugurated. All that had happened under the old covenant has now been superseded by a better covenant. It is really the implications of this new covenant which form the main aim of the letter. It will become apparent that the Son is the key figure in the inauguration of the new covenant, a mediator who cannot be bettered.

## The character of the Son

We shall first explore the character of the Son as he is set out in this letter. The presentation of Christ is undoubtedly of an exalted nature as is at once apparent in the opening verses, which not only introduce the Son, but make some extraordinary statements about him. We may conveniently summarize the Christology under three aspects: the pre-existence, the humanity and the exaltation of the Son.

*The pre-existence of the Son* is emphatically affirmed by the fact that he is said to be the agent through whom all things were created (1:2). He clearly existed before the material creation. He preceded successive periods of world history (the ages). Such an exalted Christology is therefore the starting-point for the argument of the epistle. The pre-existence theme is also supported immediately by the character of the agent in creation – as the glory and image of God – and by the fact that he continues to uphold all things by his power. In the course of the epistle there are further hints which agree with this concept of Christ's pre-existence. In the writer's application of Psalm 8 in 2:9 there is the implication that Jesus was made to adopt a status – lower than the angels – which he did not naturally have. In 7:3 Melchizedek is made like the Son of God, not *vice versa*, which must mean that Christ predated Melchizedek. It is possible also that 10:5ff. bears witness to the fact that in the incarnation a body was prepared for the Son.

It seems evident that when the writer speaks in terms of the Son's pre-existence he is thinking of the Son as sharing the divine nature. Such expressions as the *reflection* (*apaugasma*) and *very stamp* (*charaktēr*) of God's nature (1:3) are sufficient to demonstrate this. Moreover, the fact that the Son plays a part in creation shows that he performs the same function which is elsewhere in Scripture attributed to God. Further, the upholding of all things is said to be 'by his word of power', which parallels the many references to the power of Yahweh in the Old Testament. It may be said, in fact, that the whole argument of the epistle rests on the fact that the Son holds a unique position in relation to God, which undergirds his effectiveness as mediator and intercessor. It shows the basic reason for the superiority of Christ as high priest. That the writer has not just invented this is seen from the Old Testament support which he collects in chapter 1, particularly the passage from Psalm 45:6, 7 which he attributes in 1:8 to Christ, although the wording is addressed to God.

Our next consideration must be *the humanity of the Son*. This follows directly from the necessity for the incarnation. Clearly a high priest who was divine could not otherwise represent mankind. To be a true representative the Son must become man. This is grasped in 2:17 where the writer shows that the Son had to be made like his brethren in order to fulfil the function of a merciful and faithful high priest. If the pre-existence and divine nature of the Son is a basic assumption of the writer, so is the true humanity. It is not without significance that the name Jesus, which carries with it allusions to the human life of the Son, occurs nine times in this letter. In most cases where it occurs it stands at the end of the clause and therefore attracts added emphasis (*cf.* 2:9; 3:1; 6:20; 7:22; 10:19; 12:2, 24; 13:12, 20).

Some of the clearest references to the earthly life of Jesus outside the Gospels occur in this epistle. The agony in Gethsemane seems to be directly alluded to in 5:7ff., where Jesus' loud cries and tears are mentioned. The sufferings of Jesus are of vital importance to the argument of the whole epistle and are mentioned various times. These sufferings are specifically said to have taken place 'in the days of his flesh'. The ministry of Jesus is alluded to in 2:3. The hostility which he roused against himself is mentioned in 12:3. Such events as the cross (12:2), the resurrection (13:20) and the ascension (1:3) are assumed to be basic knowledge.

In addition, we may note what the writer says about the attitudes and reactions of Jesus. By implication through an Old Testament quotation (Is. 8:17–18), he is said to have exercised faith in God (2:13). He is also seen to be a man of prayer (5:7) and to have shown godly fear (5:7).

The question must next be faced whether the Son of God in becoming man became fallen man and the answer according to our author must be emphatically in the negative. He twice affirms the sinlessness of Jesus (4:15; 7:26), while at the same time he agrees that Jesus was tempted in all points as we are. This shows that he does not consider the sinlessness to be the result of non-exposure to the normal trials and tensions of life, but rather to be an evidence of a positive conquest over sin.

Another aspect of the humanity of Jesus in this letter is the emphasis on his perfection. Although the concept of his being made perfect through suffering (2:10) raises problems, these are lessened if the idea of perfection is seen to consist in bringing a process to completion. The writer cannot conceive that the whole plan of salvation could stand if Jesus had not suffered, and he sees this as part of the process of consummation. Another passage which brings out the same thought is 5:8–9 where the author says that though Jesus was a Son he learned obedience. This does not mean that he was reluctant to obey or that there was a time when he was not obedient, but it affirms that the experience of Jesus showed the Son to be obedient. It was only because of this that he has become the source of eternal salvation to all who obey him.

There are many passages in this letter which point to the representative nature of Jesus Christ, an important feature if he is to be an effective high priest. He is said to have shared the same nature as men in order to defeat him who held men in bondage to death (2:14). It is for the same reason that the incarnation is said to be fitting (2:10). The main qualification for the high priest was to be like his brethren (2:17). In no clearer way could the writer establish his point about the necessity for the true humanity of Jesus. To be a representative he had to experience what man experiences. None other than a true man could possibly have done this.

We need to pass from a consideration of his humanity to the theme of *the exaltation of Jesus*. At strategic points in the argument the Son's status at the right hand of the majesty on high is mentioned. We meet the exalted Son first in the opening verses as if, even before he dwells on the humiliation involved in the incarnation, the writer wants his readers to know about the exalted position of the Son. Moreover, the fact that the Son is seated shows that his work is already completed. The focus falls on his post-resurrection achievement. It is the writer's way, not only of referring to the ascension, but also of showing the positive advantages of the whole mission of Christ. To be seated in so exalted a position gives the Son the most advantageous status for his work of intercession, although the high-priestly work is not actually mentioned until a later stage. Before going on to discuss the new covenant in chapter 8, the writer again reminds his readers that our high priest is seated at the right hand of God (8:1). The same applies to 12:2, just prior to the passage on discipline.

In addition to these references to the session of the Son at the right hand of God, we discover various descriptions of the Son which assume his exaltation. He is described as heir of all things (1:2), which does not simply point ahead to a future inheritance, but indicates what he has already entered into. There is a sense in which the Son's full realization of his inheritance is yet unfulfilled until he has put all his enemies under his feet. Yet even believers are said to inherit the promises (6:12) and some aspect of present realization cannot, therefore, be denied to the supreme heir of all things. Another aspect of the Son is the idea of the forerunner, which comes into the description of Jesus as high priest in 6:20. This is of particular interest for the writer, for he is concerned throughout with man's approach to God, and it serves his purpose well to show that Jesus has already gone into the heavenly sanctuary. Christ as forerunner is at once seen to be superior to the Jewish high priests, but this superiority is a theme which occupies the writer in several sections of the epistle. It was clearly of great importance to him to demonstrate in a preliminary way the infinite advantages which Christ by nature had in his work as high priest.

*The superiority of the Son over others*
So far we have been concentrating on what the letter says about the nature of the Son. We come next to note the various ways in which the superiority of the Son is illustrated. First of all there is a stress on the Son's *superiority to angels* (1:5 – 2:9). It may not at first be evident why the writer is concerned to establish this. It may be supposed that the readers had a par-

ticularly high regard for angels and had not been able to appreciate to what degree our high priest is so much superior. It seems likely that many were contending that angels were superior to Jesus Christ, in which case their problem was not that Jesus was made a little lower than angels, but that he was always superior to them. The fact that this comparison with angels supplies the main thrust of chapters 1 and 2 shows the importance which the author placed on the whole comparison.

But he then goes on to affirm the Son's *superiority to Moses*. He does this in 3:1–6, where having compared Moses, the faithful one who was nevertheless only a servant, with Christ as a Son, he has no hesitation in declaring the superiority of the latter. As he develops his Moses theme to include the wilderness wanderings of the Israelites, this leads him to show that our leader is *superior to Joshua*, who was unable to give the people rest.

The superiority theme is further developed by showing our high priest's *superiority to Aaron*. This will be particularly demonstrated in our next section on the Son as high priest. Not only does the writer show the superiority of Jesus, because of the insufficiencies of the Aaronic line with its constantly repeated sacrifices and its ever-changing succession of priests, but also because he belonged to the superior order of Mechizedek. Indeed, the Melchizedek theme is introduced largely in order to demonstrate a viable alternative order of priesthood, which would at the same time be superior. To those who revered the Aaronic priesthood as the only legitimate means of approach to God, the demonstration of Christ's superiority to Aaron would be an indispensable line of argument.

*The Son as high priest*
Although this theme is of prime interest to the writer, he does not introduce it at once. In fact, he introduces it gradually in order to build up his argument to a climax. It is mentioned almost incidentally in 2:17 and 3:1 and then not again until 4:14. Even then the theme is briefly touched on to introduce the Melchizedek theme, only to be delayed once more by the diversion over apostasy, which then leads to a return of the theme at 6:20. This somewhat truncated handling of the theme cannot

be accidental and must, therefore, be designed to concentrate the readers' attention on its paramount importance.

In the early references certain features are brought out in passing. The high priest had to be like his brethren (2:17); he had to be merciful and faithful (2:17); he had to make expiation for the sins of the people (2:17); above all he had to be able to sympathize with the people he represented (4:15). In the first more extensive passage in 5:1ff., the main qualification stressed is that of being appointed by God. The writer has no doubt that Jesus, the Son, fulfils all of the above-mentioned requirements. The fact that Jesus is seen, on grounds of these qualities, to be eligible for the office of high priest leads into the main discussion over Melchizedek, for whatever qualities he possessed, Jesus lacked one essential qualification for eligibility to the Aaronic priesthood: he belonged to the tribe of Judah, not Levi. There was no way, therefore, of maintaining that Jesus was a high priest of the Levitical type. If he was to be a high priest at all it would have to be of a different kind, and the writer's inspiration leads him to identify that new order of priesthood with Melchizedek. He was probably led to this idea from the explicit statement of Psalm 110:4 which then led him back to the original reference in Genesis 14:17–20. Since we know there were speculations about Melchizedek in the Qumran literature, it is not impossible that the readers may already have been primed about Melchizedek, although the writer raises issues and applies the idea in a way which is totally new.

The particular aspects of Melchizedek's high-priesthood which he brings out may be briefly summarized under the following headings. First, it is *different from Aaron's*. The difference does not simply reside in its superiority. Nor does it lie in the priestly functions, for by definition the function of the priest is to act for God before men and for men before God. Both Aaron and Melchizedek did this. But where Melchizedek differs radically from Aaron is in the order to which he belongs. The former is in a class of his own. It is different in that it rests on a different quality of life (the power of an indestructible life, 7:15, 16).

Secondly, we note that Melchizedek's order is *timeless*. His priesthood is 'for ever' and therefore not subject to the many limitations which affected the Aaronic priests. This timeless element is strangely developed from the silence of the Genesis account in relation to the beginning or ending of Melchizedek's life. But the writer is convinced that the Scripture means to support this enduring quality.

Thirdly, the order of Melchizedek is *royal*. Not only does the Genesis account call Melchizedek king of Salem, but the writer to the Hebrews adds his interpretation 'king of peace'. The main point is that unlike Aaron's order, another exists which is royal. This provides a further aspect which demonstrates the superiority of the latter. Far more effectively than Aaron ever could, Melchizedek provides a 'type' for the royal priesthood of Christ.

Fourthly, we may note that Melchizedek's order is *changeless*. It is in strong contrast to the constantly changing personnel of the Aaronic order. Provision had to be made for the continuance of a line of succession, so that when one high priest died another was raised up to take his place. Such constant change was not necessary with the order of Melchizedek.

In so many respects the order of Melchizedek is seen to be superior to that of Aaron that it may be wondered why no effective use had been made of the idea in the intervening centuries between Melchizedek and Christ. The reason must be that Melchizedek comes into his own only when the anti-type is seen. In other words Melchizedek gains his significance through Christ, not *vice versa*. Indeed, Melchizedek himself is said to be made like the Son of God.

*The Son's work as high priest*
Against the background of our high priest after the order of Melchizedek, the writer thinks of the service he performs and is particularly influenced by the ritual followed in the Levitical order on the Day of Atonement. This was the day of greatest significance for the Aaronic high priest, for it was the day on which he and he alone was permitted into the holy of holies. It was necessary for him to take in sacrificial blood as an atonement to be sprinkled seven times on the mercy seat (Lv. 16). This sacrificial idea provides a remarkable illustration of the significance of the sacrificial death of Christ.

The fact that the writer goes into some detail in describing the holy of holies (9:1ff.) shows that for him there was a close connection between the Aaronic ritual and the self-offering of Christ. The Levitical cultus was seen to be 'a copy and shadow' (8:5) of the heavenly sanctuary. The thought moves from the earthly tabernacle to the heavenly.

But not only is the location of the offering different, the offering itself is of a different kind. The high priest, in a quite unprecedented way, offers himself. It does not worry the writer that the Old Testament analogy breaks down, for the self-offering of Christ is the climax of his exposition and at once makes Christ's high-priestly work totally unique. In 9:14 he affirms that Christ's offering is through the eternal Spirit, which marks it out as incomparable when set alongside the shedding of the blood of hapless animals. He also shows that Christ's blood can purify the conscience, which the Levitical offerings could not.

Of paramount importance to the writer is the effectiveness of the sacrificial death of Christ. He several times emphasizes that it was 'once for all' (7:27; 9:12, 26; 10:10). There was never any question of a repetition. It was totally inconceivable that such an offering could ever be inadequate, nor would the re-offering of such a sacrifice be intelligible (cf. 9:26). The writer is convinced that the uniqueness of Christianity rests in the central act of Christ in giving himself as an offering on the cross for the sins of his people.

Much of the section 8:1–10:18 is taken up with the demonstration of the superior sacrifice that Christ has made. Nowhere else in the New Testament is the sacrificial aspect of the work of Christ brought out so forcefully. Any doctrine of the atonement which is based on the New Testament must take full account of the testimony of this epistle on the significance of the blood of Christ. There are certain results from the self-offering of Christ which are brought out, which have a bearing on the application of his work.

First, we note *the purification for sins*, which not only appears in the introduction in 1:3, but recurs at other times (cf. 9:23; 10:2f.). The removal of the guilt of sin which is integral to the idea of atonement is a particular interest of this epistle. The writer is faced with the fact that the old Levitical order could not remove sins (10:4), but he is convinced that what is lacking in the old is amply covered in the new through Christ. The cleansing theme reaches its climax in 10:22 where the readers are exhorted to draw near to God because their hearts have been cleansed from an evil conscience (*cf.* 9:14).

Secondly, we find that stress is laid on the *perfection* theme. Through Christ's single offering he is said to have 'perfected for all time those who are sanctified' (10:14). This is another feature of the superiority of Christ's offering, for the law could make nothing perfect (7:19). It should be noted, however, that this feature of Christ's work lends no support to the theory of sinless perfection. The perfection theme in Hebrews runs parallel to Paul's doctrine of justification, although approaching it from a different angle.

Thirdly, the concept of *sanctification* needs further emphasis, for it occurs not only in the passage just cited (10:14) but also in 2:11; 10:10, 29; 13:12. Sanctification and purification are closely linked, but the former is specifically concerned with setting apart for a holy purpose, for which a process of becoming holy is indispensable. But it is important to note that in the references mentioned above it is not the individual who sanctifies himself. This is the work of God through Christ. This emphasis on sanctification shows that although the offering of Christ is once for all, his work on man's behalf is nevertheless continuing, as is also his work of intercession (4:15; 7:25).

*The Son's inauguration of the new covenant*
No survey of the theology of Hebrews, however brief, would be complete without some mention of the new covenant. Since at the heart of the Christian memorial to Christ's death in the Lord's supper, there is reference to the new covenant, the teaching of this epistle on the theme has special significance. Although the writer states that the old is obsolete (8:13), there is some continuity between the old and the new. The old, like the new, was ordained by God. It was God's provision for his people. Immediately after mentioning the obsolete character of the old covenant, the writer goes on to speak with evident appreciation of the furniture of the centre of worship under that covenant (9:1ff.).

Moreover, both old and new covenants were provisions of God's grace for those who could not make any provision for themselves. The recipients of the new covenant had no greater claims upon God than those of the old. The greater significance of the new did not rest in an agreement between God and a better people. It is superior entirely because it has a better mediator. It is based on a more effective removal of sins.

The extended quotation from Jeremiah 31:31–34 in Hebrews 8:8–12 draws attention to the inward character of the new covenant. Its results will, therefore, be of a high ethical order. When God's laws are written on men's hearts they will work out in men's lives. This inward character, therefore, marks out the new covenant as clearly superior to the old.

But how does the writer think of the application of his rather theological debate about the nature of the Son, the high priest and the sacrificial system? When he reaches the conclusion of this part of his letter, he makes a threefold exhortation in 10:19–25, which shows that he has a distinctly practical approach. 10:22 mentions *faith*, 10:23 refers to *hope*, and 10:24 to *love*. These three responses sum up the Christian's reaction to all that Christ has done (*cf.* Paul's treatment of the same three qualities in 1 Cor. 13). In addition to these specific exhortations, the writer devotes a whole chapter (11) to illustrations of faith. He further assures his readers that their new position will not absolve them from the need for discipline (12). There is in fact a nice balance between doctrine and practical living in this epistle, which makes it valuable and relevant not only for the original readers, but also for their modern counterparts.

It is within the context of the new covenant that the warnings against falling away (2:1–4; 6:1–8; 10:29) have relevance. To turn one's back on such a marvellous covenant would be tantamount to re-crucifying the Son of God, amounting to a total rejection of Christianity. These passages must not be isolated from the epistle as a whole. They are intended to warn against the serious consequences of rejecting the gracious provisions of God.

The writer makes much of the concept of faith and it is important to compare his teaching on the subject with other New Testament writers, especially the apostle Paul. The statement in 11:1 that faith is the assurance of things hoped for, the conviction of things not seen, shows the main idea is a close connection between faith and hope. This is undoubtedly the most distinctive feature of the heroes of faith listed in chapter 11. These great men of the past were forward-looking. The basis of their exploits was seen to be trust in God who would turn their present distresses into ultimate victory. There is, therefore, a close connection between Old Testament piety and faith in God. Faith provided the confidence in God which was so needed in times of Israel's stress. As the writer contemplates the history of the past he is not unmindful of the existence of unbelief, as he shows so vividly in chapters 3 and 4.

But we need to enquire in what ways the writer brings out the specifically Christian aspect of faith. Clearly Christ has made a difference. He is described as the pioneer of our faith as well as its perfecter (12:2). The readers are exhorted to look to him. This Christ-centred quality of faith is a development of the Old Testament trust in God. Yet the rewards of faith are to be shared alike by the faithful people of old as well as the present Christian believers (cf. 11:40).

It is noticeable that there is an absence of the characteristic Pauline view of faith as personal commitment to Christ. That does not mean to say that this writer conceives of any other way to appropriate the benefits of salvation other than through faith. But he assumes it rather than expounds it. He is concerned about the understanding of those who have already become partakers of the Holy Spirit (6:4). He wants to ensure that they remain steadfast (cf. 3:6; 10:23).

## Conclusion

We cannot better conclude this brief outline of the main teaching of the epistle than by drawing attention to the magnificent prayer with which the epistle itself concludes (13:20–21). It sums up the close connection between the doctrinal and ethical aspects of the whole theme. It mentions the nature of God (God of peace), the resurrection of Christ, the function of Christ (shepherd), the blood of the covenant, and the practical application (that you may do what is pleasing in God's sight). It is both a prayer and a statement rolled into one.

# ANALYSIS

## I. THE SUPERIORITY OF THE CHRISTIAN FAITH
### (1:1 – 10:18)

A. GOD'S REVELATION THROUGH THE SON (1:1–4)

B. THE SUPERIORITY OF THE SON TO ANGELS (1:5 – 2:18)
   (i)   *Christ is superior in his nature (1:5–14)*
   (ii)  *An exhortation against drifting (2:1–4)*
   (iii) *The humiliation and glory of Jesus (2:5–9)*
   (iv)  *His work on man's behalf (2:10–18)*

C. THE SUPERIORITY OF JESUS TO MOSES (3:1–19)
   (i)   *Moses the servant and Jesus the Son (3:1–6)*
   (ii)  *Focus on the failure of God's people under Moses (3:7–19)*

D. THE SUPERIORITY OF JESUS TO JOSHUA (4:1–13)
   (i)   *The greater rest which Joshua could not secure (4:1–10)*
   (ii)  *The urgency to seek for that rest (4:11–13)*

E. A SUPERIOR HIGH PRIEST (4:14 – 9:14)
   (i)    *Our great high priest (4:14–16)*
   (ii)   *Comparison with Aaron (5:1–10)*
   (iii)  *A challenging interlude (5:11 – 6:20)*
   (iv)   *The order of Melchizedek (7:1–28)*
   (v)    *The minister of the new covenant (8:1–13)*
   (vi)   *The greater glory of the new order (9:1–14)*

F. THE MEDIATOR (9:15 – 10:18)

   (i)   *The significance of his death (9:15–22)*
   (ii)  *His entrance into a heavenly sanctuary (9:23–28)*
   (iii) *His offering of himself for others (10:1–18)*

# II. EXHORTATIONS (10:19 – 13:25)

A. THE BELIEVER'S PRESENT POSITION (10:19–39)

   (i)   *The new and living way (10:19–25)*
   (ii)  *Another warning (10:26–31)*
   (iii) *The value of past experience (10:32–39)*

B. FAITH (11:1–40)

   (i)   *Its nature (11:1–3)*
   (ii)  *Examples from the past (11:4–40)*

C. DISCIPLINE AND ITS BENEFITS (12:1–29)

   (i)   *The need for discipline (12:1–11)*
   (ii)  *The avoidance of moral inconsistency (12:12–17)*
   (iii) *The benefits of the new covenant (12:18–29)*

D. CONCLUDING ADVICE (13:1–25)

   (i)   *Exhortations affecting social life (13:1–3)*
   (ii)  *Exhortations affecting private life (13:4–6)*
   (iii) *Exhortations affecting religious life (13:7–9)*
   (iv) *About the Christian's new altar (13:10–16)*
   (v)  *Final words (13:17–25)*

# COMMENTARY

## I. THE SUPERIORITY OF THE CHRISTIAN FAITH
### (1:1 – 10:18)

Christians who had come from a Jewish background would naturally compare their new-found faith with the richness of their Jewish heritage. This letter sets out to show them the greater richness of their Christian position. At every stage of the argument the keynote is that their new faith is better.

Although the drift of the argument would have special value for former Jews who had become Christians, the theme of the superiority of the Christian faith would have significance also for those converted from a pagan background, in view of the fact that Gentile believers as well as Jews accepted the authority of the Old Testament scriptures and would need a true interpretation of them.

### A. GOD'S REVELATION THROUGH THE SON (1:1–4)

In this brief introductory section, God's revelation through his Son is seen to be not only superior but final. Bearing in mind that such a conclusive revelation requires a very special means, the writer introduces his readers to the superior nature of the Son and also links what he is with what he has done.

**1.** The letter begins with a statement of fact, that is, that *God has spoken*. At least the writer sees no need to demonstrate this fact. He does not prove that God speaks; he asserts it. Does this mean that the letter has no relevance for those who do not accept that God has spoken to man? The answer must be yes. Faith not only in the existence of God, but also in the communication of God is taken for granted. It is one of the planks on which the whole argument of the letter rests. It is useless to read further if God makes no revelation to men. The letter provides, on the other hand, some help towards a better understanding of what God has done.

Another assumption which the author makes is that what has happened in the past has a bearing on the present. Such an assumption would be rejected by many contemporary thinkers. There is in fact in the secular world a reaction against the past as if any appeal to its lessons is inadmissible. There is however always a section of society which lives in the future and is against the present and the past – a sort of permanent anti-establishment attitude. But the wisest of men recognize that some continuity is inescapable. This principle is basic to the New Testament and is nowhere brought to focus so clearly as in Hebrews. What strikes the writer is the variety of ways in which God had spoken in the past. He does not list them, but uses the expression *In many and various ways*. Anyone acquainted with the Old Testament would at once be able to fill in the details – the different modes (visions, angelic revelations, prophetic words and events) and the different occasions (stretching across the whole vista of Old Testament history).

The most illuminating revelations came through *the prophets*. These were men raised up by God to challenge their own time. Their badge of office was the unshakeable conviction that they spoke from God. Their ability to say, 'God says', gave their words a unique authority. They were ill-treated (as Heb. 11:33ff. shows) and yet they persisted with their message. Their stories make heroic reading, but what they said was incomplete. The writer knows that it needed a better method of communication, and he recognizes that this has come in Jesus Christ. If this is so we might wonder why the old cannot be forgotten. After all, what Jesus reveals is better than the prophets. Nevertheless the continuity is kept. What was said *in the past* (*palai*) prepared the way for the most important communication of all (*i.e.* revelation through a Son). This is the real theme of the whole letter: the past has given way to better things.[1] This is the reason why the

---

[1] F. F. Bruce, *Comm.*, p. 2, distinguishes sharply between the evolution of the idea of God, which he rejects, and the idea of progressive revelation which he sees demonstrated here.

past (Old Testament religious ideas) keeps coming into the picture in this epistle, only to fade out again as better ideas fulfil and expand it. It is easy to see why the writer begins as he does. He sees value in the past (for God spoke through it), but he also sees its imperfections. What he says cannot fail to throw light on the Christian approach to the Old Testament. This makes his letter valuable for today as well as for his own time.

**2.** *In these last days* could be understood to mean *at the end of these days*, which points most clearly to a crisis, a new decisive revelation contrasted both with the variety of modes and the necessity in the past for repetition. A once-for-all revelation is clearly superior. The writer may have been thinking of the last days as the concluding days of the pre-Christian period, much as the Jewish teachers divided time between the present age and the age of the Messiah. According to this view, since Christians believed that Jesus was the Messiah, the 'last days' were the end of the old era. But in view of the corresponding expression 'at the end of the age' in 9:26, it is more probable that 'these last days' refers to the Christian era, which involves a new era compared with the old. When God spoke to men by a Son, it was meant to mark an end of all imperfect methods. The curtain had finally fallen on the previous age and the final age had now dawned.

When, in the Greek text, the writer says *a Son* rather than *his Son*, he does this to show the superior means used.[1] He is certainly not saying that God has more than one Son. He is implying that the finest of the prophets cannot stand comparison with a Son as a means of revelation. Of course, the idea of God's Son coming to men is a stumbling-block to many, but the writer does not defend his statement. He sees no need to do so, in spite of the fact that his own contemporaries would have been no more used to the idea than we are. The pagans thought sometimes of the offspring of the gods, but this is a very different idea from Jesus as Son of God. Our writer must have assumed that his readers would acknowledge this without question. But he does not say at first that he is thinking of Jesus.

[1] A. Nairne, E. Riggenbach and C. Spicq all agree that the omission of the article must be intentional. Westcott, *Comm.*, p. 7, attempts to express the idea in English as 'One who is God's Son'.

That comes later in 2:9.

There is naturally a language problem here. For it may be questioned how meaningful the father-son idea is in reference to God, however valuable it is in human affairs. But in the attempt to put divine truth into human language, the best that can be done is to use the nearest approximation; so long as this is borne in mind, it becomes full of meaning. The essence of the Christian revelation is that God is best seen in his Son. The human analogy is of course imperfect, because no human father is completely reflected in his son. But Jesus Christ perfectly shows all that is knowable about the Father. No wonder our writer is struck by the superiority of this kind of message compared with the means used in the past! He knows that if men cannot learn about God from the Son, no amount of prophetic voices or actions would convince them.

Before he identifies the Son as Jesus Christ, he gives a description of the Son. It is a profound description for it tells us about what he is and not about his appearance. The writer wants us to know first of all about the Son's relationship to the world of nature. It is understandable that he should begin with this, for the world of nature is our environment, our home. For many this is true to such a degree that they feel themselves encased in it and cannot conceive that anyone could be more powerful. This author's view of the world agrees with that which is seen throughout the New Testament. It is a view which begins with God as creator and goes on to see Jesus Christ as closely linked with him in the creative act. In this way the impersonal universe at once becomes personal. The writer declares that God has *appointed* his Son, which is an act of personal initiative here (the Greek aorist *ethēken* must be regarded as timeless). The important truth in this passage is that everything goes back to God.

Why is it said that God appointed the Son *the heir of all things*? Does this mean that he became what he was not before? Time elements are apt to confuse. It is best to think of the created order as it is, and then to be reminded that it belongs to Jesus Christ.[1] It is the present reality of the appointment that the

---

[1] F. F. Bruce, *Comm.*, p. 3, sees here an allusion to Ps. 2:8, a psalm cited in verse 5. The 'all things' go beyond the world and include the universe and the world to come.

writer is concerned about, and not about when it was made. Indeed, it is clear that the writer wants us to understand that there was never a time when the Son was not the heir. The two ideas, Sonship and heirship, are closely linked. In human affairs the eldest son is the natural heir. In the analogy a more profound thought is introduced. The heir is also the creator. He is not inheriting what he has not been connected with. He inherits what he himself made. The writer has at once plunged us into deep thinking about the origin of the world. Yet his interest in it is not theoretical but practical, reminding us of the teaching of Jesus about God and creation. It is his creation; he even notes the falling of the sparrows. It is reassuring to know that the Son has the same personal interest in the world around us. What this letter proceeds to say about Jesus Christ is clearly based on a high view of him.

The statement that God *created the world* through the Son is staggering. There is no denying that God could have made the universe apart from his Son, but the New Testament is at pains to show that he did not do so. The Christians were convinced that the same person who had lived among men was the one who created men. A letter such as Hebrews, written from this conviction, could not fail to present a more than human picture of Jesus Christ. It is noticeable that this writer uses the word for 'ages' (*aiōnes*) and not the usual word for worlds (*kosmoi*) when speaking about God's creative acts. The reason is that the word for 'ages' is more comprehensive, including within it the periods of time through which the created order exists. The more science discovers about the universe, the more marvellous is the thought that Christ is the agent through whom it was made. Rationalists may contend that scientific discovery makes the New Testament view of the world untenable, but the Christian claims the opposite. The greater man's understanding of the marvels of the universe, the greater the need for an adequate understanding of its origin. The belief in a personal creator is not less credible as man's penetration into space grows.

3. Having already plunged his readers into deep theological thoughts, the writer now goes yet deeper as he comments on Christ and God. What is the relation between them? We are told three things in answer; the first may be summed up as the

Son and the glory of God. *He reflects the glory of God*. To understand this claim we need to recapture the background to the
thought. The idea is of the radiance which bursts out of a
brilliant light.[1] It is a striking picture, like the sudden appearance
of a glorious dawn at sunrise. The rays of light pierce every
shred of darkness to shatter it. Even this picture poorly explains
the sense in which Jesus Christ reflects his Father's glory, because rays of light, however splendid, are after all impersonal.
Perhaps some of the readers would have remembered that in
the Jewish Book of Wisdom (7:26) the same word was applied
to wisdom, thought of as personified. At all events our writer
wants them to know that the glory of God could be seen in
Jesus Christ.[2] A similar idea comes in John 1:14 where an eye-
witness claims to have seen the glory. This can only mean that
the whole ministry of Jesus was evidence of God's glory. John
actually says this about the first miracle that Jesus performed
(Jn. 2:11). It was clearly a firm conviction among the early
Christians that in some way the glory of God was seen in a
human life. The most obvious occasion was when Jesus was
transfigured, but his whole mission, including his death, was
glorious for those who came to believe in him. To reflect the
glory of God in this way presupposes that the Son shares the
same essence as the Father, not just his likeness.

The second statement about the Son is that he *bears the very
stamp of his nature*. This goes considerably beyond the first statement, although it is bound up with it. This specifically brings
out the fact that the one who reflects God's glory shares his
nature. The word used here for stamp (*charaktēr*) is the word
for a die or an engraving. It is highly expressive since a stamp
on a wax seal will bear the same image as the engraving on the
seal. The illustration cannot be pressed too far, for it must not
be supposed that the Son is formally distinct from the Father as
the stamp is from the impression it creates. There is nevertheless an exact correspondence between the two. This statement

[1] The Greek word *apaugasma* is used by Philo in describing the Logos in his relation to
God, *De Opficio Mundi* (Loeb edition 136, pp. 114f.). For a discussion on this word, *cf.* R.
Williamson, *Philo and the Epistle to the Hebrews*, p. 36.

[2] On the concentration of ideas here expressing the becoming Visible of the Invisible and
of the becoming Intelligible of the Unintelligible, *cf.* Wickham, *Comm.*, p. 4.

itself contains a deep truth, for the exact resemblance relates to God's nature (*hypostaseōs*). The statement is not unimportant to the theological thinker, for it supports the view that Jesus was of the same nature as God. If so, no difference can be made between the nature of the Father and the nature of the Son. The writer has rapidly plunged his readers into profound theology, but he does not tarry to discuss it. He assumes that his readers will accept this view of Jesus Christ without question.

The third statement is about the Son's present part in creation. He is said to *uphold the universe by his word of power*. Two questions at once arise. In what sense is the upholding to be understood, and in what way does the word convey power? The word for 'upholding' (*pherōn*) has the sense of bearing up or sustaining, which shows that Jesus Christ is seen at the centre of the continuing stability of the universe. There is no place here for the deist's idea of God as a watchmaker who, having made a watch, leaves it to run on its own mechanism. The New Testament view is that God as creator and the Son as agent in creation are dynamically active in the created order. Yet how does the Son exercise his power?[1] It should be noted that the word *his* (*autou*) could refer either to the Son's power or to the power of the Father, but it makes little difference to the interpretation. The *word* is reminiscent of God's command at creation (*e.g.* 'Let there be light') and the idea in John 1:1–3 that all things were made by the Word (*Logos*), by which term Jesus Christ himself is meant. In the same way as the Word created, the Word sustains. The amazing stability of the created order is witness to the 'power' behind it.

After this series of great sayings about Jesus Christ, the writer now gives a clue to the predominant theme of his letter. *Purification for sins* is an agelong religious quest. Wherever there is any sense of sin there is generally present a strong desire to be cleansed from it. Man's varied attempts to obtain such purification present a wide spectrum of ideas ranging from the most desperate self-efforts to the suppressing of all effort and even of desire. Most systems begin with man and rely on his own strength of will. Notorious among such systems current in the

---

[1] G. Zuntz, *The Text of the Epistles* (London, 1953), p. 45, considers that the powerful word refers to the Logos, although the Greek word used is *rhēma*, not *logos*.

time of Jesus was that of the Pharisees who generally made good works and self-effort the measure of religious devotion. The idea that sins could be purified without such effort was foreign. Certainly the idea that Jesus Christ could purify sins was regarded as incredible. Jesus came up against this when he forgave a man's sin and was told that only God could forgive sins. But in this letter the idea goes further than forgiveness, for purification involves cleansing, in the sense of making pure.

It is strange that the writer of this letter gives no hint at this point about the way Jesus Christ has purified our sins. There is nothing to show how sin was dealt with, although as the letter goes on this becomes increasingly clear. It seems as if at this stage it is sufficient for him to mention a completed act (the aorist tense (*poiēsamenos*) demands this[1]) to summarize what the Son has done for men. The linking of the idea of sustaining the universe with that of purifying sins is most striking. The remoteness and awesomeness of the former is offset by the amazing intimacy of the latter. With a canvas as big as the universe, it is remarkable to find any mention at all of sins. But it is the latter theme which is to dominate the whole letter. It must be borne in mind that the Old Testament shows that provision is made for atonement by sacrifice, and since this letter is addressed to 'Hebrews' it is no doubt assumed that the readers would connect up 'purification' with the Day of Atonement, when it was emphasized that the cleansing of the people's sins could only be done through sacrifice. The writer shows later that the blood of bulls and goats cannot take away sins (10:4). For the time being he is content with the concisest possible summary.

After dealing with sins, the Son ascends the throne. Again the action is specific. It happened *after* the event of purifying sins, suggesting that the importance of the enthronement finds its key in the act of purifying.[2] Again we are dealing with the

---

[1] The Latin Vulgate translates this aorist with a present tense. This, however, is plainly incorrect. It is misleading because it appears to support the view that in his present position at God's right hand, Christ continues to atone for sins. The force of the aorist points to a finished work.

[2] Some see here a parallel with contemporary enthronement ideas. O. Michel, *Comm.*, p. 54, sees in Heb. 1 a similar sequence of exaltation, presentation and installation. He compares with 1 Enoch 71:14–17; 3 Enoch 10:3; Test. Lev. 5:2–7.

briefest of summaries. The *right hand* was traditionally the place of honour. The idea here is drawn from the practice of oriental kings to associate the heir with them in the exercise of government. Nevertheless, the idea of Messiah being seated at the right hand of God comes from Psalm 110:1. The association with this passage must have been in the writer's mind, since several times he quotes from this psalm later in the epistle. Indeed it may be said that this psalm forms an important part of the background to the whole letter. The writer had evidently been meditating on it, for it is from it that he develops the idea of a different order of priesthood. For the moment, however, he has other things on his mind before coming to that. The act of sitting (*he sat down, ekathisen*, aorist) carries a strong sense of fulfilment, for a sitting position is more suggestive of a finished task than a standing position. Indeed, this emphasis on Christ seated, which is supported by other New Testament evidence, shows conclusively that the sacrificial work is done. There is no longer any need for such sacrifice. The sitting position may also denote a position of high honour.[1] There is only one reference to Christ standing in heaven: when Stephen saw the Son of man in heaven he saw him standing at the right hand of God (Acts 7:56). This refers to his work of intercession, not his work of sacrifice. Sin has been dealt with, but the people of God still need an intercessor to plead for them – another theme developed later in this letter.

It is worth noting that *the Majesty on high* is a particularly respectful way of speaking of God. It reflects the Jewish reverence for the name of God which led devout Jews to avoid using it, and to substitute some phrase of respect. The writer uses an almost identical phrase in 8:1. The present statement is but a sign-post to the fuller exposition to follow. The writer clearly has a majestic view of God.

**4.** This verse serves two purposes: it concludes the introductory statement and sets the scene for the first main section. In view of all that has already been said, the Son's superiority to angels comes as no surprise. But why the comparison is made with angels at this point is not so clear. It may be that the writer

---

[1] *Cf.* P. E. Hughes, *Comm.*, p. 47.

had been meditating on the passages from the Old Testament which he proceeds to quote, with special interest in Psalm 8 (quoted in ch. 2) and Psalm 110, because he regarded them as Messianic. On the other hand the idea of Christ's superiority to angels may have occurred to him first and the relevant passages may have then sprung to mind. This latter suggestion is probable in view of the great Jewish interest in angels. It is understandable that, in an age when angels were highly regarded, the writer wished to show that God had now spoken through his Son in a much more effective way than through them.

Modern man is not so sure about angels, and the relevance of this passage requires some discussion. Angels appear several times in the Gospel stories and there is no denying that the evangelists regarded these supernatural beings as real. Indeed Jesus himself spoke of the guardian angels of children. Much modern criticism dispenses with angels by calling them mythical, *i.e.* some kind of personification of the messages of God. If this view is right there would be little relevance in the discussion of the Son's superiority to angels, except to demonstrate the ineffectiveness of mythical beings. But if there are spiritual dimensions represented by angels which cannot be regarded on the same level as natural experience, it at once becomes relevant to define the position of the Son in these spiritual spheres. The man of faith can sometimes penetrate into spheres which are blocked from many because of their unbelief. The 'angel' in the New Testament is invariably a messenger of God and it is this feature which is important to the writer's present argument.

He concentrates first on the *name*, which is again surprising. The modern saying, 'What's in a name?' certainly did not apply then, for names were more than a means of distinguishing people; they were means of saying something about those people. The name described the nature. But what is the name which *he has obtained*? Since Jesus Christ has already been introduced as the *Son* and this idea is the theme in the following Old Testament quotations, it is clear that the more excellent name is that of *Son*, which implies the closest and most intimate relationship. Since to the world at that time the name of 'angel' was so highly honoured as symbolic for a divine messenger, it may be that some were calling Jesus Christ by the name of 'angel' and making him no higher than the spiritual beings who were believed to influence the affairs of men. The idea of him as Son is much more exalted. Clearly Christianity would have taken on a very different complexion if Jesus' status had been no higher than an angel's. The readers may have belonged to a group similar to those at Colossae who were actually worshipping angels (Col. 2:18), or to a group who had previously been under the influence of Qumran, where angels were highly respected. It was essential for the Christian gospel to be rescued from this kind of approach. The excellence of the name given to Jesus Christ is found also in Philippians 2:9ff., where it is regarded as a sign of high honour.

## B. THE SUPERIORITY OF THE SON TO ANGELS (1:5 – 2:18)

Jewish readers would certainly have had a high regard for angels and the writer considers it necessary to show Christ's superiority to these revered heavenly messengers. The exalted character of Christ presupposed his superiority to angels, but a problem would arise over his manhood. In this section the writer leads his readers to recognize why Jesus had to become a real man if he was to be effective as a high priest on man's behalf, a function which no angel could perform.

### (i) Christ is superior in his nature (1:5–14)

**5.** Now begins a list of Old Testament quotations which set out to show the extent of the Son's superiority. The writer does not use his quotations in precisely the same way as in the original context. For example, he takes words which applied originally to an Israelite king and applies them to Jesus Christ. He regards this as a legitimate procedure. In this he is not alone, for there are other examples among the New Testament writers. Matthew's Gospel contains several. Matthew 2:5f. and 22:44 are instances where Old Testament passages are cited Messianically. Some of Matthew's fulfilments, however, are passages which the Jews never regarded as Messianic (*e.g.* Matthew 2:15 which quotes Hosea 11:1), but which the Spirit led the early Christians to recognize as such. It is clear that the Old Testament Scriptures possessed considerable authority for the

New Testament age and indeed the whole of this letter to the Hebrews testifies to this. It is further to be noted that the writer introduces the quotations in this chapter with the simple formula 'He says', which must refer to God. The Scriptures for him are the voice of God.

For an appreciation of the Christian approach to the Old Testament, it is necessary to bear in mind this flexible view of the fulfilment of prophecy. The idea of an immediate and a remote fulfilment is common and this explains how a prediction which had relevance in the past could have a more complete fulfilment in the future. This is in line with the nature of God who sees time in a way different from man's view of it. For him a thousand years is but a day, not to be regarded as an exact correlation, as some millenarians suppose, but as an indication of an essential difference of reckoning.

The first passage quoted comes from Psalm 2:7, a psalm which reflects a wartime environment and probably belongs to the historical situation described in 2 Samuel 7. Our writer is not, however, interested in the historical event, only in the suitability of the words to apply to the Messiah.[1] In the psalm, the words *You are my son* apply to David but clearly have only an imperfect application to him. The early Christians recognized the words as Messianic. They are quoted in Paul's address at Antioch in Pisidia (Acts 13:33). The Jews in his audience would have appreciated the force of this quotation; it added scriptural authority to the claims that Paul was making. What impresses the writer to the Hebrews is that, whereas the words apply to Jesus Christ, they cannot apply to an angel. If God addresses the Messiah in this way, the Messiah must therefore be superior to angels. But in what sense are the words *today I have begotten thee* to be understood? As applied to David they may refer to the anniversary of his coronation. Or, perhaps the word 'begotten' (*gegennēka*) is to be understood of the paternity of God, without indicating any specific point of time. When applied to Jesus Christ as Messiah the same applies. It could refer to the incarnation or to the resurrection. Indeed it is in the latter sense

---

[1] Héring, *Comm.*, p. 8, has pointed out that in spite of the forced interpretation of the Old Testament, the themes treated in the epistle lose none of their value. He considers that the author's shrewdness in culling suitable texts from the Bible is to be admired.

that it is applied in Acts 13:33. On the other hand it is not clear that in Hebrews any importance is attached to the time element. The writer is clearly more concerned to demonstrate the significance of the begetting in terms of the Son's status, rather than to tie it down to a specific occasion.[1]

The second quotation is another passage which was widely accepted as referring to the Messiah. It comes from 2 Samuel 7:14, from an oracle given to David. There is a close link between this passage and the last. The idea contained in it caught the imagination of many Old Testament writers, as seen in their belief in a coming Messiah. The father-son relationship is again the key idea for our writer, for it marks the Messiah as distinct from the creator-creature relationship between God and the angels. Historically the words may be said to find a partial fulfilment in Solomon, the son of David, who completed the building of the first temple. But the perfect fulfilment did not come until the time of David's greater Son. Both the kingdom and the temple needed re-interpreting in spiritual terms and it was one of the main burdens of our writer to do this in reference to the tabernacle which foreshadowed the temple. It is worth noting that there is some mention of a father-son relationship in Psalm 89:26f., followed by a reference to the first-born, a combination of ideas which is also found in verses 5 and 6 of this chapter. Since our writer is deeply versed in the Old Testament it is probable that his acquaintance with Psalm 89 has also influenced his selection of some of the other Old Testament passages cited here.

**6.** The words *And again, when he brings the first-born into the world*, which introduce the next quotation, themselves echo the Old Testament passage mentioned above (*i.e.* Ps. 89:27). There the word *first-born* is used ('I will make him the first-born') of David. It is clear that in the writer's mind the 'first-born' (*prōto-tokos*) of verse 6 is the *Son* of the previous verses. It is suggestive that the same term is used of Jesus Christ by the apostle Paul (Col. 1:15, 18; Rom. 8:29), qualified in the following way: first-

---

[1] Bruce, *Comm.*, p. 13, takes 'this day' to refer to the occasion when Jesus was 'vested with His royal dignity as Son of God'. Hughes, *Comm.*, pp. 54f., points out that Augustine regarded the begetting as eternal, not temporal, but Hughes thinks the primary reference here is to the resurrection.

born of all creation, first-born from the dead, first-born among many brethren. The expression clearly becomes invested with profound meaning when applied to Christ. The writer here does not, as Paul does, go on to enlarge on the superiority of Christ. He is content rather to make statements which will produce a profound impression of superiority. The primary reference must be to the incarnation to draw attention to the fact that when Jesus Christ was born the function of angels was to worship. In the writer's view the angels' homage is proof that they regarded the Son as superior. His meaning is clear enough, but a problem arises over the quotation.

The formula *he says* (*legei*), which introduces the quotation, is a familiar one in this epistle. The subject is omitted, but God is clearly meant. The scripture quotations are not simply formal Old Testament statements, but God himself speaking personally out of the text. This gives an indication of the view of the inspiration of scripture held by the writer. He intends it to be understood that the quotation he makes comes with authority, although no such precise quotation as *Let all God's angels worship him* appears in the Hebrew Bible. In two passages in the Septuagint (Ps. 97:7 and Dt. 32:43) there is a close approximation; the latter passage includes the conjunction 'and' (*kai*) which is present in the Greek original of our verse, but omitted in most English translations. Deuteronomy 32:43 is part of the song of Moses which looks ahead to the triumph of Israel's Lord over his adversaries.[1] Our writer transfers the triumph from this song to the Messiah, whom he sees as the 'first-born'. The same Old Testament passage is quoted by Paul in Romans 15:10 where the Gentiles are called on to rejoice. It is worth noting that Paul introduces his quotation from Deuteronomy 32:43 with the same formula (*legei*) as used in Hebrews, all the more significant because it is not usual for the apostle to use the formula without stating the subject. Another interesting parallel between the two New Testament passages is the double use of the word *again* (*palin*) in successive quotations as if intended to heighten

---

[1] There was a tradition that when Adam was created the angels were invited to worship him; they refused to do so until Michael set the example (*cf.* also *Life of Adam and Eve*, xiii–xiv). *Cf.* C. H. Dodd, *The Bible and the Greeks* (London, 1935), pp. 156f., and W. D. Davies, *Paul and Rabbinic Judaism* (London, 1945), p. 42.

the close connection between them. The practice of heaping up scriptural quotations in the manner of both Paul and the writer to the Hebrews can be paralleled in Jewish literature. In the passages under comparison, Paul finds a link word in 'the Gentiles', while Hebrews does so in the idea of *angels*. The statement that angels are commanded to worship the first-born suggests that this is their proper duty.

7. Having established the superiority of Jesus Christ over angels, representing the most exalted of God's creatures, the writer presses home his point with further references to the Old Testament. The first comes from Psalm 104:4, but not in the sense found in the Hebrew text, which makes no reference to angels. The writer clearly recognizes the authority of the Greek text which has interpreted the Hebrew text in the same way as rabbinical writers did. The words *Who makes his angels wind*, are intended to show a strong contrast between the angels and the Son. Whereas the Son is said to be begotten, they are said to be made. The distinction is not accidental. The angels, as creatures, can function only within the limits for which they were created, that is to carry out the wishes of their Creator. Both angels (*angeloi*) and servants (*leitourgoi*) have a very different function from the Son. Their task is one of service. The Son's task is one of rule (as verses 8 and 9 show).

It is suggestive that the description of the angels is in terms of the natural world. *Winds* and *fire* are best seen as representative of powerful natural agencies, rather than as illustrative of what is insubstantial. There are Old Testament parallels to the idea of supernatural agencies behind the elements of nature (*e.g.* Pss. 18:10; 35:5). There is some suggestion of irresistible power in the imagery used, for both wind and fire can be irresistibly destructive, or, if properly harnessed, powerfully constructive. But the writer's main thought in this epistle is the angels' acknowledgment of a power greater than themselves, indeed the power which appointed them. Whereas these spiritual agencies are more powerful than men, they are nevertheless surpassed by the power of the Son. If it be thought that behind this idea is an outmoded view of the world as subject to invisible personal influences, rather than the modern idea of cause and effect which leaves no room for supernatural manipulation, it should be remembered that the writer is not here giving a scientific comment on such natural phenomena as 'wind' and 'flame'. His purpose is wholly spiritual, a demonstration of the supreme importance of the Son over all creatures. At the same time what he says is not in conflict with a scientific view of the world.

**8–9.** The contrast between the angels and the Son is brought out unmistakably in the construction of the Greek sentence (*men . . . de*). The quotation setting out the sovereignty of the Son comes from Psalm 45:6–7. The original context of the psalm was quite different, referring to the marriage feast of some king of Israel. Yet it was widely recognized to have a much more extended meaning and was in fact regarded as Messianic. It is in this latter sense that it is here quoted. The opening words, *Thy throne, O God, is for ever and ever*, cause a problem, for they can be taken either as a direct address to the Son in which case the implication cannot be avoided that the Son is being described as God,[1] or less probably the words can be understood to mean 'The throne of your God', or 'God is your throne', in which case the implication that the Son is God is avoided. If the historical context is borne in mind it is difficult to imagine an earthly king being directly addressed in this way, except in a restricted sense, and it is better therefore to regard the statement as finding its only true fulfilment in Christ. It should be noted, however, that the deification of the king finds parallels in pagan literature (*cf.* also Jn. 10:34f.). Nevertheless, since in Hebrew thought the occupant of the throne of David was regarded as God's representative, it is in this sense that the king could be addressed as God.[2]

The next words, *the righteous sceptre is the sceptre of thy kingdom*, focus on the character of the Son's sovereignty. The Old Testament frequently emphasizes the idea of righteousness, not only the righteousness of God, but also the need for righteousness on the part of the people. The theme is particularly relevant to the main subject of this epistle. The Son gives no grudging acceptance of a righteous standard. It forms the centre of his

---

[1] F. Rendall, *Comm.*, p. 10, considers that *ho theos* can be regarded only as vocative here.

[2] For a fuller discussion, see Leslie C. Allen, 'Psalm 45:7–8 (6–7) in Old and New Testament settings' in *Christ the Lord*, ed. Harold H. Rowdon (Leicester, 1982), pp. 220–242.

affection. It is part of his nature – *Thou hast loved righteousness.* Such a positive approach to righteousness involves a definite rejection of its opposite, *lawlessness* (*anomia*). It is typical of Hebrew poetic style for an idea to be stated, followed by a denial of its opposite. Those who love righteousness have no alternative but to hate lawlessness, and yet only Jesus Christ the Son has ever perfectly fulfilled both objectives.

The anointing of the Son is not to be thought of in connection with coronation rites, but as symbolizing the joy of festival occasions, when the practice of anointing was followed. This accounts for the expression *oil of gladness.* The word used (*agalliasis*) expresses a strong sense of gladness. The same idea occurs in Psalm 23:5, where the anointing is a sign of favour. The words *beyond thy comrades* in the original psalm probably refer to other kings and stress the superiority of the king being addressed (*cf.* Ps. 89:27).[1] It may, however, be less formal and refer to the companions at the feast. Whichever it is, it here serves the purpose of focusing attention on yet another aspect of the superiority of the Son. The transference of the idea to the Son needed no explanation, since the familiar title 'Christ' (as the corresponding title Messiah) means 'the Anointed One'. Peter fastened on this thought in his exposition to Cornelius (Acts 10:38). Moreover the idea of anointing is important in an epistle whose theme is the high-priesthood of Christ, for all the priests of Aaron's line were anointed on taking up their office.

**10–12.** The next three verses create a problem because the passage cited from Psalm 102:25–27 contains no reference to the Son. In the Septuagint verses 1–22 are addressed to God, but verses 23–28 consist of the answer. The writer understands God to be the speaker here. In his mind it was legitimate to transfer to the Son what applied to God, since he has already drawn attention to the eternal character of his throne. The passage has many interesting features which are apt when applied to Jesus Christ. The writer has already spoken of the Son's part in creation and in view of this the Psalm 102 passage is appropriate. In applying the passage, the writer draws attention to a pro-

---

[1] Bruce, *Comm.*, p. 21, sees a reference to the 'many sons' of 2:10, and the *metochoi* (the sharers in Christ) in 3:14.

found idea about the Son, *i.e.* his changelessness. The earth and heavens seem substantial enough, yet *they will perish*. There was a widespread belief in the Graeco-Roman world that the world and indeed the universe was indestructible.[1] The Christian view expressed here would be in stark contrast. This transitoriness of the apparently changeless material creation serves to heighten the contrast with the divine stability. There is a majestic ring about the words: *but thou remainest*. This statement focuses attention on unshakeable stability, which is further enhanced by the striking picture of God rolling up the heavens and earth, now tattered like a worn-out garment, as if they are of no further use. This magnificent glimpse by the psalmist into the winding up of the present age is intended to lead to the climax: *But thou art the same*. In face of the disintegration everywhere else, the unchangeable character of the Son stands out in unmistakable contrast.

Christian readers would find no difficulty in applying the words quoted to the Son, although in the psalm they refer to the Father. It would be different for Jewish readers since there is no evidence that the psalm was ever considered by them to be wholly Messianic. Nevertheless the writer's conviction that Christ is timeless is an essential feature of his theological approach throughout this epistle. It is one of the most dramatic distinctions between the order of Melchizedek and the order of Aaron, which forms the key to the central part of his argument.

**13.** It has already been noted that Psalm 110:1, which is next quoted, has been in the writer's mind at the opening of his epistle when he speaks of the Son sitting down at the right hand of the Majesty in heaven (verse 3). The idea of enthronement is now repeated to bring out the most obvious contrast between Jesus Christ and the highest order of created beings. At no time are angels ever conceived of as sitting, and therefore the enthronement of Jesus at once establishes his superiority. Not only is his sovereignty stressed, but also his absolute power over his enemies. That this idea is prominent in the writer's mind is clear from his repeating the statement in chapter 10:12, 13. In both chapters 1 and 10 the enthronement and victory are

[1] Héring, *Comm.*, *ad loc.*

linked with Jesus Christ's atonement for sins. Moreover, this theme is found elsewhere in the New Testament. It occurs in Peter's sermon at Pentecost (Acts 2:34f.), where it is again set over against the Jewish action in crucifying Jesus. Whatever men do, God has appointed Jesus both Lord and Christ. It was this claim of Peter's, based on this same psalm, which resulted in the remarkable mass conviction in the minds of Peter's audience. Those who responded on the day of Pentecost would have cause to remember Peter's cogent use of this psalm. Not only so but Paul echoes the same idea in his letter to Corinth (1 Cor. 15:25) in the course of proving that Christ must have absolute sovereignty, even over death itself. A reminiscence of Peter's use of the psalm may be noted in his first letter (1 Pet. 3:22). The idea of God's supremacy over his enemies is also found in Psalm 8:6, which Paul, in fact, quotes in conjunction with Psalm 110:1 in 1 Corinthians 15. There is no doubt, however, that Psalm 110 has a special place in the thought of this writer since it recurs several times in his exposition.

**14.** There is a marked contrast between the enthroned Son and the ministering angels. The function of the latter is essentially one of service and the *all* (*pantes*) significantly includes all ranks of angels. Even the noblest are *sent forth to serve*. There is here a contrast between the temporary servant position of the Son in his ministry (*cf*. Phil. 2:7) and his discarding of that position following the completion of his mission. The angels, on the other hand, are committed to constant service and will never be enthroned.

The writer is certainly not wishing to belittle the function of angels, for he notes that their service is *for the sake of those who are to obtain salvation*. It may seem strange that no definition of salvation is given, which suggests that the readers already knew what was meant. It was not even defined as Christian salvation, although that is clearly assumed. The gist of the whole letter is bent on explaining salvation in terms of offerings and what they achieve. Indeed, the writer echoes the theme almost immediately in the next passage. What is important at the moment is to observe that heavenly messengers are occupied in a ministry directed towards the salvation of men. The focus of God's plan of salvation is on people, thought of as heirs. The idea of inheritance does not come out clearly in the RSV, although it is present in the Greek (*klēronomein*). NIV has 'those who will inherit salvation'. It is familiar in New Testament thought, for Christian salvation is thought of as something worth possessing. Believers are called heirs, even joint-heirs with Christ (*cf.* Rom. 8:17). The inheritance idea, moreover, recurs in Hebrews 3 and 4 (under the metaphor of a rest), in Hebrews 9 (under the imagery of a will) and in Hebrews 11 (in relation to the promises to faith).

It may justly be claimed that in this first chapter of Hebrews are met many of the dominant ideas which recur in the epistle. Although these are not expressed in a formal sense, they are nevertheless an effective introduction to the following discussion.

## (ii) An exhortation against drifting (2:1–4)

**1–2.** Although it is early yet in the course of the discussion for the writer to give a definite exhortation, it is nevertheless characteristic of him to include brief asides. One interesting detail is the introducing phrase (*therefore, dia touto,* on this account). No break is intended between the discussion of chapter 1 and the beginning of chapter 2. The connection is not, however, at once transparent. The real link seems to be salvation which becomes the crucial challenge of this exhortation (verse 3). Moreover the part played by angels in establishing the dignity of the message is another link. *The message declared by angels* is reminiscent of what Paul says of the law in Galatians 3:19, that 'it was ordained by angels'. In both cases the agency of angels is intended to show that God's message is too important to be ignored – it does not come from men. In the present statement the dignity of the Law[1] is demonstrated by the fact that any transgression of it will certainly be punished. The word rendered *retribution* (*misthapodosia*) is peculiar to Hebrews. In 10:35 and 11:26 it means 'reward'. The writer's purpose is to awaken the conscience to the grave consequences of neglecting the message of God. He has no doubt that retribu-

---

[1] Bruce, *Comm.*, pp. 28–29, shows that in this letter law is not presented as the antithesis of grace in relation to salvation. He calls it an anticipatory sketch of Christ's saving work.

tion, when it comes, will be *just*.

The challenge to the readers to give heed is strongly expressed in verse 1. In view of the importance of what has been heard, the readers are urged to *pay the closer attention*, words which indicate a careful observance of what has been said.[1] It is not surprising that the exhortation is followed by a solemn warning, the first of many in this epistle. It shows clearly that the writer has no intention of writing a purely academic treatise, but aims throughout to emphasize the practical significance of the points he makes. He is conscious that he is dealing with a situation which could empty the gospel of its essential meaning. He is not thinking of a deliberate refusal to heed, but of an almost helpless slipping away – literally to flow past like driftwood in a river. Hence the words, *lest we drift away*.

**3.** The crucial question is then introduced, which provides a clue to the understanding of the author's purpose. *How shall we escape if we neglect such a great salvation?* There was evidently a serious danger of neglect on the part of the readers, for otherwise this challenge would not have been introduced so early. But what was the nature of the neglect? It is defined only by way of contrast. In some way or other the greatness of the salvation was being affected. Indeed, it is highly probable that in the writer's mind the readers were in danger of turning their backs completely on the Christian gospel. If this is so the greatness of the salvation only increases the tragedy. The kind of rhetorical question used here is typical of this epistle. The answer is assumed: there is no *escape*. The idea of *escape* linked with salvation expresses salvation in terms of deliverance, a concept found elsewhere in the New Testament. It recurs in Hebrews 2:14–15 in the sense of deliverance from the power of the devil. In common with other New Testament writings, Hebrews sees the non-Christian life as a life of continual bondage.

The details given to explain how the writer and his associates came to know about salvation supply valuable information about the writer's experience. The basic originator of the mes-

---

[1] Westcott, *Comm.*, p. 36, takes the adverb as expressing an absolute rather than a relative excess. It would have the sense 'with most particular attention' rather than 'with more attention'. The former is clearly the stronger and more effectively heightens the distinction between what Christ offers and what the readers had previously known.

sage is the Son, here described as *the Lord*, a significant New Testament title for Jesus Christ which links him with the Old Testament name for God (*Kyrios*). There is here no doubt that Jesus himself first declared the meaning of his own mission. His message, because personal and direct, was superior to the message conveyed through angels. But the writer had clearly not been a hearer of the Lord himself, which distinguishes him from the twelve apostles and indeed from all those who accompanied Jesus during any part of his ministry. The message had apparently been passed on by others, *it was attested to us by those who heard him*. According to the most natural understanding of this statement, they were no doubt the apostles, although other reliable witnesses are not excluded. Most scholars consider these words to be conclusive against Paul being the writer, on the grounds that he would not have admitted receiving his gospel from others. Moreover, it could be argued that the words suggest that the first generation of Christians has now passed and that the writer and his associates depend on that earlier generation for their understanding of the gospel.

4. There was divine confirmation of the message through *signs and wonders and various miracles and by gifts of the Holy Spirit*. In the Synoptic Gospels there are many instances of 'wonders' and 'miracles' happening in the ministry of Jesus, while John's Gospel describes in a distinctive way the supernatural happenings as 'signs'. These three words thus present a comprehensive description of the miracles in the Gospels. What is important to note is that these supernatural events have a definite value as confirmation of the message. There is no suggestion that the miracles prove the basic facts of the gospel, such as the exalted character of Jesus Christ. Some apologists have based their claims about the divinity of Jesus on the abundance of miracles, but this is inadequate. Jesus would still have been divine if he had performed no miracles. Indeed he refused to give signs when asked to do so. Men must first come to believe in him before the miracles become in any sense 'signs'. Nevertheless, as John shows so clearly in his Gospel, the signs have a confirmatory value, pointing to the glory of Jesus Christ. It is impossible to excise all miracles from the message, as some seek to do, because the message itself is a supernatural communi-

cation of God to men. Moreover, the signs and wonders continued to be performed during the first Christian era as the first witnesses told the message. The book of Acts cannot be denuded of its miracles without impoverishing the history of early Christianity. If these miracles were no more than myths the writer to the Hebrews must have been grossly mistaken in recognizing in them the witness of God. The verb translated 'bore witness' (*synepimartyrountos*) means 'bearing witness together with' and must refer to God bearing witness to us. Indeed, the writer would not have appealed to miracles if there had been any possibility of the readers maintaining they had neither seen nor heard of them.[1] He treats them as common knowledge.

The *gifts of the Holy Spirit* are in a rather different category, although closely allied. The writer is conscious that the first witnesses did not declare the message in their own strength or by their own ingenuity. The word used here for gifts is not the usual New Testament word (*charismata*), but the more general word for distributions (*merismoi*). The emphasis thus falls on the distributor. The gifts of the Spirit are also mentioned in Acts and especially by Paul in 1 Corinthians, and were a prominent characteristic of early Christianity. They were evidences of God's approval of the proclaiming of the gospel. There is a hint of both diversity (*distributed*) and sovereignty (*according to his own will*). Our writer has a high view of the activity of the Spirit and this first mention of him will be followed by several other important statements (*cf.* 3:7; 6:4; 9:8, 14; 10:15, 29). The stress on the gifts removes all justification for human pride among the early Christians since distribution did not depend on man's capabilities, but on the Spirit's sovereign will (*cf.* the similar statement in 1 Cor. 12:11).

*(iii) The humiliation and glory of Jesus (2:5–9)*

**5.** The writer next reminds his readers that, in spite of the dignified status of angels, it is not to them that the coming world is to be subjected. This is intended again to enhance the superiority of the Son as the following quotation from Psalm

---

[1] *Cf.* Bruce, *Comm.*, pp. 30f.

8:4–6 shows. The key thought is that God *subjected, i.e.* he took the initiative. The subject of the sentence is missing from the Greek, but is clearly carried forward from verse 4, as the opening word *for* (*gar*) shows, and must therefore be God. The meaning of *the world to come* is a matter of debate. The Greek expression (*hē oikoumenē hē mellousa*) can be understood in various ways, as for instance (i) of the afterlife, (ii) of the new order inaugurated by Jesus Christ, *i.e.* the fulfilment of the looked for 'age to come' which was now come in the present kingdom of God, or (iii) of the end of the present age. There may be truth in all three, but the second seems to be brought most clearly into focus by the context. It is worth noting that the word used here for 'world' is not *kosmos* (the world as a system), but the world of inhabitants (*oikoumenē*). The writer is more interested in the personal than the abstract. He sees salvation as a corporate reality (*cf.* verse 10 'many sons').

**6.** The formula used to introduce the quotation from Psalm 8 is surprising. *It has been testified somewhere* may suggest that the writer could not remember the reference, but it may simply be used because precise reference was unimportant. Against the latter view is the fact that it is not used to introduce the other Old Testament quotations in the present context, but in support of it is the fact that Philo on occasions uses a similarly vague formula (*de Ebrietate 61*). What seems to be clear is the great importance attached to the words of Scripture, irrespective of their human author or historical context. There is no doubt that for the writer the very words of Scripture are authoritative.

The use of Psalm 8 is nevertheless interesting, for this passage was never considered to be Messianic. The original context is man, yet not in his ordinary state but in his ideal state, indicated by the use of the title 'son of man'. At creation man was given dominion over the earth, but ever since the fall that authority to subject has been lacking. The psalm is only perfectly fulfilled, therefore, in the ideal Man, Jesus Christ, who alone has that authority. The writer sees a fulfilment of this psalm in a way that the Jews never foresaw. The same psalm is cited by Jesus (Mt. 21:16) and Paul (1 Cor. 15:27),[1] both in a way which points

---

[1] There may well be here a reference to the idea of Christ as the last Adam, which Paul mentions in 1 Cor. 15, and alludes to in Rom. 5. Some see it also in Phil. 2. *Cf.* C. K.

to its fulfilment in Jesus himself.

*What is man?* The question which forms the basis of this quotation here is more dramatic when placed in its original context. The psalmist thinks of man against the background of the glory of the created order generally. The contrast is so marked that man's stature is seen in its true perspective, as a special concern of the Creator, yet in a sense overshadowed by the glory of God in the universe. The *son of man* becomes for the writer an idealized man and serves as an admirable introduction to Jesus Christ since he used the title so many times of himself. Indeed the only other person ever to use the title of him was Stephen (Acts 7:56). This identification of Jesus as Son of man leads to the development of the idea in the next statement. Our author is not interested in actually calling Jesus by this title, but he clearly recognized the appropriateness of the reference in the psalm to him. It is remarkable that when at length he introduces a name in 2:9 it is the name of Jesus he chooses.

7. *For a little while lower than the angels* is intended in the psalm to be a mark of man's dignity. It points to the distinctive superiority of man over all other created beings except angels. This dignity does not accord too well with the evolutionary theory of man's development, for the psalmist sees man's dignity to be directly due to God's initiative. There is no suggestion of a gradual process. What the psalmist and indeed the writer to the Hebrews are mainly concerned with is man's present status. Yet the crowning with glory and honour and the subjecting of all things is clearly seen ideally rather than actually. In fact it was accomplished only in one man – Jesus Christ. He was certainly crowned with glory, as Paul points out in Philippians 2:9ff., and to him all things are to be subjected, as Paul shows in 1 Corinthians 15:27f. The writer here recognizes that man generally does not possess authority over all things, so he proceeds in the next section to concentrate on Jesus.

8. The words *nothing outside his control* have meaning only

---

Barrett, *From first Adam to last* (London, 1962) and R. Scroggs, *The Last Adam* (Oxford, 1966) for a general discussion of the Adam theme, but neither mentions this Hebrews passage. Ps. 8 contributed to this viewpoint as is clear from Paul's citation from the Psalm in 1 Cor. 15:27.

when applied to the Son of man, the perfect fulfilment of Psalm 8. Since Hebrews has already said that the Son sustains all things by his word of power (1:2–3), it is not to be wondered at that all things are under his control. In this respect Jesus has superiority over the angels. Yet in his incarnation it did not appear to be so, a thought brought out by the words *we do not yet see everything in subjection to him*. This subjection is regarded as still future but the writer has no doubt regarding its ultimate fulfilment. Some regard the subjection to be 'to man' rather than 'to Christ', but since the former can be achieved only through the latter it makes little difference to the meaning.[1]

**9.** The point has now been reached for Jesus to be introduced by name, and it is significant that the name chosen is his human name. After the exalted concepts in the first section, the writer shows him to be one who is closely identified with man. There is a curious mixture of seeing and not seeing in this epistle. The writer acknowledges some things which are not seen (*cf.* 2:8; 11:1f.). He presents a firm basis for present faith in what can now been seen, hence the importance of the words, *But we see Jesus*. Moreover, in order to leave no doubt about the character of the one seen he combines two ideas which appear at first to be opposite: *the suffering of death* and *crowned with glory and honour*. The specific idea of the suffering of Jesus comes into the epistle here for the first time, although it is indirectly implied in the reference to the purification of sins in 1:3. Suffering is to be a dominant theme throughout the letter. Indeed, the present combination of suffering and glory supplies the key to the writer's understanding of the Christian faith. The suffering of death is a major problem to all men, but is a particular problem for the Son of God unless some explanation of it can be given. The suffering itself belongs to a less exalted status than that of the angels, hence the statement applied to Jesus, *who for a little while was made lower than the angels* (which could also be rendered 'a little' instead of 'a little while'). This present section of the letter is complementary to the first section. The glory and honour bestowed on Jesus is the direct result of suffering. The combi-

---

[1] As Westcott remarks, 'In "the Son of man" (Jesus) then there is the assurance that man's sovereignty shall be gained.'

nation between the two ideas, which is alien to natural thought, is nevertheless central in the New Testament. It is not only Jesus himself who gains glory through suffering, but all his followers (cf. Rom. 6:8ff.; 2 Tim. 2:11–12). The problem of the passion of Jesus becomes transformed into a path to glory once it is recognized that the God who bestows the glory is the one who permits the suffering.

The result of the sacrifice and glorification of Jesus is stated to be *so that by the grace of God he might taste death for every one.* Since the tasting of death is synonymous with the suffering of death, this statement poses an enigma for the interpreter and many suggestions have been made. The question is complicated by an alternative reading, *chōris* (apart from God) instead of *chariti* (by the grace of God), which is capable of various interpretations.[1] Taking 'grace' as the better attested reading, the emphasis in the tasting of death must fall on its result, that is 'for every one'. It is important to notice that the death of Jesus is related to man, not just corporately, but individually. Although the Greek could be understood to refer to 'everything', the main thought in the present passage is so clearly personal that 'everyone' is the more likely meaning.

If the alternative reading is considered, it would introduce a strange statement, for the tasting of death would then be said to be 'apart from God'. This would presumably mean that Jesus died apart from his divinity (the sense in which the Nestorians took it), or as a reference to God forsaking him in the sense of his cry of abandonment on the cross (Mt. 27:46), or that God alone was excepted from the results of the death of Jesus (cf. 1 Cor. 15:27). Even if the reading itself were better attested, the possible explanations are less in line with the context than the reading 'by the grace of God', which explains the provision made for Jesus while he was tasting death.

---

[1] Héring, p. 17, prefers the reading 'apart from', although it is not supported by many MSS, because it is the more difficult reading. But the alternative is so much better supported that it must stand. The variant no doubt arose because of the problem of thinking of grace as an instrument of death. R. V. G. Tasker, *NTS* 1 (1954–5), p. 184, regards this reading as a correction based on 1 Cor. 15:27. Cf. also J. C. O'Neill, 'Hebrews II.9', *JTS* 17 (1966), pp. 79–82, who takes it to mean 'far from God' in a spatial sense.

*(iv) His work on man's behalf (2:10–18)*

**10.** There is a direct connection between the statement just made and the words which follow, *i.e. For it was fitting*. It may not at first seem obvious why the death of Jesus was fitting. Indeed this has always presented a problem to theologians who have endeavoured to explain the fittingness of the sufferings of Jesus. It must be remembered that to Jews the idea of a suffering Messiah was abhorrent and the Christian claim that it was fitting must be viewed against this background. Moreover, from the point of view of man, with his sense of need, it was highly fitting that the grace of God should be extended towards him, whatever the reason for the method used. Some may feel that to judge what is fitting is too subjective a business, but this is not so with God, who can never do anything unworthy or inappropriate. Whatever the reason for the cross, there is no doubt that it is most revealing of the nature of God. It is in this sense that it was fitting.

The expression *he, for whom and by whom all things exist* could refer either to God the Father or to Jesus, but in view of the statement that the agent of creation made Jesus, the pioneer (*archēgos*), perfect, the former must be the right interpretation. The same expression is applied to God in Romans 11:36. The idea of the exalted position of Jesus (as in chapter 1) adds tremendous significance to his sufferings (as here), as if the whole created order was designed on the principle that glory could be secured through suffering. It is further important to note that the creative activity of God is extended from the material creation to the spiritual and personal realm (*bringing many sons to glory*).[1] The sequence of thought expresses the multiplications of glory. Not only was the Son crowned with glory, but his glory is shared with those he saves. The expression here is suggestive, for the purpose of the sufferings of Jesus is seen to be vicarious, that is, it reaches its climax in its effect upon others.

The idea of Jesus as the *pioneer of salvation* is another suggestive figure of speech, for the word means one who goes before

---

[1] A problem arises, however, over the tense of the word 'bringing' (*agagonta*, aorist participle). The aorist seems to be used with the force of a present tense, expressing a simultaneous action.

and leads the way. The implication is that if Jesus had not blazed the way there would have been no salvation. The pioneer in this sense is more than an example for others to follow. His mission is to provide the basis on which salvation can be offered to others. The word *archēgos* (pioneer) occurs again in Hebrews 12:2, where as here, it is linked with the idea of perfection. It is clear that this concept was important in the mind of the writer. It occurs also in Acts 3:15, 5:31, on both occasions as a description of Jesus. In the latter instance it is stated that God had exalted Jesus to this position. The title 'pioneer' is therefore a title of honour. It is significant moreover that in Acts 5:31 it is linked with the title 'Saviour', a combination of ideas which is closely paralleled here. The idea of perfection is prominent in this epistle, but its meaning when applied to Christ is different from that applied to believers. In his case he was already perfect. Some interpreters claim that God brought his Son to a perfection he did not previously have.[1] But this seems to imply degrees of perfection, a concept which raises considerable difficulties when applied to Jesus Christ. The meaning is rather 'to bring to completion' in the sense that suffering was necessary before Jesus could be the complete pioneer of salvation, or the perfect high priest.[2] He did not need suffering for his own salvation, but it was indispensable if others were to be saved. Without any theoretical explanations, the writer assumes, in common with all the New Testament writers, that the sufferings of Christ and man's salvation are inextricably bound up together.

11. Another recurring theme in this epistle is that of sanctification which is first introduced here (cf. 9:13; 10:10, 14, 29; 13:12). It is important to establish the precise meaning of the idea. The common use of the term 'to sanctify' is to make holy, but this cannot apply to Jesus Christ. Nor is this meaning the original meaning of the word, for it is used in the Old Testament with reference both to the Levitical offerings and to the people

---

[1] Cf. Héring, Comm., p. 18.

[2] For the idea of perfection in this epistle, cf. A. Wikgren, 'Patterns of Perfection in the Epistle to the Hebrews', NTS 6 (1959–60), pp. 159ff. Cf. also P. J. du Plessis, TELEIOS: The Idea of Perfection in the New Testament (Kampen, 1959), and C. Spicq, Comm. 1, pp. 64ff., who sets out in a detailed way parallels between Hebrews and Philo in the use of such a term as teleios.

to whom the offerings applied. In that case to sanctify meant to set aside for a holy purpose, a sense which is certainly more applicable to Jesus Christ. *He who sanctifies* is here the pioneer of salvation, who has nonetheless first sanctified himself (*cf.* Jn. 17:19). When he sanctifies others he is leading them into an experience through which he himself has passed. He is setting them apart for salvation. Here the focus of attention is not, however, on the act of sanctification, but on the common *origin* of both sanctifier and sanctified, *i.e.* God himself. In this way the work of Christ is seen to be effected, both in its completion and its application, by God himself. Moreover the sending of the Son on a mission of suffering arose from the same source – from God's love for mankind and his desire to provide an effective means of salvation.

The close connection between the sanctifier and the sanctified is further seen in the fact that the former is *not ashamed* of the latter. Indeed the sanctified are regarded as *brethren*. This follows the similar idea in Romans 8:29 (*cf.* also Jn. 20:17), and the further thought that believers are fellow-heirs with Christ (Rom. 8:17). It may be wondered why the idea of being ashamed is introduced to be dismissed. A similar rejection of shame is found in Hebrews 11:16 where God is not ashamed to be called the God of the patriarchs who died in faith. By way of contrast we may note that Jesus said that the Son of man would be ashamed of those who are ashamed of him (Mk. 8:38). Those identified with Jesus will share his glory. Far from being ashamed of them, he will be delighted to regard them as 'brethren'. There could be no greater contrast between the destiny of believers and unbelievers. Shame and glory are mutually exclusive.

**12.** Three quotations follow, all designed to show the close relationship between Christ and his people. The first comes from Psalm 22, which was recognized by the early Christians to be Messianic. Its most powerful application was the quotation of its opening words by Jesus on the cross. The cry of abandonment fitted perfectly the pathos of the just dying for the unjust. But the part of the psalm here quoted is the opening statement of the more triumphant conclusion (verse 22). In spite of the sufferings of the former part, the psalmist now breaks into a confident assertion, *I will proclaim thy name to my brethren*. The parallel with Christ is at once apparent. He too was identified with his brethren as well as passing through suffering for them. The early Christians did not fail to see the remarkable suitability of this psalm when applied to Jesus Christ. That a psalm which begins with a cry of desolation should end with a song of praise is significant for the present writer's purpose, for he sees suffering in the light of the ultimate glory. The words *in the midst of the congregation* are significant because the Septuagint, which is here quoted, uses the word *ekklēsia* (church) to describe the company of the brethren.

**13.** The second quotation may have come from Isaiah 8:17 or 2 Samuel 22:3, but in either case an emphatic 'I' (*egō*) is added. Clearly when applied to Christ the personal emphasis has a different meaning from the original contexts. It is, in fact, a remarkable statement on the lips of the Messiah – *I, even I the Messiah, will put my trust in him*. In this respect the Messiah places himself on an equality with his brethren, which prepares for the later statement in verse 14 that he shares their nature. This attitude of trust is amply seen in the life of Jesus and is particularly evident in the Gospel of John, where all the facets of his movements and thought are seen to be in accordance with God's will.

It seems certain that the writer had the Isaiah passage in mind in this second quotation, for he follows it up with another from the same passage (Is. 8:18). The precise purpose of the third saying, *Here am I, and the children God has given me*, is not at first obvious, for the words originally referred to the prophet's own children. Isaiah saw himself as linked with his children in the service of God, for he recognized that the children were 'signs' given by God. This identification of the prophet with his children as signs is paralleled in the writer's thought by the close link between Christ and his people, which leads naturally into the next important section.

**14.** The writer reflects on the incarnation and mission of Jesus. His becoming man was necessary because his 'children' were *flesh and blood*, a somewhat unexpected way of putting it. Nevertheless the idea is clear enough. It is worth noting that in the Greek text the order is *blood and flesh*. It has been suggested that 'blood' alludes to Christ's shedding of blood, which is then given as the reason for his becoming flesh, *i.e.* the atonement required the incarnation. To deliver man, Jesus Christ had to share his nature. We are in the presence of a mystery here. The fact that *he himself partook of the same nature* sums up the perfect humanity of Jesus. When this statement is set over against the statements in chapter 1 about the divine Sonship of Jesus, the mystery deepens. His superiority to angels is set against his equality with man. There can never be a wholly satisfactory explanation of these two facets of his nature, because man has no suitable frame of reference in which to consider it. There are no human analogies. The writer is not concerned with theological debate, but with showing how closely Jesus Christ is identified with his people. It is significant that a different verb (*meteschen*) is used to describe what Jesus shared from that used (*kekoinōnēken*) to describe what the children shared. Although there is no essential difference in meaning, the change of tense from the perfect to the aorist suggests that Christ's taking on human nature is a specific act in time; he became what he was not before (*i.e.* a man).

Once again *death* is mentioned. A statement is made that *through death he might destroy him who has the power of death*, which plainly brings out the powerful effect of Christ's death compared with the deaths of all other men. In Scripture death is the result of sin. The Genesis story bears this out. It is supported in the Pauline epistles (*cf.* Rom. 5:12). It is basic to the New Testament teaching on the death and resurrection of Christ. Because of Christ's resurrection, death has now lost its 'sting', which shows that it possessed a sting (1 Cor. 15:55), identified by Paul as 'sin'. It is no wonder that Hebrews speaks of 'fear of death'. It is, therefore, paradoxical that Christ used death as a means of destroying the maliciousness of death. But the difference between his death and all others lies in the fact of his sinlessness. Death for him was caused by other men's sins. It is difficult to imagine the complete transformation which came to the minds of the early disciples in assessing death when they came to explain why Jesus died.[1]

---

[1] As F. F. Bruce, *Comm.*, p. 49, points out.

The idea that the devil has *the power of death* is in complete agreement with other New Testament passages regarding his power. Death is the worst enemy of man, but many other human woes are seen to proceed from the same origin (*e.g.* the woman with the bent back is said to have been bound by Satan, Lk. 13:16). The power thus exercised is not absolute and applies only to man in his unredeemed state, as is clear from the fact that the death of Christ has brought deliverance to man and destruction to the devil. Both are potential rather than actual, for the devil is still active and most men still fear death. Nevertheless, the death and resurrection of Jesus have demonstrated once and for all that the devil is no longer master of death. For a variation of this victory theme, *cf.* Colossians 2:15. In this epistle salvation involves more than release from sin, for it includes complete deliverance from the bondage of the devil.

**15.** The deliverance which Jesus Christ has brought is for *all those who through fear of death were subject to lifelong bondage.* The idea of bondage is familiar in various parts of the New Testament, but the word used here (*douleia*) occurs elsewhere only in Romans (8:15, 21) and Galatians (4:24; 5:1); in none of these cases does it refer to the bondage of death.[1] Most men reject the notion that they are in bondage, as the Jews did when in debate with Jesus (Jn. 8:33). It offends their pride. This is one of the main reasons why the subject of death is so often avoided, for honest men would otherwise have to admit their bondage to fear of it. It is the one fact which is universally admitted to apply to all men. All men know they must die, but not all men admit themselves to be sinners. Moreover, death is no respecter of persons. It is the great leveller. Any power, therefore, which removes its terror is a boon which is applicable to all mankind. The Christian approach to death brings complete deliverance. Only those who refuse the gift of deliverance are still in its grip.

**16.** The thought of the writer swings back to the theme of angels, and he realizes at once that what he has just said has

---

[1] E. Käsemann, *Das wandernde Gottesvolk* (Göttingen, 1939), pp. 99–100, claims to find here gnostic influence, because he maintains that the gnostic redeemer myth did hold out hope of deliverance from fear of death. But for the gnostic the imprisonment was an imprisonment to matter, from which death brought release.

no relevance for them. He is reminded of Isaiah 41:8–9 where 'the offspring of Abraham' is mentioned as the chosen servant of God. In other words, one bondage is exchanged for another, but the exchange is most unequal since those who serve the devil have no status as *the descendants of Abraham* have. Angels are not included in the act of deliverance since they have no need of it. The writer may have concentrated on the descendants of Abraham because the epistle is addressed to Hebrews. It should be remembered, however, that when Paul wrote to the predominantly Gentile Roman church he could speak of Abraham as 'our forefather according to the flesh' (Rom. 4:1), while Jesus pointed out that Abraham's children were those who do what Abraham did (Jn. 8:39). In a spiritual sense Abraham's offspring includes all who share his faith and this must be the sense in which the present passage should be understood (*cf.* also Rom. 4:11). It must also be noted that both Matthew and Luke show that Jesus himself was historically a descendant of Abraham (Mt. 1, Lk. 3 in the respective genealogies).

**17.** Possibly it was the thought of Psalm 22:22, which he had already cited (verse 12), that led the writer to re-emphasize the need for Jesus Christ *to be made like his brethren*. This is essentially a restatement of verse 14, the significant addition of the words *in every respect* drawing attention to the complete and perfect manhood of Jesus. Its restatement at this point permits the author to introduce the main subject of the letter, the *high priest* theme, although it is not developed until chapter 5. The intervening passage prepares for the same theme by another route. Certain important aspects of the high priest's character and work are mentioned, but are not expounded here as they are later on in the letter.

With respect to his character, our high priest (*i.e.* Jesus) is said to be both *merciful and faithful*. The former word occurs only here in this letter. Indeed its only other occurrence is in the beatitudes, where the merciful are promised mercy. Nevertheless the idea of showing mercy (the verb rather than the adjective) is frequent and may be said to be a predominant characteristic of God's attitude to man. Mercy was not, however, a quality required from those who served in the Aaronic order of priesthood, although, according to 5:2, the high priest was expected to have some capacity to deal gently with the wayward. The idea of faithfulness is even more dominant in the New Testament and recurs in four other places in this epistle (3:2, 5–6; 10:23; 11:11), in all except one place referring to the faithfulness of God. Utter trustworthiness is indispensable if the mission of Jesus is to be enduring and the writer has no doubt that he is completely dependable. He enlarges on this theme as he extends his discussion in the next chapter.

The faithfulness in the case of our high priest is specifically related to the things of God (*ta pros ton Theon*), *i.e.* those aspects of a priest's work which are Godward, the most notable aspect of which is his *expiation for the sins of the people*. The verb used (*hilaskomai*) is not generally followed by an object which denotes the thing propitiated. This is therefore a striking usage. The meaning is 'to make propitiation for sins'. The verb occurs elsewhere in the New Testament only in Luke 18:13, although there are many instances of its use in the Septuagint. In Luke it is used in the tax-collector's cry to God for mercy. When related to sins its function is to provide a common footing for the sinner and the One sinned against. It is worth noting that the propitiation (an idea expressed in typical sacrificial language, highly appropriate for the priesthood idea) is said to be for *the sins of the people* rather than for 'sin' in the abstract. The plural makes the provision more personal. Many scholars object to the rendering 'propitiation' for the Greek *hilaskomai*, because it conjures up ideas of placating an angry deity. But this is never in view in the New Testament usage where it is God himself who provides the propitiation (*cf.* Rom. 3:25) out of his deep love for mankind (Rom. 5:8).

Cognate nouns are used in Hebrews 9:5; Romans 3:25 and 1 John 2:2; 4:10. In all these instances the purpose of propitiation is the restoration of a previously broken relationship between God and man occasioned by man's sin.[1]

**18.** Another thought altogether concludes this chapter, although it follows on from Jesus Christ being made like his brethren. The problem of temptation is ever present with man,

---

[1] On the whole idea, *cf.* L. Morris. *The Apostolic Preaching of the Cross* (London, 1955), pp. 125ff.; J. Herrmann and F. Büschel, *TDNT* 3, pp. 300ff. C. H. Dodd, *The Epistle to the Romans* (London, 1932), pp. 54f., strongly favours expiation against propitiation.

but to what extent is it possible to think of Christ being tempted in the same way? Our writer is convinced that Christ's ability to help those tempted depends on his experience of temptation. To understand the present statement (*because he himself has suffered and been tempted*), it is essential to note that the tempting is linked with the suffering. It has been suggested that Jesus' sufferings were those caused by human weakness: fear, grief and pain caused by the infliction of physical injury.[1] But the sufferings of Jesus were mainly those involved in his Messianic office and included more than physical suffering. Since the suffering is special, so is the temptation. The point of contact between Jesus Christ and his people is not so much in parallels with the nature and form of the temptation but in the fact that both sustain an experience of temptation. The point is brought out most clearly in 4:15. In commenting on that verse the theological problem raised by the temptation of Christ will be discussed. For the time being the important thought is that *he (i.e.* Christ) *is able to help*, for the main burden of this early part of the epistle is to demonstrate the perfect suitability of Christ to be the representative of his people in their approach to God.

## C. THE SUPERIORITY OF JESUS TO MOSES (3:1–19)

Because of the great importance of Moses as the lawgiver, a comparison of him with Jesus would have been of great significance to both Jewish and Gentile Christians, but particularly to the former. The writer shows that Moses' status as servant was greatly inferior to Jesus' status as son. Moreover, in spite of his greatness, Moses never achieved his aim of leading the Israelites into the promised land; this too is in strong contrast to the completed work of Christ, which is so strongly stressed later in the epistle.

### (i) Moses the servant and Jesus the Son (3:1–6)

**1.** There may at first sight seem very little connection between the Moses theme and the theme of chapter 2. Nevertheless, the writer intended to connect the two ideas for he begins

---

[1] *Cf.* Montefiore, *Comm.*, p. 68.

with *Therefore, holy brethren*, which follows on from his statement about Jesus as high priest. There is also a sequence in the mention of 'brethren' in 2:11, its repetition in 2:12, 17 and the description of the readers by the same word here. Twice more the same description is used (10:19 and 13:22), but only here is the adjective 'holy' added. It is surprising in this context. It shows at once both familiarity and respect. It is a combination which Christians would do well to cherish. Indeed there are other things or persons described in this epistle as holy (*cf.* the many instances of the Holy Spirit being mentioned, the holy place, the holy sanctuary, the holy of holies). The writer is not using the word lightly of the brethren. It is, of course, used ideally, as it is when it becomes a noun for describing believers (the saints), as in 13:24.

This description of the brethren is then followed by a definition to exclude all possibility of confusion. They are the people *who share in a heavenly call*. This in fact introduces another characteristic theme of this letter, the word 'heavenly'. The writer speaks also of the heavenly gift (6:4), the heavenly sanctuary (8:5), heavenly things (9:23), the heavenly country (11:16) and the heavenly Jerusalem (12:22). In all cases the 'heavenly' is contrasted with the earthly, and in all cases the heavenly is the superior, the real as compared with the shadow. If the heavenly call is understood in the same sense, it must mean a vocation which has a spiritual and not a material direction. This word for 'call' (*klēsis*) is specially characteristic of the apostle Paul who uses it nine times. Otherwise it occurs only in 2 Peter 1:10. There is no support for the view that the call comes from within a man, for in all cases the call comes from God. Man's part is to become a co-operator by responding to it. The idea of sharing recurs in 3:14 where Christians are said to be 'sharers of Christ'. The phrase that the writer uses in the present context is pregnant with meaning. To share in a heavenly call is to become closely identified with the caller, *i.e.* God. No wonder such people are called 'holy'. The New Testament implies that this is the norm for Christians. They are a called out people.

In the following statement about Jesus the readers are exhorted to *consider* (*katanoeō*) him, that is to direct the mind carefully towards him (the same verb is used in 10:24). For a

97

similar idea although with different verbs, we may compare
12:2–3, where again the object of the considering is *Jesus*. In
some sense the writer is giving in epigrammatic form his whole
intention – to direct his readers to examine the claims of Christ
to be the superior high priest. For the moment he is content to
describe Christ as *the apostle and high priest of our confession*. Not
only is this the only occurrence of the word 'apostle' in this
letter, but it is the only occasion in the New Testament where
it is used of Christ. It is striking that the same term used of the
men whom Jesus had chosen is used of Jesus himself. It is not,
however, so unexpected when Jesus' own words are considered: 'As thou didst send me into the world, so I have sent
them into the world' (Jn. 17:18); indeed, it is worth noting that
the idea of Jesus being sent is frequent in the New Testament.
In other words they became apostles because he was an apostle.
He is the perfect fulfiller of the office. All others are pale
reflections.

There is moreover a close connection between the apostle and
the high priest. Both were 'appointed' and did not take the
office on themselves. Both were representative offices, in which
the holders were acting on behalf of others. The apostle represented Jesus Christ, and the high priest represented God before
men and men before God. Since a comparison between Christ
and Moses immediately follows, it is noticeable that Moses
performed the function of an apostle in acting as God's representative to the people and the function of intercessor before
God on behalf of the people. He is never specifically called
either apostle or priest. His brother Aaron was in fact appointed
to the office of priest instead of him. Christ is seen to be superior
to Moses in perfectly fulfilling both functions.

But why are the offices qualified by the words *of our confession*?
The noun *homologia* (confession) is not frequent in the New
Testament, occurring once in 2 Corinthians (9:13), twice in
1 Timothy (6:12–13) and three times in Hebrews (here and 4:14;
10:23). In the present statement it is used subjectively, *i.e.* Jesus
whom we profess. Some outward acknowledgment of our
allegiance to Jesus is evidently intended, although this is to be
thought of as a constant confessing of Christ and is not restricted to a single act. Hebrews 4:14 is a similar use of the

word, for the readers are to hold fast their confession, again in reference to Jesus as high priest. Similarly in 10:23 is another exhortation to hold fast. The dominant idea in Hebrews is that believers have a wonderful confession to make, and must carefully watch lest they neglect what God has provided for them.

2. Another characteristic of our high priest is that he was *faithful.* This comes into special focus at this stage in the discussion, having already been mentioned in 2:17. A comparison is made between the faithfulness of Jesus and the faithfulness of Moses. Such a comparison would carry great weight with readers who had come from Judaism and would have carried over into Christianity a high respect for the ancient lawgiver. Indeed even Gentile Christians would soon learn from their growing acquaintance with the Old Testament that Moses is a name to conjure with in ancient Old Testament history. Moses' faithfulness is implied in Numbers 12:7, where the Lord mentions that Moses was entrusted with all his house. It is this feature which provides a suitable comparison with Jesus Christ.

The words *who appointed him* (*i.e.* Jesus) are literally 'who made him' (Greek *poiēsanti*). It may be that the verb was suggested by 1 Samuel 12:6 where the Septuagint uses it in the sense of 'constitute' which seems to be the meaning here. Moses' faithfulness is said to be *in God's house*, which seems to be a figurative expression for all the responsibilities committed to him for the theocratic community. An alternative reading, although not so strongly attested, has *in all his house*, which would highlight even more the extent of Moses' faithfulness. Nevertheless this faithfulness gains its greatest renown when it serves as a pattern for, although exceeded by, the faithfulness of Christ.

3. There is a direct connection between verse 3 and the previous verse, as is shown by the conjunction *for*, AV (*gar*). The words *Jesus has been counted worthy* give the reason why the readers should consider (*katanoēsate*) him (verse 1). He is a worthy object of thought. If Moses was so highly respected by Jews and Jewish Christians alike, how much more should Jesus be honoured! The comparison is heightened by the claim that *the builder of a house* is greater than the house itself. Although

the glory of Moses is indisputable and is brought out in other New Testament passages (especially 2 Cor. 3), he was not the innovator of the legal system, but simply the agent through whom it was given. The vivid Old Testament description of the law tablets being written by the finger of God at once puts Moses in his right perspective, almost as a spectator who was himself intimately affected by what he saw.

But who is *the builder* who has more honour than the house he builds? There are two interpretations. (i) It may refer to Jesus since he is being compared with Moses. In this case the comparison is between Jesus, the builder of the house, and Moses, the house which he built. But this interpretation raises difficulties for it implies a concept of the pre-existence of Jesus and of his identification with the giving of the Law, which introduces a new thought not prepared for by the previous chapters. The glory and honour attributed to Jesus is through suffering and death (2:9), not through creative power (although this is referred to in 1:2). (ii) The alternative interpretation identifies God as the builder, which is supported by verse 4. Although (ii) fits the context better than (i), there is truth in the idea of Jesus Christ as founder of his house, *i.e.* the church. Bruce thinks no distinction can be made between Father and Son here, for it is God who founds his own household, but he does so through his Son.[1]

It should be noted that the combination of *glory* and *honour* in this verse corresponds not only with the quotation from Psalm 8 in 2:7, but also to the ascription to the Lamb by the heavenly creatures in Revelation 5:12–13 (*cf.* also Rev. 4:9, 11; 7:12). Nevertheless in the present verse 'glory' is applied to the persons and 'honour' to the building and the builder, presumably because 'glory' would be a less suitable idea to apply to a building or its builder.

4. This verse is placed in parenthesis in RSV because it makes a general statement intended to back up what had just been said. The conjunction *for* (*gar*) shows the connection. *Every house is built by some one*; this is a generic statement which hardly needs to be made at all unless there are grounds for disputing

---

[1] *Cf.* Bruce, *Comm.*, p. 57.

it, and those grounds may be found in what may well have been a current approach to the Law. There was certainly danger in some Jewish quarters of excessive respect for Moses at the expense of recognizing that God was the originator of the Law. But the present context in which God is spoken of is much wider than that. He is *the builder of all things*, not merely of the 'house'. It is God-like to be the innovator of all things. We may reject the view that the second part of the verse is a gloss which disrupts the context.[1] The writer's purpose in making this point is to enhance the glory of Jesus who was appointed by such a God to his office (verse 2). Some restrict the 'all things' to matters related to the church,[2] but it is better to take it more comprehensively of the whole material creation, as well as of the establishment of the new spiritual community.

**5–6.** Another line of argument is now introduced to strengthen the superior position of Christ over Moses – the difference between a Son and a servant.[3] Again Moses' faithfulness is emphasized in a way which suggests no more than a *servant*. The word for servant here is not the usual term *doulos* used elsewhere in the New Testament, but *therapōn*, which occurs only here. It refers to a 'personal service freely rendered'.[4] It is a more tender word than *doulos* and does not imply the latter's overtone of servility. Even so the personal attendant cannot share the same status as the son. In Moses' case the servant had an important task to perform, to bear testimony to what was to follow. In other words what Moses represents in Jewish history is not in itself complete. It was pointing forward to a fuller revelation of God at a later time, *i.e.* it concerns *things that were to be spoken later*, which must point to the time of Christ. The mission of the servant, great though it was, prepares the way for the far greater mission of the Son.

[1] *Cf.* Héring, *Comm.*, p. 25.

[2] Calvin, *Comm.*, p. 36.

[3] It may be wondered why the author goes to the trouble of showing Christ's superiority to Moses. Some think that the answer may be found in the development of an inadequate type of Christology based too narrowly on the prediction of the coming prophet in Dt. 18:15ff. For this kind of Moses-Christology, *cf.* E. L. Allen, 'Jesus and Moses in the New Testament', *ExT* 17 (1955–56), pp. 104ff.; H. J. Schoeps, *Theologie und Geschichte des Judenchristentums* (Tübingen, 1949), pp. 87ff.

[4] Westcott, *Comm.*, p. 77.

The faithfulness of Christ is repeated to bring out its superiority over Moses' by virtue of his Sonship. *As a son* echoes the main theme of the opening part of the epistle. The writer is impressed by the thought that our high priest is none other than God's Son. This will be evident at several points in the development of his discussion. To him the Sonship of Jesus adds incomparable dignity to the high-priestly office.

As he still thinks of God's *house*, he becomes more specific and identifies his readers with the house, but makes an important condition in doing so; *if we hold fast our confidence and pride in our hope*. The conditional statements in this epistle are significant. The writer wishes to make it clear that only those who are consistent with what they profess have any claim to be part of the 'house'. The word for 'confidence' (*parrēsia*), sometimes translated 'boldness', is another characteristic idea in this epistle. Here the implication is that we have a solid assurance to hold fast to. The New Testament word for 'hope' is much stronger than the normal English use, in which it almost means no more than a pious wish that may have no real basis in fact. That kind of hope would hardly provide a satisfactory basis for pride. No-one is going to boast in a thing which is not certain to happen. The writer is sufficiently convinced of the certainty of Christian hope to use a strong expression (*to kauchēma*, exultant boasting) to describe the Christian's attitude towards it. It is worth noting that the confidence spoken of here is referred to again at the end of the theological discussion and the beginning of the application (*cf.* 10:19). The same idea of 'holding fast' which is used here occurs there in the form of an exhortation.

## (ii) Focus on the failure of God's people under Moses (3:7–19)

**7.** The idea that a new interpretation of the house illustration is possible – a transference from the Israelites as Moses' house to the church as Messiah's house – caused the writer to reflect further on Israel's failure to inherit the promises. This is obviously intended to back up the importance of the condition just imposed, *i.e.* of holding fast to our confidence. The writer is mindful of the fact that some of his readers were in danger of doing what the Israelites had done. A brief historical interlude is not, therefore, out of place.[1]

He begins with a scriptural quotation from Psalm 95:7–11 introduced by the words *as the Holy Spirit says*. This and 10:15f. are clear indications that the writer regards the words of the Old Testament as inspired by the Spirit. Although he does not explicitly state so in introducing other quotations, it may be assumed to underlie his whole approach to the Old Testament. Indeed, his doctrine of the Spirit in relation to Scripture reaches to the significance of the imagery used, as 9:8 shows. By introducing the scriptural text in this way, he gives tremendous authority to the words he quotes, containing as they do a strong warning.

The first words of the quotation have particularly caught the writer's imagination for he repeats them three times (verses 7–8; 3:15 and 4:7). He sees the opening *Today* as significant, allowing him to apply the words to his present readers. Although he goes back in history, his mind is on the contemporary scene. Indeed the words *when you hear his voice* emphasize this present relevance, his voice being the voice of God in Christ. Moreover the context in the Psalms is particularly appropriate, for Psalm 95:7 says 'we are the people of his pasture, and the sheep of his hand', which fits well into the Christian view of the church as the flock of God. But the subsequent exhortation against following the example of the rebellious Israelites introduces a stern note of warning.

**8–9.** The idea of hardening the heart occurs frequently as a description of Israel's disobedience, and is a permanent reminder against adopting a fixed attitude of disobedience to God. That hardening is in fact seen in various phases of Old Testament history. It began, as the passage quoted makes clear, during the wilderness wanderings. *The rebellion* refers to such incidents as those recorded in Exodus 15:22–25; 17:1–7 and 32:1ff. Indeed the Hebrew text of the Psalm cited mentions

---

[1] It is this section which forms the core of Käsemann's theory of a Gnostic background to this epistle (*cf. Das wandernde Gottesvolk*). O. Hofius, *Katapausis: Die Vorstellung vom endzeitlichen Ruheort im Hebräerbrief*, denies a Gnostic origin and claims an apocalyptic background. Hofius' thesis is that the place of rest spoken of in this section is the holy of holies. G. Theissen, *Untersuchungen zum Hebräerbrief*, pp. 128ff., criticizes Hofius' appeal to apocalyptic. Many exegetes would agree with the interpretation of God's people as a wandering people seeking rest, without subscribing to Käsemann's Gnostic theory.

Meribah and Massah. These were two classic occasions which stand out in Israel's history as instances of rebellion against God. The word used for rebellion (*parapikrasmos*) occurs in the New Testament only here and in verse 15 and comes from the root *pikros* (bitter); it may have been suggested by the Meribah incident where the water was found to be bitter. It appears to be of Septuagint origin to express in a pointed way provocation against God. It is to be distinguished from the parallel word in verse 10 (RSV *provoked*), which means 'to be disgusted with, abhor', MM).

*The day of testing* may perhaps refer to the beginning and the *forty years* to the duration. What appeared on a particular occasion as a symptom developed into a settled habit of mind; this led to an attitude of abhorrence on the part of God, in spite of the fact that in the Old Testament God is revealed as the one who is not easily provoked, but one who is 'slow to anger'. It has been suggested that the writer of this epistle may have read into the 'forty years' the period which had elapsed since the crucifixion of Jesus, during which the Jewish people generally had continued to reject him. But he does not draw special attention to this part of the quotation. The gist of the whole passage is to serve as a warning against a repetition of similar rebellion against God. Another suggestion is that the forty years may have held special significance for the writer, as it appears to have done among the Qumran Covenanters. The latter related their future to a period of forty years following the death of the Teacher of Righteousness.[1]

**10–11.** If it be thought strange that God can be *provoked*, it should be remembered that many difficulties arise when any sort of emotional response is attributed to God. Human analogies are the only means of expression available, but are fraught with the danger that God will be reduced to human terms. When God is provoked it is entirely different from much human provocation, for anger never arises in the mind of God without just cause, whereas it so frequently does in the minds of men. The description of the recalcitrant Israelites is twofold: their habitual straying from God and their ignorance ('*They always go*

---

[1] Cf. Bruce, *Comm.*, p. 65, n. 57 for details.

*astray in their hearts; they have not known my ways'*). The one plays on the other. Ignorance of God's ways will naturally lead to people straying away from them. But the writer of the psalm mentions them in the reverse order, as if the habitual attitude of straying had contributed to their ignorance. A hardened state of mind becomes impervious to God's voice and leads to increasing ignorance of his ways, not because God does not make them known, but because the hardened mind has no disposition to listen. What was true of the Israelites is a commentary on all who resist the claims of God.

The verdict on the rebels in the psalm is conclusive, expressed in the form of an oath. An Old Testament passage which seems to be reflected here is Numbers 14:21, where God gives his word by an oath. The context of this Old Testament passage is the occasion when the spies returned to Kadesh-barnea and the majority report was unfavourable. The words of the oath, *They shall never enter my rest*, are introduced in the Septuagint by an if clause (*ei*), which because it has no then clause serves as a strong negative. What is meant by 'rest' is further discussed in chapter 4. What is important here is that rebels effectively place themselves outside the provision of God. They are not eligible.

**12.** Now follows a discussion, based on the quotation, which is clearly related to the historical situation of the readers. It appears most likely that among them were some who were tempted to fall away from God. *Take care* (*blepete*) as an exhortation to the readers occurs again in 12:25 and in both cases there is a serious issue involved. As the Israelites had fallen a prey to unbelief, so their successors, the Christians, must watch out that they do not fall into the same trap.

The writer sums up the state of mind of the Israelites in the psalm as that of *an evil, unbelieving heart*, and sees the possibility of the same condition in some of his readers. The order of words in the original is 'evil heart of unbelief', which leaves open whether the evil precedes the unbelief or vice versa. The writer is not interested in such niceties. What bothers him is that unbelief invariably leads to evil consequences. Unbelief leads people *to fall away from the living God*. The word used for falling away (*apostēnai*) is the root from which 'apostasy' comes. It involves a deviation from the truth. To fall away from *the living God* is the greatest defection possible. This particular title for God, which is familiar in the Old Testament, occurs several times in the New Testament, frequently, as here, without the article. The form without the article draws attention more vividly to the adjective 'living'. The Christians in pagan environments would warm to the contrast between the living God, whom they worshipped, and the dead idols of paganism (*cf.* Acts 14:15). The title was of equal appeal to a Jewish disciple, as in Peter's confession at Caesarea Philippi (Mt. 16:16), or to a Jewish high priest as the oath in Matthew 26:63 shows. There are other places in Hebrews where the same title is used (9:14; 10:31; 12:22). The words convey the idea of a dynamic God and are particularly significant in any comments about men falling away from him (*cf.* especially 10:31). Such a God is, moreover, in constant communication with men.

If the apostasy envisaged is a return to Judaism, in what sense could this be described as a falling away from the living God, since Jews did acknowledge God? The answer must be that 'apostates' in this sense would not find God in Judaism, having turned their backs on the better way provided in Christ.[1] If the writer regards Jesus as God, as he does, to reject Christ would be regarded as apostasy from God.[2]

**13.** In thinking of the passage just quoted, the writer at once transfers the *today* of the psalm to the time of his own contemporaries. In this way he makes the psalm relevant to them. This assumes a double meaning: an immediate and an extended application. Indeed the *today* is stretched to stand for the whole of the present age of grace, since modern readers of this epistle are able to extend it still further to themselves. The advice *exhort one another every day* shows the writer's practical turn of mind in applying an Old Testament quotation. This is an invitation to constant vigilance against the possibility of 'hardening'.

The writer recognizes that his contemporaries are as liable to this hardening process as the Israelites had been. He attributes it to *the deceitfulness of sin*. Sin here seems to be personified, using deceit as a means of developing a hardened attitude in

---

[1] *Cf.* Bruce, *Comm.*, p. 66.
[2] *Cf.* Montefiore, *Comm.*, p. 77.

its adherents. If some of the Hebrew Christians were deceiving themselves into thinking that Christianity could be contained within the old wineskins of Judaism, they would be adopting a similar inflexible position, which would be contrary to the revelation of God through Christ. A hardened attitude is not a sudden aberration, but a habitual state of mind. Sin uses the cloak of deceit with devastating effect on those inclined to fall under its spell. It was the deceitfulness of riches which choked the seed in the parable of the sower (Mt. 13:22). An important aspect of the warning against the deceitfulness of sin is that it is addressed to the individual – *that none of you may be hardened*. It is certainly easier for individuals to be misled in isolation from other Christians than when sharing in fellowship with others. The fact that there was a tendency for the readers to forsake assembling with others (Heb. 10:25) throws light on the present passage. It is impossible to *exhort one another* unless one is part of a fellowship. In the present case a hardening of heart is linked closely with 'sin' and this must have been a tendency in the case of the Hebrews who were tempted to turn away from Christianity.

**14.** By way of contrast to this hardening of heart is the position of those who are established in Christ. They have a firm and stable basis, for the writer says *we share in Christ*. The word *metochoi* (partakers) could be understood to mean either 'partakers of Christ' or 'partakers with Christ'. The latter is certainly better suited to the context where the believer's close connection with Christ has already been stressed (*cf.* 3:6, 'we are his house'). Moreover the use of *metochoi* with the genitive (as here) has the meaning 'confederate with' in both the Septuagint and koinē usage (*cf.* MM). It has the same sense in Luke 5:7.

It is generally agreed that 'partakers with Christ' is not equivalent to the more expressive 'in Christ' in Paul's epistles. Nevertheless although their way of expressing union with Christ is different, the basic idea is the same. It may be preferable to think of the sharing as participation in the heavenly kingdom.

It is noticeable that no indication is given of the manner in which we share in or with Christ, for the writer is more interested in the terms on which we share. He expresses it as an if clause: *if only we hold our first confidence firm to the end*. The Greek conjunction *eanper* which introduces this clause occurs only twice in the New Testament (here and in 6:3). It means 'if at least' or 'if indeed'. It is an intensive particle (MM), which draws special attention to the condition. Although the sharing is spoken of as a completed act, yet it assumes that those concerned would continue in fellowship with Christ. This proviso is understandable in view of the writer's vivid recall of the Israelites' lost inheritance, which he comments on in the following passage.

The word translated *confidence* (*hypostasis*) occurs in 1:3 and 11:1.[1] It appears in the present context to be connected with the assurance an owner of property may have because he possesses the title-deeds, a sense which is possible in 11:1 (*q.v.*). But 1:3 has a different sense (*i.e.* 'nature'). We may pursue further this imagery by suggesting that the idea is to make sure the deeds do not slip from our possession. The writer three times in this epistle uses the same expression 'hold fast' (*katechō*, *cf.* 3:6 and 10:23). It is moreover strengthened by the word *firm* (*bebaios*), another favourite word in Hebrews 2:2 (RSV 'valid'); 3:6 WH (RSV mg. 'firm'); 6:19 (RSV 'steadfast'); 9:17 (RSV 'takes effect'). It is not without significance that its usual meaning relates to a legally guaranteed security (MM). Hence in this context it brings out the need for holding securely on to our 'share' in Christ. So long as we exercise faith we have the assurance that our share cannot be taken from us, any more than another can claim ownership of our property if he does not possess the deeds.

**15-17.** The last verse was really a qualifying parenthesis, for the thought now returns to the quotation from Psalm 95. Indeed the crucial words are repeated from earlier in the chapter (verses 7b, 8). This not only serves to emphasize their importance, but provides the writer with an opportunity to add his comments upon them. He asks a series of five questions in which the second and fourth virtually answer the first and third, while the fifth contains its own answer. This method provides a fascinating example of New Testament exegesis. The writer clearly

---

[1] Héring, p. 28, considers that the genitive *hypostaseōs* could mean 'beginning of faith' or 'principle of faith' or as explanatory, *i.e.* 'the basis, which is faith'.

assumes that his readers will not need explanation of the general historical background to which the psalm refers, but his first question, *Who were they that heard and yet were rebellious?*, concerns the identity (or rather, extent) of the rebellious hearers. The second question, *Was it not all those who left Egypt under the leadership of Moses?*, rhetorical in character, merely points out what the readers must already have known, *i.e.* that the revolt was total. It could not but reflect on the leadership of Moses compared with the superiority of Jesus. Moses was honoured in being the deliverer of his people from Egypt, but the very people he delivered turned in rebellion against God. The *all* is not affected by the fact that two, Joshua and Caleb, in fact entered the promised land. It was the sheer mass of the rebellion which impressed the writer.

The next two questions put the same point. Based on the next section of the psalm, they fasten on the *forty years* to draw attention to the extended duration of the provocation. So persistent was the rebellion against God that it lasted the entire period of the Israelites' wilderness wanderings. *Was it not with those who sinned?* is a question which nails down the attitude of the Israelites as 'sin' (the verb occurs again in this epistle only at 10:26). Sin is the root cause, of which rebellion and provocation were particular manifestations. The result for the sinners is vividly summed up: *whose bodies fell in the wilderness*, a decisive evidence of God's displeasure with them. The writer in this way brings out that it was not only unbelief, but the deeper reality of active rebellion which was responsible for the Israelites' failure.

**18.** The fifth question, *to whom did he swear that they should never enter his rest?*, is answered by the qualifying addition *but to those who were disobedient?* The provokers, having been identified with those who sinned, are now described as disobedient. This latter concept implies a standard of law from which they had wilfully deviated. The writer is building up a vivid picture of the sad state of those who act against God's provision for them. He is illustrating from Israel's past the impossibility of winning through by any other means than faith and obedience – a striking comment on 2:3. It should be noted that the idea of an oath of God, culled here from Psalm 95, occurs in 6:13, 16f.

and 7:21 (a quotation from Ps. 110:4) (*cf.* also 4:3). Clearly the idea held considerable importance for the writer and spoke of the absolute veracity of God's word. The 'rest' (*i.e.* the inheritance) mentioned here is regarded as of sufficient importance for its loss to be serious. It is expounded and applied in the following passage.

**19.** The last part of the quotation from the psalm, concerning entering God's rest, is expanded more fully in the next chapter, but a summary statement is made to bring to focus the real reason for the debate. Their inability to enter was traceable to *unbelief.* This goes back to verse 12 where the readers are warned against having 'unbelieving hearts'. It is instructive to note that throughout this epistle the exegesis is made relevant to the readers and constantly echoes their immediate state. By saying *So we see that*, the writer assumes that his reasoning will be self-evident. His readers could hardly question the reality of the Israelites' unbelief and he clearly hopes that they will equally clearly see the dangerous consequences of similar unbelief on their part.

## D. THE SUPERIORITY OF JESUS TO JOSHUA (4:1–13)

Since Moses was unable to lead the Israelites into Canaan, the writer reflects on the position of Joshua, who did lead them in. But he shows that even Joshua did not secure for his people true rest. Joshua failed for the same reason as Moses, that is, through the people's unbelief. This leads the writer to exhort his readers to seek that superior rest, which he goes on to imply is found in Christ.

*(i) The greater rest which Joshua could not secure (4:1–10)*

**1.** Having shown the failure of the Israelites to possess their inheritance under the leadership of Moses, the writer next turns to his successor Joshua. Although the men of the wilderness failed to obtain the 'rest', the promise of it still remained for their children. Indeed the assumption is made that the promise is timeless and is available still to the writer and his readers, hence the further exhortation. It is important to note that the first words according to the Greek text are 'Let us fear, therefore'

(*Phobēthōmen oun*). The position of the verb gives it special emphasis. It would be salutary for Christians seriously to consider the failure of the Israelites and their incurring the displeasure of God, and to fear lest a similar calamity should befall members of the new community, the spiritual Israel. The writer accepts without question that *the promise of entering his rest remains*, presumably because his doctrine of God is such that no word of his can be conceived to fail. In view of this an element of godly fear is invaluable, for it brings home the solemn consequence of underrating God's provision for his people.

The writer assumes for himself and for his readers that some kind of rest is attainable. In the following verses he gives an explanation which helps us to know the nature of the rest which is still available. There is some doubt about the precise meaning of the words *lest any of you be judged to have failed to reach it*, since the word rendered 'judged' (*dokeō*) could mean 'seem', in which case the warning is against even the appearance of failure. Moreover, it could mean 'lest any of you think', in which case the emphasis falls on a wrong assessment of the whole situation. It is, of course, possible that some of the readers were thinking too literally that the 'rest' referred to Canaan and therefore had no relevance to them. But a warning of the kind which abounds in this epistle would be best suited to the first meaning, 'be judged', with the agent of the judging left open.

2. In ascribing to his readers a parallel position to the Israelites, the writer uses a verb which is highly important. Including himself in the statement he says, *For good news came to us just as to them*, which means literally 'the gospel has been preached to us as to them'. Of course, the content of the message greatly differed, but the common factor is that in both cases God was communicating with men. When the revelation of God to the Israelites is singled out, the *message* is expressed by the word *logos*, already used in 2:2 in a similar sense. It is a favourite New Testament word for the revelation of God. In this case it is qualified by the phrase *which they heard* (*tēs akoēs*, literally 'word of hearing'). The expression could be understood to mean the message which has been simply heard, but not responded to, and this understanding of it would well fit the context. Whichever meaning is adopted, it is clear that the hearing found

111

no response, at least from some. The reason given, *because it did not meet with faith in the hearers,* is also capable of different interpretations. To begin with there is a problem about the text. The two most supported textual streams read either 'meet with' (*synkekerasmenos,* referring to the message), or 'united with' (*synkekramenous,* referring to 'them'), in which case the meaning would be 'because they were not by faith united with those who truly heard'. Either reading would emphasize the lack of faith on the part of the hearers, but the former would be more natural from the point of view of grammar. Both would bring out the fact that hearing alone is not enough, although the first does this more effectively. W. Manson[1] thinks that the second reading here implies that the group addressed in this epistle may have separated from the main group over a matter of 'faith'. But this interpretation would have no relevance to the Israelites mentioned in the context, even if it applied to the readers of the letter. *To us just as to them* would seem to exclude this view.

**3.** Believers are in an entirely different position from the ancient Israelites to whom Psalm 95 refers. Nevertheless the writer quotes once again the emphatic judgment of God which forbade the Israelites to enter Canaan, for by so doing the superior position of believers is brought into sharper focus. When he says, *we who have believed* (past tense) *enter* (present) *that rest,* he is stressing that the rest he is thinking of is an experience already in process of being fulfilled. It is not something simply to be hoped for in the future. It is an essential part of the present reality for Christians. It is strange that the word 'believe' is not in the present tense, but the writer evidently intends to refer to the event of conversion. The warning in verse 1 is clearly intended for those whose experience has fallen short of God's provision for them. Presumably the original readers would have recognized the spiritual nature of the 'rest', which the writer has so far not defined. He does, however, give some hint in the next statement – *although his works were finished from the foundation of the world* – as if he wants his readers to switch their minds back beyond the wilderness wanderings to

---

[1] W. Manson, *The Epistle to the Hebrews,* p. 70, n. 4.

the creation itself. The *my rest* of the quotation and the *his works* of the comment are clearly closely connected. What believers can now enter is none other than the same kind of rest which the Creator enjoyed when he had completed his works, which means that the rest idea is of completion and not of inactivity (but see comment on verse 10). It is important to note that the 'rest' is not something new which has not been known in experience until Christ came. It has been available throughout the whole of man's history. This reference back to the creation places the idea on the broadest possible basis and would seem to suggest that it was part of God's intention for man. 'Rest' is a quality which has eluded man's quest, and in fact cannot be attained except through Christ. Jesus himself invited men to come to him to find rest (Mt. 11:28–30).

**4–5.** Two quotations follow which confirm the points which have already been established: the reality of the rest and Israel's failure to obtain it. The first quotation comes from Genesis 2:2, but is introduced by the very general formula *he has somewhere (pou) spoken*, closely parallel to the formula used in 2:6. The authority of the passage has greater significance than the precise context. The allusion to the *seventh day* follows from what has been said in verse 3 and prepares for the further mention of a sabbath rest in verse 9. This reference to the seventh day led some ancient exegetes to maintain a view of history split into 6000 years during which God would bring things to completion followed by 1000 years of rest (so *Ep. of Barnabas* 15:4ff.).[1]

The second quotation, introduced by the formula *again in this place* (*i.e.* Ps. 95), repeats what has already been quoted in 3:11 and echoed in 3:18. It is obviously important to the writer to impress this idea on his hearers. It highlights so emphatically that God himself has the last word – not the unbelievers and provokers.

**6–7.** Although the deduction made from these quotations is not stated with logical clarity, yet the implications are clear enough. *Since therefore* connects verse 6 with verses 4–5 and the deduction is made that *some* were to enter. The line of argument

---

[1] Bruce remarks that Barnabas goes on to confuse the Jewish schema of the millennial sabbath with the Christian idea of an eighth millennium (p. 74, n. 20). For a modern exponent of a view similar to that of Barnabas, *cf.* G. H. Lang, *Comm.*, pp. 73ff.

must be that since the Israelites never entered (*i.e.*, *those who formerly received the good news*), someone else must, if God's promise is not to be rendered void. It is strange that at this point the writer takes no account of the entry into Canaan of the second generation Israelites, although he introduces Joshua later (verse 8). The contrast is still between Moses, chief representative of the old covenant, and Christ, the inaugurator of the new covenant. Again the thought focuses on the fact that the Israelites *failed to enter* and the readers are once again reminded that the cause was *disobedience*. They had only themselves to blame. But this shift from Moses to Christ involves another reinterpretation of the *today* of Psalm 95 which was already reinterpreted some centuries after the wilderness events. The writer re-introduces this *today* theme by another unusual explanation, *again he sets (horizei) a certain day*. The verb, which means to set the limits of, is admirably suited for the introduction of the extended meaning which the writer puts upon the quotation. Although the subject of the action is again left undefined, God himself is clearly intended.

*Saying through David* is literally 'in (*en*) David', *i.e.* in the person of David. This brings out vividly the combination of the divine and human in the production of the Scriptures. Although the quotation is said to be David's words, yet it is the Spirit of God who speaks through them. Moreover, whereas the hardening took place in the wilderness, David applies it *so long afterwards*, which shows the writer's firm conviction that the words of God have continual validity. This is why he is concerned to find some contemporary relevance for them. The repetition of the first part of the passage from Psalm 95 quoted in chapter 3 adds a solemnity to the warning contained in the words, as if it were like a bell constantly tolling: 'Today, harden not; today, harden not.' As Bruce says, 'By dint of repetition our author endeavours to bring home to his readers the fact that the divine warning is as applicable to them as it was in the days of Moses or David.'[1]

**8–9.** It seems likely that at this stage the writer considers a possible objection, which he assumes rather than states. An

[1] Bruce, *Comm.*, p. 16.

objector might say that although Moses could not lead the people of Israel into Canaan because of their unbelief, *Joshua* did so and the 'some' of verse 6 must therefore be the people whom he led in. In that case, of course, Joshua would be on a par with Christ who leads his people into a spiritual rest. But the writer does not think in this way. He argues, on the basis of God speaking *of another day*, that the day of Joshua's action could not have been the fulfilment of the promise. Indeed, the psalmist, in recalling this rest and applying it to his own day, was clearly not thinking of the rest which Joshua obtained. After all what Joshua did had a merely transitory importance compared with the unchanging creation rest of God. Indeed, God's idea of 'rest' is wholly different from man's idea and the writer here uses the psalmist's words to turn his readers' minds towards a spiritual idea, the kind which can truly be called God's rest.

Verse 9 introduces the conclusion with the words *So then* (*ara*), suggesting that it is indisputable. The description of the rest as *a sabbath rest* is important because it introduces a word (*sabbatismos*) which occurs nowhere else. It may have been coined by this writer (so MM), for it effectively differentiates between the spiritual kind of rest and the Canaan rest (the psalm has the word *katapausis*).[1] Those who are eligible for this sabbath rest are called *the people of God*, which distinguishes them from the unbelieving Israelites. This is, in fact, a comprehensive term, suitable for the universal community, which embraces both Jews and Gentiles (*cf.* a similar use in 1 Pet. 2:10). This possessive aspect of God is remarkable. He delights to call the believers his people. A new community, devoted to hearing God's voice and obeying it, has displaced the old Israel which failed in the time of testing.

**10.** This verse gives an explanation of the sabbath rest. It is *God's rest* and therefore has no lesser pattern. God's people share his rest. What he did, they do. By becoming identified with him, they enter into his experiences. There is no doubt that the writer is implying that the believer's present sabbath

[1] There is scant support for Käsemann's appeal to gnostic usage of *sabbatismos* as an emanation, since the only probable indication of this is in the pseudo-Clementine homilies. *Cf.* Hofius' discussion of this concept (*op. cit.*, pp. 102ff.).

rest is as much a reality as God's rest. It is not some remote hope, but a hope immediately realizable. Nevertheless the writer still fears that some of his readers will miss the promised rest altogether, hence the exhortation in verse 11.

The glorification of rest (*katapausis*) does not imply that work is therefore a misfortune. 'Rest' here is not to be thought of as inactivity. Indeed this whole passage suggests that after the act of creation, God began his rest, which presumably still continues. There is no suggestion that God withdrew from any further interest in the created order (as the Deists maintained). Héring comments, '*katapausis* must not invoke merely the notion of repose, but also those of peace, joy and concord.'[1]

*(ii) The urgency to seek for that rest (4:11–13)*

**11.** Here is another of the many exhortations with which this epistle is studded. *Let us therefore strive to enter* is expressed in a form which suggests that some considerable effort is needed. It cannot be taken for granted. The verb (*spoudazō*, strive) involves some degree of haste and this is in line with the various solemn warnings which the writer gives. The example of the people of Israel is again cited as the main motive for the exhortation. The writer clearly thinks that there is a grave danger of history repeating itself, although it should be noted that he gives no indication that his readers had as yet been guilty of *the same sort of disobedience*. The Greek (*en hypodeigmati*) here is capable of being understood in two ways, 'falling into the same example' or 'falling after the same example'. The former is the more natural, and supports the RSV. But the difference in meaning is very slight. There are several indications in the New Testament that the early Christians discerned parallels between the experience of the early Israelites and their own (*cf.* for instance 1 Pet. where the Exodus motif is strong).

**12.** A strong connection undoubtedly exists between this verse and the last. The warning was based in fact on the nature of the divine revelation. It was of such a character that its claims could not be dismissed as of no consequence. Indeed the powerful qualities of the Word are described by means of an impres-

[1] *Cf.* J. Héring, *Comm.*, p. 32.

sive metaphor, which emphasizes not only the activity, but also the effectiveness of *the word of God*. First, the meaning of this phrase must be established. There are two possibilities. It is used either in a general sense of the revelation of God or else in a particular sense of Jesus Christ himself in his function as Logos, according to John's usage. These two aspects are closely linked together, but the immediate context would suggest that it is in the more general sense of God's message to man that the expression is intended to be understood. Strong appeal has been made to God's revelation to his people and the implication is that no-one can enter into true rest except the one in whom the Word of God has taken full control in every part of his experience. Nevertheless, it is in the fullest sense possible only through that complete revelation of God in his Son which has already formed the basis of the introductory statement in this epistle (1:1ff.).

The qualities and activities attributed to the Word – living, active, sharp, piercing and discerning – are only partially applicable in a personal manner. Moreover, the *sword* imagery may at first give the impression of judgment, which is not, however, the main feature here. The idea of the Word (*logos*) dividing is found in Philo (*Quis rerum divinarum heres sit*, Sections 230–233). But Philo's idea differs from the idea in this epistle in that his logos does not distinguish things on a moral basis, but leaves man's reason to accomplish the task. The personification of the Word as God's authentic command is found in Wisdom 18:15f., in a sense much closer to Hebrews than Philo. Yet here the idea is more fundamental. It is nothing short of the permeation of the Word into every aspect of a man's being.

That the Word is *living* shows that it reflects the true character of God himself, the source of all life. This kind of life is full of energy to achieve its declared end. This living quality is particularly appropriate to the idea of the Word, especially when applied to the record of revelation, for the notion might easily degenerate into a dead code, as undoubtedly the Law had become for many Jews. But a revelation which is living has constant application to the minds of the recipients. When Jesus declared that the words which he spoke were spirit and life (Jn.

117

6:63), it was this life-giving constituent of his revelation which was being emphasized. The second characteristic, *active* (*energēs*), serves to underline the same idea. A thing may be alive but dormant, but the nature of true life is that it springs into activity and challenges on every front those who fall short of its standards. The Word of God, in its intellectual and moral demands, pursues men and cries out for personal decision to be made in response to its exhortations. No doubt the writer is thinking of the ever present character of the spiritual challenge he has just culled from his reading of Psalm 95.

The comparison of the Word of God to a sword is found also in Ephesians 6:17 and recurs in Revelation 1:16, where the idea of a *two-edged sword* is used to describe the nature of the words which proceed from the mouth of the glorified Son of God. It is also found in Isaiah 49:2 and Wisdom 7:22. The reference in Ephesians is in a context of spiritual armoury and is specifically applied to the attack against the forces of evil. Here, however, the emphasis falls on the penetrating character of the Word. This is expressed in the comparative description, *sharper*. It is the ability of a two-edged sword to penetrate which has struck the author most forcibly. But even that fails to do justice to the activity of the Word.

The following description elucidates this penetrating aspect of the Word. *Piercing to the division of soul and spirit* draws special attention to the divisive action of the Word of God, but in what sense is it here intended? Although it has been suggested that the division is of soul (*psychē*) from spirit (*pneuma*), it seems better to suppose that the penetration is into soul as well as spirit, *i.e.* its action brings out the true nature of both.[1] In this case the Word would be seen as penetrating the whole person, both soul and spirit. If the former were adopted it would mean that the penetration was so thorough as to reach to the notoriously obscure dividing-line between soul and spirit. Both the word for 'piercing' (*diïkneomai*) and for 'division' (*merismos*) are peculiar to this writer in the New Testament. The latter word occurs also in 2:4 where it relates to the distribution of spiritual

---

[1] C. Spicq, *Comm.* 1, pp. 52ff., sees a Philonic distinction here between soul and spirit, in which the latter is superior to the former and is alone able to comprehend divine teaching.

gifts, but clearly the meaning is different here. The New Testament use of *pneuma* for the human spirit focuses on the spiritual aspect of man, *i.e.* his life in relation to God, whereas *psychē*
refers to man's life irrespective of his spiritual experience, *i.e.*
his life in relation to himself, his emotions and thought. There
is a strong antithesis between the two in the theology of Paul.

When the divisive activity is extended to *joints and marrow*
and *thoughts and intentions*, it is again clear that the idea of
thoroughness is in mind. The theme that the Word of God
affects us to the extent of discriminating our intentions is challenging. Nothing, not even our innermost thoughts, is shielded
from the discernment of the message of God. It affects in a most
comprehensive manner the whole man, as the next verse so
clearly brings out.

**13.** What has just been said is now backed up by a more
general statement about the relation between the creation and
the Creator, although God himself is not named. There is no
doubt that the expressive description, *him with whom we have to
do*, is a reference to God. A literal understanding of the words
would be 'to whom to us is the account', *i.e.* to whom we must
give account. This reminds us of the final reckoning, in the light
of which the whole verse must be understood.

It is a salutary warning that nothing and no-one can be hidden
from the sight of God. Every creature is said to be *open* (*gymna*,
literally 'naked'), which stresses complete exposure before God.
In addition it is said to be *laid bare* (*tetrachēlismena*), a colourful
term, which occurs only here in the New Testament and does
not occur in the Septuagint. It means 'to bend back the neck'
(as in wrestling); but its secondary sense is 'to lay bare', either
in being overcome or forced to fall prostrate, or as here in the
metaphorical application of 'lay bare'. It is as if God ensures
that no-one can hide his face from the eyes of God: his head is
pushed back so as to be in the full view of God. This solemn
thought prepares the way for the second main part of the epistle
in which the purpose and effectiveness of the high-priestly
work of Christ is expounded. The fact that nothing can be
concealed makes all the more pressing the need for an effective
representative who can act on behalf of men.

## E. A SUPERIOR HIGH PRIEST (4:14 – 9:14)

The Law of Moses had recognized and made provision for a high priest who could mediate between God and man. But the priesthood of Aaron had several weaknesses and the writer shows that the high-priesthood of Christ is of a superior kind. In a challenging interlude, the writer warns the readers about the consequences of turning away from the Christian faith. The question of what order of priesthood Christ belongs to leads the writer to discuss the superior order of Melchizedek. Closely linked with this theme is that of the New Covenant which is shown to be superior to the old.

*(i) Our great high priest (4:14–16)*

**14.** Although it has been stated a number of times (*cf.* 1:3; 2:17; 3:1) that the high-priest theme occupied a prominent place in the writer's mind, only now does the full explanation of it begin. It is probable that the conjunction, *Since then (oun)*, which opens this verse links directly with 2:17–18, the intervening section being something of an interlude which nevertheless sets the tone by calling the attention of the readers to the importance of the theme.

There are three statements made about our *high priest*. First he is *great*, which marks him out as superior to other lesser priests. The writer thinks primarily of his superiority to the Aaronic order of priesthood which he deals with in the subsequent passage. This greatness extends not only to his character but also to his work.

The second characteristic is that he *has passed through the heavens*. Since the plural 'heavens' is used, it is suggested by some that the Jewish idea of an ascending series of heavens is here in mind. Paul in 2 Corinthians 12:2 speaks of being caught up into 'the third heaven'. Clement of Alexandria refers to seven heavens. But since it was the regular practice in the Old Testament for the plural to be used for heaven, it is unlikely that the Jewish idea of successive heavens is in mind. It is most likely that the idea is general and is intended to contrast with the limited entrance of the Aaronic high priest within the veil. Our high priest penetrates to the very presence of God. The words suggest that no hindrance obstructs his passage. We may compare the statement here with that in 10:19 which declares that, in view of our high priest's work, we now have confidence to enter 'the sanctuary'. We share the access of our high priest.

The third statement about him gives his name, *Jesus, the Son of God*. The former of the two names has already appeared in 2:9 and 3:1 where it identifies him in his human nature to show his eligibility for the office of high priest. The name is again used in connection with the high-priestly theme in 6:20; 7:22; 10:19; 12:24; 13:12. Indeed the name Jesus without any other titles occurs as frequently in this epistle as the single title 'Christ' (9 times each). The writer does not appear to use the different names indiscriminately. It is highly important for him to establish without question that our high priest is none other than the historical Jesus. At the same time he reiterates what he has already made clear, that this Jesus is also Son of God. Although the Sonship of Jesus is assumed in the preceding part of the epistle, the title *Son of God* is not used until this point in the discussion, and it is no doubt intentionally introduced here to combine the humanity and divinity of Jesus as the perfect qualifications for a high priest who was to be superior to all others. It is used again in 6:6; 7:3 and 10:29; in the first and last of these references Son of God describes the one who is treated with ignominy by those who apostatize.

After the introduction of so great a high priest, it is not surprising that an exhortation is at once added: *let us hold fast our confession*. The verb used here (*kratōmen*) means 'cling to', as if it requires some determination on our part. The idea, but with a slightly different verb (*katechōmen*), recurs in 10:23 in relation to the same object, *confession*. This latter word has already been met in 3:1 and may be considered a key idea in this epistle, since there is a direct link up between the present passage and 10:19–23. Indeed 4:14–16 may be regarded as the prologue to the high-priestly theme and 10:19–23 as the epilogue. In both passages there occur the ideas of holding on to the confession, of drawing near to God through a great high priest and of a confidence (*parrēsia*) in doing so. The parallels are too striking to be accidental. They reflect the writer's purpose in the structure of his epistle. His interest in expounding his high priest theme is not theoretical but practical, *i.e.* to exhort his readers to draw near.

**15.** Although the ability of our high priest to sympathize with the tempted has already been pointed out (2:18) the same idea is now expressed in a negative way, *we have not a high priest who is unable to sympathize.* Why does the writer change from the positive to the negative form? It seems most likely that he is aware of an objection, perhaps that in some way Jesus Christ was too remote from man's need. If so, he hastens to dispel this fear. The statement here is given as a reason for holding fast, as the conjunction *For* (*gar*) shows. Our confidence is directly related to the ability of our high priest. Only in this epistle (here and in 10:34) is the verb *sympathize* (*synpatheō*, literally 'suffer along with') used in the New Testament. Here it relates to Christ's sympathy with his people, and in 10:34 to the Christian's compassion for prisoners. The Christian's capacity for sympathy is based on Christ's ability to sympathize. In the present case the object of the sympathy is *our weaknesses.* This idea of weakness (*astheneia*), implying a consciousness of need, occurs elsewhere in the epistle in reference to the weakness of Aaron's order of priesthood (5:2; 7:28), and stands in marked contrast to the absence of such weakness on the part of our great high priest. It is, in fact, because in this sense he stands above such need that he, being strong, is in a position to sympathize. The word *weakness* is sufficiently comprehensive to include any form of felt need. There is sympathy for the needy, but not for the self-sufficient.

In case any should think that even if our high priest is able to sympathize he cannot know the temptations which assault other men, the temptations of Jesus are now specifically referred to. He is *one who in every respect has been tempted as we are.* This is a more specific development of the statement in 2:18, where the fact of the tempting of Jesus is given as a guarantee that he is able to help others in their temptations. There are here two further assertions which raise a penetrating problem: that his temptations are like ours (*as we are*), and that they extend to all points (*in every respect*). The first statement could be understood in the sense that his nature is like ours, rather than his temptations, but this would not avoid the implication of the second statement. *In every respect* (*kata panta*) places Jesus in the same category as ourselves when it comes to temptation. This conveys an aspect which is tremendously encouraging. We may take great comfort from the fact that his experience matches ours.

But the problem arises from the excepting clause, *yet without sin*. Since we are tempted and we sin, and he is tempted and does not sin, how can his temptations be the same as ours? If he has no bias to sin as we have, is he not by that fact in a privileged position which at once distinguishes his temptation from ours? For a solution to this difficulty we must note that temptation in itself is not sinful. The idea is rather of exposure to testing or seduction. This is clearly possible without sinning. While there may certainly be a sense in which the exposure to temptation on the part of Jesus was on a different plane from man's temptations because he was free from the bias of sin, yet in another sense his own testing was in all respects similar to ours. The experience of Jesus was not confined to the three recorded temptations in the wilderness; it affected the whole of his mission. It is enough to know that he passed through stresses and strains which no other man has ever known. The greater in this case includes the lesser. What are my temptations, even faced with a bias which a perfect and divine person did not experience, compared with what he endured? His sinlessness is not set out for his people as an example so much as an inspiration.[1] Our high priest is highly experienced in the trials of human life.

With this important and specific statement about the sinlessness of Jesus, we may compare Paul's comment in 2 Corinthians 5:21. It is an integral feature of New Testament teaching and particularly important for this writer's high-priest theme (*cf.* the further statements in 7:26ff.), that Jesus, though a man, nevertheless was without sin.

**16.** Another exhortation follows, which, as already noted above, recurs in 10:22f. It is the possibility of drawing near to God which has particularly caught the imagination of the writer. There are here a number of features which are worth noting.

---

[1] Westcott, *Comm.*, p. 107, comments that Christ shared our temptations, but with the exception 'that there was no sin in Him to become the spring of trial'.

First the Christian's approach to God is to be characterized by *confidence* or boldness (*parrēsia*), by a freedom of expression and deliverance from fear. This is one of the most striking features about the Christian way to God, that it is unencumbered even by a man's sense of awe in God's presence. It is perfectly reflected in the Lord's prayer, where the use of an address like 'Our Father' reveals a marvellous boldness. The second feature is the expression *throne of grace*. The throne stands for royalty and could certainly be overawing were it not that its main characteristic is grace, *i.e.* the place where God's free favour is dispensed. In 8:1 and 12:2 Jesus Christ is seen to be seated at the right hand of the throne. He is the guarantee that it is a place of grace. A third feature is the combination of *mercy* and *grace* as special favours dispensed from the throne. Already our high priest has been described as merciful (*cf.* 2:17). This is a prominent New Testament theme and is especially characteristic of the Pauline epistles. The fourth point is the help which is forthcoming *in time of need*. The supply of grace is unrestricted, the only condition being a willingness to receive it, a sense of its indispensability.

*(ii) Comparison with Aaron (5:1–10)*

1. The first four verses of chapter 5 are historical and relate to the order of Aaron. If the epistle is addressed to Jewish Christians, the statements would come by way of reminder to serve as the background for the introduction of a superior order. Having already claimed that Jesus Christ is a great high priest, some comparison with the Aaronic order is unavoidable and may in fact have two aims. It may demonstrate that Jesus fulfils all the conditions of high-priesthood and it may further demonstrate how much superior he is to Aaron's line. If the latter aim had not been included, the real significance of the order of Melchizedek would have been missed.

The discussion begins with a quite general statement regarding the high-priestly office. This moreover is seen to have some connection with the introductory section at the end of chapter 4 as the opening conjunction, *For* (*gar*) shows. Indeed, the ability of our high priest to help depends on the extent to which he fulfils the conditions. There are several specific characteristics mentioned. (i) The high priest is essentially a representative of man; he is *chosen from among men* (literally 'taken from men'). It is because he is identified by nature with men that he can act and plead on their behalf. This was fundamental to the Aaronic priesthood. There was no question of the task being entrusted to a superhuman being. It needs a man who can understand and feel for men. (ii) He *is appointed* (*kathistatai*). As the verb is passive, it is implied that the appointment of the high priest is made by God. The Aaronic order did not provide for democratic election, but only for authoritative theocratic assignments. (iii) His appointment is *in relation to God* (*ta pros ton Theon*). His work as mediator, to act on God's behalf towards men and on man's behalf before God, is clearly seen here. This is an essential function of priesthood. (iv) His purpose is *to offer gifts and sacrifices for sins*. This clause (a *hina* clause) brings out the result of his being so closely identified with both God and men. The two things offered are closely allied. Indeed the two words are sometimes used interchangeably, but here they are distinguished. In this case the *gifts* (*dōra*) must relate to the meal offerings and the sacrifices (*thysias*) to the blood offerings. The Aaronic high priest, in fact, was making an approach to God on the score of man's sins. Here the statement 'for sins' is significant, for it is not restricted to sacrifices, but also relates to gifts. It is best therefore to understand this as referring to the full range of the high priest's work. His whole performance as a representative of his people has value as an expiation, *i.e.* it has to do with the sins of the people whom he represents.

**2.** After these general functions of the office, the more personal aspect is brought into focus: the high priest's ability to *deal gently* (*metriopathein*) with the ignorant and the wayward.[1] Although nothing is said in the Old Testament about moral qualities, the writer has deduced this quality of gentle understanding from the basic fact that the high priest is essentially a man among men. It is much easier to dispose of, or at least ignore, the ignorant and wayward. They are a nuisance in any

[1] It is worth noting that the quality of gentle moderation mentioned here would not have been valued in Stoic circles, where it was regarded as a second best to the absence of passion. *Cf.* Williamson, *Philo and the Epistle to the Hebrews*, pp. 26f.

well-ordered society. But in a theocratic society they cannot be ignored. Provision must be made for them. The high priest was not only representative of the better sections of society, but also of the worse. The two descriptions – *ignorant (agnoousi) and wayward (planōmenois)* – may point to the origin and characteristic of the kind of sin with which the high priest can deal. Sins of ignorance were carefully distinguished from wilful sins, for which the law made no provision. The wanderers are those who have strayed from God's path, but want to get back. They are not the hardened rebels. The high priest had a special ministry of gentleness towards those conscious of their need. It is these with whom he could identify himself in his own *weakness*. Yet in this feature Aaron's line differs from our high priest who is even more able to deal gently with his people because of his strength rather than his weakness. He was never ignorant nor wayward, but has perfect understanding of those who are. Nevertheless the words translated *beset with weakness* may be understood in the sense 'wrapped around with weakness'. In this case the high priest may be thought of being clothed with the weaknesses of his people; if this is the meaning, there is a closer parallel with our great high priest. Yet the former sense, which contrasts Aaron's weakness with Christ's strength, is the more likely.

**3.** There is even more evident divergence in this verse between Jesus Christ and Aaron's order. Being a sinful man himself the Aaronic high priest is *bound to offer sacrifice for his own sins*. It was an important part of the whole process on the Day of Atonement for the high priest first to offer sacrifice as an atonement for his own sins (*cf.* Lv. 16:11ff.). In the writer's mind there appears to be a close connection between weakness and sin, although the one does not necessarily follow from the other. In the case of men, however, *i.e.* every man except the perfect man, weakness issues in sin. The perfect example of a sinless form of physical weakness is the cross. But the Aaronic order made no provision for that kind of weakness in its priests, except perhaps ideally, in its sacrificial system. Yet as this epistle will go on to show, whereas Aaron had to offer an animal, Christ offered himself. There is clearly a common factor between the high priest's sins and those *of the people*. He was in the same needy condition as they were. But again our high priest stands out in marked contrast. Being without sin he had no need to offer for himself and this at once places him in a different category.

**4.** A most important factor in the high priest's office is its origin. It was a divine appointment and not a self-appointment or a human appointment: *one does not take the honour upon himself*. The case of *Aaron* is now specifically mentioned, for he was set aside by God. The calling of God is an important factor in the New Testament as it was in the Old Testament, drawing attention as it does to the divine initiative. When comparison is made with our great high priest, it is evident that he also was appointed to his office. We are reminded that he recognized that God had given him the work he had come to do (*cf.* Jn. 17:4).

**5.** The next six verses explain the relationship between Christ and the order of Aaron and introduce the order of Melchizedek, which is then developed further after the interlude in 5:11 – 6:20.

The writer first of all explores the divine appointment of Christ, a characteristic which is in direct line with Aaron's position. It is noticeable that the title *Christ* is here used rather than Jesus (which is preferred in 4:14). This suggests that the writer is deeply impressed by the thought that the anointed one, the Messiah, in his office *did not exalt himself* as he might well have done. The New Testament picture of the Messiah, however, is always of one whose mission is to serve, never of one who has snatched at positions of honour. In John 8:54 Jesus maintains that he does not honour himself, but is honoured by the Father. The fact that he was *appointed* is supported from Psalm 2, from a passage which has already been cited in Hebrews 1:5. This recurring theme, which is here linked with another citation from Psalm 110, suggests that these psalms had been meditated on and formed a vital part of the structure of the epistle. They are like recurring airs in a piece of music, each new introduction of which comes with variations. The writer wants the high-priest idea to be linked closely with his exalted view of the Christ as Son of God. The appointment by God is an indication that our high priest is wholly acceptable to God. Had he been man-appointed there would always have been doubt.[1]

**6.** The second quotation, from Psalm 110:4, is introduced with a very general formula, *as he says also in another place*, presumably to distinguish it from the first quotation. It is nevertheless quoted as authoritative, for 'he says' clearly refers to God. The divine appointment to the office of *priest* is supported by this quotation, but two entirely new features are also introduced which show the priesthood of Christ to be different from Aaron's. First, it is *for ever*, because it can never be improved upon. Being already perfect, it never reaches the point when it gives way to a better. Secondly, it is *after the order of Melchizedek*, because, as will be expounded later, it has no succession as Aaron's order had. It was once for all, and yet constantly applicable. In this sense it is timeless.

Melchizedek, unlike Aaron, is a mysterious person. The fleeting mention of him in Genesis 14:18–20 shows him as a historical person whose priesthood was accepted by Abraham. It is remarkable that the author of this epistle makes nothing of the fact that the Genesis account says that Melchizedek brought out bread and wine. He might have attached symbolical importance to this, since the bread and wine are so highly significant in reference to the Lord's supper. But he concentrates instead on the historic fact that Abraham offered tithes to Melchizedek (see ch. 7). He might further have cited and enlarged on the oath mentioned in Psalm 110:4, especially as he has already mentioned a divine oath in chapters 3 and 4. But he reserves such comment until 6:13 when the significance of the oath is expounded. The author's method of introducing the strange figure of Melchizedek is as mysterious as the figure of the priest himself. There is a certain aura about him which is fitting in view of the exalted high priest whom he is seen to typify.

**7.** In this epistle there are many surprises in the sudden introduction of different themes which do not at first seem to follow naturally from the context. The next section (verses 7–10) is an example of this. The writer introduces what may be called a historical reminiscence from the life of Jesus. We may wonder what this has to do with Melchizedek, whose order of

---

[1] As Montefiore says, *Comm.*, p. 96, 'Only a high priest who is Son of God can have his rightful place at God's right hand.'

priesthood is mentioned again in verse 10. It may be that the repeating of the quotation of Psalm 2 reminded the writer of his earlier sequence of thought where he concentrates on the divine Sonship (chapter 1) and on the humanity of Jesus (chapter 2). He seems to want to dispel any idea that Jesus is a mystical non-historical figure by abruptly reminding the readers what happened *In the days of his flesh*. The expression is interesting because it draws attention to the reality of his human life. The writer has already made this clear in chapter 2 (see verses 14 and 17), but the present reference much more vividly introduces a clear allusion to the historical record of the life of Christ. Indeed this is one of the most vivid examples in the New Testament outside the Gospels. In the Greek text the possessive *his* is not identified, but it must refer to *Jesus*, who is the subject of the whole of this section (*cf.* verse 5).

The main statement about the human life of Jesus concerns his powerful prayers. The two words used for this, *prayers and supplications,* are closely akin, but are nevertheless distinct. The former (*deēsis*) is the general New Testament word for prayers, but the latter (*hiketēria*) has a stronger element of entreaty and is derived from the ancient practice of holding out an olive branch as a sign of appeal. These are remarkable words in describing the Son's prayer to the Father, but they show how completely identified he is with his people. The *loud cries and tears* seem to be an undeniable allusion to the agony of Jesus in the garden of Gethsemane, where his prayer was accompanied by sweat of blood, revealing the inner intensity of the struggle through which he passed. The accounts in the Gospels do not mention tears, but tears would not be out of keeping with those accounts. He who could weep at the grave of Lazarus would not be beyond expressing himself similarly on other occasions of deep emotion. Although tears are usually regarded as a sign of weakness, they nevertheless have healing properties. Our high priest was not so far above us that tears were beyond him at times when his mind was sorely distracted.

In describing the person to whom these intense prayers were addressed, the writer purposely uses a descriptive phrase to draw attention to God's ability to save: *who was able to save him from death*. This idea of God as deliverer is so characteristic of the New Testament that it is not easy to appreciate its full significance. This epistle has already drawn attention to man's constant bondage to the fear of death (2:15). The message that victory is through Christ has in the past brought challenge and new hope to many people. It is no wonder the writer returns to it when he thinks of the prayers of Jesus.

When he says, however, that *he* [Christ] *was heard for his godly fear*, it is not immediately clear how the words should be understood. Many commentators consider that the form of words means that his godly fear – his passion – was turned into the means to cast out all fear. The words would, however, seem to be a more direct allusion to the agony in the garden where the climax was the acceptance of the divine will by Jesus ('nevertheless not my will but thine be done'), in which case the word *for* (*apo*) would mean 'because of' (*his godly fear*). Another understanding of the same preposition would be the more usual 'out of', giving the meaning 'delivered out of *his godly fear*', but this thought seems alien to the context. The writer is careful about the word he uses to express fear (*eulabeia*) and does not use the more common word (*phobos*). Indeed only in this epistle does the word he uses occur in the New Testament (*cf.* also 12:28 where the meaning is 'reverence'). On its use here Westcott remarks: 'more commonly it expresses reverent and thoughtful shrinking from over-boldness, which is compatible with true courage.'[1] The idea is therefore applicable to the Gethsemane experience. A problem has been thought to arise over the fact that the Synoptic accounts clearly state that the Gethsemane prayer for the removal of the cup was not pressed. In what sense therefore was Jesus heard? The answer surely lies in his perfect acceptance of the divine will.

**8.** This reminiscence from the earthly experience of Jesus, which is an essential contribution to his qualification as a great high priest, leads the writer to reflect on the paradox of his sufferings. It would not be entirely unintelligible that sons usually learn obedience by what they suffer, *i.e.* at the hands of earthly fathers,[2] but with Christ it is very different. His Son-

---

[1] Westcott, *Comm.*, p. 127.

[2] *Cf.* C. Spicq, *Comm.* 1, pp. 46f., for examples from Philo showing a close connection between learning and suffering (*mathein/pathein*).

ship was perfect and therefore raises the problem why he needed to learn obedience at all. Here we are faced with the mystery of the nature of Christ. In considering the divine Son it may be difficult to attach any meaning to the learning process (*he learned obedience*), but in thinking of the Son as perfect man it becomes at once intelligible. When Luke says that Jesus advanced in learning (2:52), he means that by a progressive process he showed by his obedience to the Father's will a continuous making of God's will his own, reaching its climax in his approach to death. The cry of acceptance in the garden of Gethsemane was the concluding evidence of the Son's obedience to the Father. No-one will deny that there is deep mystery here, but the fact of it makes our high priest's understanding of us unquestionably more real. There are certain parallels here with Philippians 2:6ff., which also stresses the obedience of Christ in the form of a servant. In both passages the suffering servant of Isaiah may be in mind.

**9.** No less impressive is the repetition of the idea of a perfecting process being applied to Christ (as in 2:10). As in the former case, there is a close link between perfection and suffering. It is through a path of suffering that perfection is achieved. In the present case it is obedience which is specially linked with perfection, reminding us of the sequence of thought in Philippians 2:8–9. Of no human high priest could it be said that he was *made perfect*. This expression must not be understood to suggest that there was a time when he was not perfect. In the course of his human life the perfection which Jesus possessed was put to the test. That perfection remained unsullied through all that he suffered. As Hughes remarks, 'His sufferings both tested, and, victoriously endured, attested his perfection, free from failure and defeat.'[1] The emphasis here is on the perfection which is an ever-present reality. It should also be noted that the verb is frequently used in the Septuagint of the consecration of the high priest to his office, an idea which has some relevance to the theme of this epistle.

The perfection of Christ is seen as the basis for our salvation. Indeed, *he became the source of eternal salvation*. The becoming

[1] Hughes, *Comm.*, p. 188.

(*egeneto*) refers to the effecting of salvation and for this reason is expressed as a past tense. Historically it appears to refer to that point of time when Jesus assumed the office of high priest. The word translated 'source' (*aitios*) occurs only here in the New Testament and means 'cause'. It can refer to a good or a bad cause but here it is wholly good and is well rendered 'source' (AV has 'author'). There is no short-circuiting the means of salvation. What does not come through Jesus is no true salvation. For our writer there is special significance in the idea of eternal things. He speaks of eternal judgment (6:2), eternal redemption (9:12), the eternal Spirit (9:14), eternal inheritance (9:15), the eternal covenant (13:20). It is obvious that he wishes to lay foundations which are permanent, contrasting with the ever-changing scene of any earthly priesthood and method of approach to God. There is something stable and enduring about the salvation which Jesus Christ provides. We might compare the frequent occurrence in John's Gospel of the idea of eternal life.

It is quite clear that there are conditions laid down for those who wish to avail themselves of this salvation. These are summed up as obedience, the counterpart of what the Son has already learned (verse 8). Obedience in that sense involves a complete acceptance of the divine will. As far as Christians are concerned this sums up a man's response to God's provision of a means of salvation. It is noticeable that those eligible for salvation are *all who obey him*, which means all classes of obeyers, Jews and Gentiles, rich and poor, learned and uneducated, freemen and slave (*cf.* for instance Paul's statement in Gal. 3:28). The universality of the gospel is reflected in the universal effectiveness of the high priest's office.

10. Another word is now used which is unique in the New Testament to describe the public giving of a name or title, which the RSV gives as *designated* (*prosagoreuō*). The announcement of a new order of priesthood is made *by God*, which draws attention to the divine appointment, as already mentioned in verses 4–5. In any case the order of Melchizedek is not an order with a hereditary succession, as the writer shows in 7:3, and therefore no-one could be consecrated in it except by God himself. It is also a unique order, in that no-one else until Christ be-

longed to it. The unusual word mentioned above is particularly appropriate to the status of our *high priest*, since he is of a wholly different order from Aaron.

At this point in the development of his argument, the author leaves his *Melchizedek* theme to deal with some serious problems affecting his readers. It seems to be a planned digression, which returns gradually to the Melchizedek theme at the end of chapter 6 by way of a discussion of the oath to Abraham.

*(iii) A challenging interlude (5:11 – 6:20)*[1]

**11.** Unexpectedly the writer suddenly reflects on the capacity of his readers to grasp what he has just been saying and what he intends to expound further. This shows unmistakably that he is addressing real people whose condition is known to him. He is aware that they are *dull of hearing*, presumably in a spiritual sense. Perhaps he thinks his discussion of Aaron's order and its inferiority to Melchizedek will sound too academic and theoretical to some of his readers. He seems, at least, to recognize that there are difficulties in his exposition thus far, and there are greater ones to come; but he knows that they ought to present no obstacles to men of mature minds. Nevertheless he has serious problems over the readers and decides to interrupt his main discourse to issue a strong warning. When he says *About this we have much to say which is hard to explain*, he is particularly referring to the Melchizedek theme which would not have been one of the more familiar themes in contemporary Judaism, though there is some mention of it in Philo's writings, and in the Qumran documents. It is noticeable here that a direct relationship is assumed between spiritual condition and understanding. The latter is not merely a matter of intellect. The difficulty is essentially a problem of communication, how to express truths in a manner which is within the grasp of the readers. Undoubtedly the problem facing the writer is one faced by every exponent of divine truth.

**12.** The criticism about being dull of hearing would sound unwarranted without some justification being given. With this in mind an explanation for the assessment is set out. The first

---

[1] On this section, *cf.* H. P. Owen, 'The "Stages of Ascent" in Hebrews v.11–vi.3.', *NTS* 3 (1956–57), pp. 243ff.

thing is the clear failure of the readers to fulfil what was ex-pected of them: *you ought to be teachers*. The reason why teaching was expected of them is that they had been Christians long enough to have acquired sufficient basic understanding to be able to pass it on to others. The question arises here of the identity of these people. It seems reasonable to suppose that all the members of a church cannot be meant, since all churches contain those who are not apt to teach. It suggests that a group of people is in mind who had the potential for teaching others, but nevertheless lacked the necessary basic understanding. They needed to go back to elementary matters themselves. They were probably a small group of intellectuals who lacked spiritual perception. It is worth observing that the verb translated 'ought' (*opheilontes*) implies an obligation and not just a desired char-acteristic. The propagating of an understanding of the Christian message in a fully-developed form depends on those who are mature instructing those who are immature. It is a serious pos-ition therefore in any community if its potential teachers are themselves at the immature stage.

The need of these readers is next specified, *i.e.* for *some one to teach you again the first principles of God's word*. Evidently these people had not merely not advanced, they had actually lost their understanding of 'the first principles'. They needed to go back to square one. The instruction required was as basic as that. It is a tragic commentary on their spiritual grasp. No wonder the writer finds it difficult to communicate his message. It is to be wondered why he did not devote his whole epistle to an exposition of the gospel rather than labour his high-priest theme. The answer may be that the high-priest theme, so in-tegral to Jewish ways of thinking, was one of the main causes of the readers' failure to develop. The phrase translated 'of God's word' (*tōn logiōn tou Theou*) literally means 'of the oracles of God' and is elsewhere used in the New Testament to describe the Old Testament (*cf.* Acts 7:38; Rom. 3:2). Here, however, it appears to mean the basic teaching of the gospel since it is used in conjunction with 'principles' (*stoicheia*), a word which is com-monly used to describe the A.B.C. of a thing. If the 'oracles' are understood in the same sense as elsewhere, the reference could conceivably be to a failure on the part of the readers to understand the basic principles of the interpretation of the Old Testament, which was leading them to wrong thinking about the uniqueness of Christianity. They needed to return to basic thinking about this.

The contrast between *milk* and *solid food* is not intended to make them mutually exclusive, but to suggest a normal development from one to the other. The milk phase is as essential as the solid food, but those who never reach the latter stage are sadly deficient. The physical has a precise parallel in the spiritual. There are various grades of understanding and it is highly desirable that the spiritually minded man should be advancing in knowledge. This metaphorical use of milk and solid food is also found in 1 Corinthians 3:1–2.

**13.** In this verse a fuller explanation of the milk metaphor is now given. The milk-Christian is one *unskilled in the word of righteousness*, an expression which deserves comment. First the word 'unskilled' (*apeiros*) means literally 'untried', hence inexperienced, and would suggest that the lack of skill was linked with lack of practice. This is distinct from a state of complete ignorance. The things of God require something more than a nodding acquaintance. The writer unhesitatingly places his readers in the milk category. They had never developed the necessary skills.

The second comment is on the phrase *word of righteousness*. In the Greek there are no articles and the phrase must be taken to mean, not any specific body of doctrine, but the kind of word (*logos*) which has the character of righteousness. This would agree with the use of the same term (*logos*) in 6:1 where it refers to doctrine. The writer may be thinking of the special use of righteousness (*dikaiosynē*), which describes what is obtained by faith in Christ, but could also refer to the more general idea of rightness. These two interpretations are in any case linked, for man can have no adequate idea of right except through the righteousness of Christ. Undoubtedly when men first believe they do not at once gain skill in appreciating this theme, but some such interpretation is an indispensable quest for anyone who desires to be mature.

The concluding description of the milk-person as being *a child* follows naturally from the metaphor used. The child should precede the man. No-one wants to remain a perpetual child. There is a parallel to this imagery in 1 Corinthians 13:11 where Paul says, 'when I became a man, I gave up childish ways'. Grown men are not sustained on a diet of milk.

**14.** There is an equally valuable comment on the *mature* (*teleiōn*). The idea of maturity is linked with perfection, although certainly not identified with it except in the case of Christ. Maturity is here seen as the desirable development from spiritual childhood. This is a familiar idea in the Pauline epistles (*cf.* Eph. 4:13ff. – note especially 'we are to grow up in every way'; *cf.* 1 Cor. 2:6; 3:1; 14:20). The New Testament presents a picture of the full-orbed Christian life as completeness. The experienced Christian knows that he needs strong meat to attain to this kind of maturity.

The thought is still further developed as the mature are defined as *those who have their faculties trained by practice*. There is a reference to habit in the Greek here. In fact the words *by practice* (*dia tēn hexin*) could be translated 'by habit', which would bring out perhaps more clearly the building up of experience through a continued process in the past. The word occurs only here in the New Testament. Spiritual maturity comes neither from isolated events nor from a great spiritual burst. It comes from a steady application of spiritual discipline. Another word without parallels in the New Testament is that used here for *faculties* (*ta aisthētēria*), which denotes those special faculties of the mind which are used for understanding and judgment. Of all men the Christian has insight into spiritual things because his mind is trained in the art of understanding. This process of training is found elsewhere in Hebrews 12:11; 1 Timothy 4:7 and 2 Peter 2:14, although in the last case it occurs in the adverse sense of training for greed. The power to distinguish between good and evil has been sought ever since the times of Adam and Eve, but the facility to do so does not come easily even for those with some knowledge of Christ. This skill at once shows the difference between the mature and the immature. It must be recognized that Christians, especially among Gentiles, would need to forge a new code of morals in order to leave themselves unspotted in the world.

**6:1.** The contrast between the mature man and the child is next developed by a description of what the spiritual child must leave behind if he is to mature. The writer introduces a two-fold exhortation: *let us leave* and *let us go on*. These include, therefore, both a backward and a forward look. All progress is like that. Those who never get beyond beginnings never mature at all. But what beginnings are in the writer's mind? In the RSV they are described as *the elementary doctrines of Christ* (*ho tēs archēs tou Christou logos*), which represents words which are capable of different interpretations. The meaning could be either 'the word of the beginning of Christ', or as in the RSV, which applies the beginning (*archēs*) to the doctrine rather than to Christ.[1] There is no doubt that the former is the most natural understanding of the Greek, because of the order in which the words occur. But what does 'the beginning of Christ' here mean? A parallel may be seen in 5:12 where the 'beginning of the oracles of God' is mentioned. Evidently some basic aspects of Christ must here be in view. The 'beginning' would therefore be the initial understanding of the Christian position which differentiated it from Judaism.

The second positive injunction, *go on to maturity*, is expressed in the Greek rather unexpectedly in a passive form, in the sense 'let us be carried on to maturity (or completeness)'. This form suggests an element of yieldedness to a nobler influence, as if the maturing process is not a matter of our ingenuity. Spiritual maturity is not the kind which can be had for the asking, but requires higher powers than man's natural endowments. Nevertheless, this writer is deeply conscious of man's own responsibility, as his subsequent statements in this chapter show. There are clearly factors in a man's spiritual experience which can effectively cut off growth. He cannot be 'carried on to maturity' if he has no desire to be mature.

There are six factors in the description of the elementary doctrines of Christ: *repentance* and *faith, ablutions* and *laying on of hands, resurrection* and *judgment*. The grouping into three couples is probably not accidental. The first two are basic to the essential character of a living Christian faith. It is important to

[1] J. C. Adams, 'Exegesis of Hebrews vi.1f', *NTS* 13 (1967), pp. 378ff., regards the genitive 'of Christ' as subjective and contends that basic Jewish religion is here in mind. But *cf.* Hughes, *Comm.*, p. 195, n. 33, for an adequate answer to this.

note that these are actually described as *a foundation*, which by its very nature does not need renewal. The folly of a builder whose work is so unsatisfactory that he must start again at the foundation is self-evident. But is the writer suggesting that his readers might not have had the true foundation at the beginning of their Christian lives? The words *not laying again* seem to militate against that. The suggestion is that the foundation has been laid and what is necessary is to develop an adequate superstructure.

The expression *repentance from dead works* is unique. Nowhere else, except in 9:14, which speaks of purifying the conscience from dead works, is the idea of deadness applied to works. It is, however, applied to faith (Jas. 2:17), to the body (Rom. 8:10) and to men (Rom. 6:11; Eph. 2:1, 5; Col. 2:13). In each case the deadness indicates a state of non-functioning. When faith is dead, it is not performing its true purpose. It might as well not exist at all for all the use it is. Dead works, on the same analogy, would be works which had only the appearance of works, but which lacked any effective power. In the present case there may be an allusion to the Jewish idea of attaining justification through works, which from a Christian point of view would be regarded as 'dead' because ineffective. All those who turned from Judaism to Christianity would need to repent of their reliance on good works. In a more general sense the first step for all those who turn to Christianity is repentance, as John the Baptist, Jesus himself and the early preachers in Acts show.

The same may be said of the basic requirement of *faith toward God* (*epi Theon*), which brings out strongly the direction of faith. The various parts of the New Testament all testify to the necessity for faith in any approach to God. This epistle in some respects has a distinctive use of 'faith' (*cf.* 4:2; 6:12; 10:22, 38, 39; 11:1–39; 12:2; 13:7). Here the meaning must be the response of faith to the provision of God. In chapter 11 the emphasis falls on the activity of faith. There is no denying the dynamic character of faith seen through this writer's eyes.

**2.** The next two elementary doctrines are by contrast external acts of a cultic kind. *Ablutions* and *laying on of hands* are both paralleled in Judaism, but clearly had a different significance when applied to Christianity. The first literally concerns baptisms (*baptismōn*). The plural shows that not simply one act, but several ritual cleansings are in mind. It is to be noted that the Qumran community observed some kinds of ritual cleansings, but there is no evidence that this sort of ritual was practised in the Christian church. It is not impossible that the writer used the plural to suggest a comparison of the Christian practice of baptism with the Jewish idea of washings,[1] as the word is used elsewhere in the general sense of cultic washings (Heb. 9:10). Since these ritual practices are introduced by the word *instruction*, which also extends to the third couplet, it would seem that the writer is denying the need for any further basic teaching on these elementary Christian facets.

*The laying on of hands*, which in Jewish procedure was bound up with the giving of a blessing, in the Christian church acquired a new meaning.[2] There are many instances where the laying on of hands is connected with healing (*cf.* Mk. 16:18; Acts 28:8, where it relates to Christian healing by this means). But the sense here is more specific. It probably included the conferring of specific gifts (*cf.* Acts 8:17; 13:3; 19:6; 1 Tim. 4:14).

The practice here is of a basic character and presumably relates to all Christians and not simply to those called to special tasks (as in ordination). It may therefore be paralleled by Acts 8:17; 19:6, in both cases being accompanied by the gift of the Spirit.

The other two factors are of a doctrinal character. *The resurrection of the dead and eternal judgment* are regarded nevertheless as an essential constituent of Christian teaching. So essential is the former that the early preachers could not preach without bringing it in. They never mention the death of Christ without including his resurrection. Moreover, the application of the same idea to believers is implicit (*cf.* Acts 23:6 and especially 1 Cor. 15:12ff.). The New Testament makes no sense if the resurrection of the dead is denied. The writer does not argue this point. He regards it as sufficiently self-evident to be in-

[1] For baptism in other Jewish schools of thought, *cf.* D. Daube, *The New Testament and Rabbinic Judaism* (London, 1956), pp. 106–140; also M. Black, *The Scrolls and Christian Origins* (London, 1961), pp. 99ff., 114f.

[2] *Cf.* Mishnah, *Sanhedrin* 4.4, for the Jewish practice. It should also be noted that laying on of hands is found in OT, in both commissioning (Nu. 27:18, 23; Dt. 34:9) and in Levitical ritual (Lv. 1:4; 3:2; 4:4; 8:14; 16:21).

cluded in the elementary doctrines. The same applies to judgment. The use of the adjective 'eternal' may be compared with Mark 3:29 where the concept of 'eternal sin' is mentioned. It is probable that the expression here is intended in a comprehensive sense to include the basic eschatological teaching which all Christians would receive. Every believer must have some knowledge of both resurrection and judgment, for both are tied up with an awareness of the demands and also the glorious provision of God. This theme of judgment is not infrequent in Paul.

Part of the problem facing the Hebrews was the superficial similarity between the elementary tenets of Christianity and those of Judaism, which made it possible for Christian Jews to think they could hold on to both. The danger of apostasy was much greater for them than for converts from paganism.

**3.** The words *this we will do if God permits* could be understood as an exhortation, as the RSV margin states, *i.e.* 'Let us do this if God permits', as some manuscripts have it. But taken as a definite resolve on the part of the writer, confidently linking with him his readers, it has more point. Surely the writer does not doubt that God desires his people to advance in the spiritual life? The only other occasion in the New Testament where a parallel phrase is used is in 1 Corinthians 16:7, where Paul employs it in relation to his proposed plans. Since the writer goes on in the next section to speak of apostasy, he may be thinking of the conditions under which God permits progress. In this case the condition is added as a reminder that going on to maturity is not mechanical or automatic, but involves taking stock of God's conditions. There could have been no doubt in the writer's mind that God desires maturity in his people. It would be contrary to the nature of God as seen in this epistle to suppose otherwise.

**4.** That there is a definite connection between the statement just made and the following discussion about apostasy is clear from the conjunction *For* (*gar*). There is at least a theoretical possibility that spiritual maturity may prove to be unattainable. It is important for a true understanding of this difficult verse to recognize this context. It is equally important to note that the statement depends on the fulfilment of a condition as the if clause in verse 6 shows.

The various ways in which this writer uses the word *impossible* (*adynaton*) are instructive. Here he uses it of the impossibility of repentance in certain circumstances; in 6:18 of the impossibility for God to prove false; in 10:4 of the inability of the blood of animals to remove sin; and in 11:6 of the impossibility of pleasing God without faith. In each case there is no provision for compromise. The statements are all absolutes. The present one, however, causes most difficulty and can be correctly understood only when all the facets of the case are thoroughly examined. There are four verbs used to describe the subjects of the impossibility: (i) *enlightened* (*phōtisthentas*), (ii) *tasted* (*geusamenous*), (iii) *become partakers* (*metochous genēthentas*), (iv) *tasted the goodness* (*kalon geusamenous*). The last three are apparently intended to make clear the sense in which the first is used. The idea of enlightenment is characteristic of the New Testament in relation to God's message to man (*cf.* also 10:32 in the other apostasy passage). Especially is this true of John's Gospel in which Jesus claims to be the light of the world (8:12; *cf.* 1:9). Another parallel is 2 Corinthians 4:4, where the world is said to be blinded by the god of this world so as not to see 'the light of the gospel of the glory of Christ'. Wherever the light has shone in individual minds there has come some understanding of the glory of Christ. Bruce[1] finds the view tempting that the enlightening may refer to baptism and the tasting to the eucharist, but he admits especially in the latter case a wider reference also. Hughes[2] cites examples of patristic writers who adopted this kind of interpretation. But he himself prefers a metaphorical sense, *i.e.* the sense of experiencing the blessing. Those spoken of here, therefore, must have some initial revelation of Jesus Christ. This is strengthened by the other three statements made.

The idea of tasting *the heavenly gift* implies more than just knowledge of the truth. It implies experience of it. This is an Old Testament usage (*cf.* Ps. 34:8). In the New Testament 1 Peter 2:3 contains the same idea. There is a development between knowing about food, even liking the look of it, and actually tasting it. No-one can merely pretend to do the latter. Of course, not all tasting is pleasurable, and in the hypothetical

---

[1] Bruce, *Comm.*, p. 120.  [2] Hughes, *Comm.*, p. 208.

case which the writer is supposing, it clearly was not so. The *heavenly gift* was not appreciated. But what is meant by this expression? Nowhere else in the New Testament is the 'heavenly gift' (*tēs dōreas tēs epouraniou*) mentioned, although the idea of a gift from God occurs several times, mainly in relation to the Holy Spirit (*cf.* Acts 10:45; 11:17). In other cases it is linked with God's grace (Rom. 5:15; Eph. 3:7; 4:7), where it embraces the whole gift of salvation. In the present statement the content of the gift is undefined, but its origin is left in no doubt. Although it has been maintained that 'heavenly' describes, not the origin, but the sphere in which the gift is exercised, it would still show that the gift is not one of human making. It should be noted that the word used here for 'gift' (*dōrea*) is exclusively used of spiritual gifts in the New Testament.

The third statement is closely linked to the last, for the sort of persons whom the writer imagines are those *who have become partakers of the Holy Spirit*, which ties up with the gift of the Spirit. Nevertheless, it is probable that this is seen as a distinctive feature in their experience. We have already met the word for partakers (*metochoi*) in 1:9; 3:1, 14 and we shall meet it again in 12:8. The only other occurrence of the word in the New Testament is in Luke 5:7 where it means 'comrades'. Since in 3:1 the writer is addressing those who share in a heavenly call, the same sense must be intended here. The idea of sharing the Holy Spirit is remarkable. This at once distinguishes the person from one who has no more than a nodding acquaintance with Christianity.

**5.** The fourth statement, *and have tasted the goodness of the word of God*, introduces yet another aspect of Christian experience. The repetition of the 'tasting' metaphor shows the importance which the writer attached to it. But this time it is a matter of tasting the *goodness* (*kalon*), a word which incorporates in it some notion of beauty. It includes outward attractiveness as well as moral goodness. It is contrasted with evil in 5:14. It describes a clear conscience in 13:18. It is something to be highly desired. This fits in well with the metaphor. It is appetising to the taste. It is also not accidental that what is tasted is not the word of God itself, but its goodness. The distinction is not unimportant in the context. It is possible to approach the word of God sincerely but without relish. In the present case those who could taste the goodness were well immersed in Christian experience. The descriptive phrase 'word of God' (*Theou rhēma*) occurs again in 11:3 and in a few other places in the New Testament, but is not as frequent as the more general but parallel expression (*logos tou Theou*) which occurs in this epistle in 4:12 and 13:7. The present phrase draws more pointed attention to a specific communication from God rather than to the general message of God. Indeed it may most probably refer to the experience of God which a person knows at conversion, when the amazing condescension of God towards sinners dawns on the soul in all its resplendent beauty.

But the tasting also reaches to *the goodness of the powers of the age to come*, which seems a strange idea. If the age to come is still future, as the words (*mellontos aiōnos*) suggest, it cannot be that the writer means to refer to a remote hope. Since he uses 'these last days' (1:1) to denote the days of the inauguration of the Messiah, he may well be thinking here of the present foretasting of an experience which will not reach its climax until the second coming. In any case, he is concerned most with the powers of the coming age, which suggests the operation of the same powerful influences as will have full sway in that future age.

**6.** At last the conditional part of the sentence is reached: *if they then commit apostasy* (in the Greek the conditional is expressed as a participle, *parapesontas*). The statement which follows applies only when the experience of enlightenment and sharing is linked with a complete falling away (as indicated by the aorist tense). The idea of apostasy is expressed by a verb which occurs here only in the New Testament. Its root meaning is falling aside, *i.e.* a falling away from an accepted standard or path. The subsequent statement in this case makes clear the irretrievable nature of the apostasy. It is said that they *crucify the Son of God*, and the compound verb used (*anastaurountas*) shows that the writer is thinking of a repetition of the crucifixion. He could not have expressed the seriousness of the apostasy in stronger or more tragic terms. As he thinks of what the enemies of Jesus Christ did to him, he actually sees those who turn away from him as equally responsible. He may be thinking that such apostates would be more culpable than those who originally cried out 'crucify him', who had never known anything of the wonder of God's grace through Christ. Anyone who turned back from Christianity to Judaism would be identifying himself not only with Jewish unbelief, but with that malice which led to the crucifixion of Jesus. The words *on their own account* make clear that they must take full responsibility for the crucifying. Moreover, the writer explains that the effect of this action is to *hold him* [Christ] *up to contempt* (*paradeigmatizontas*, another word found only here in the New Testament). In no more vivid way could the position of the apostatizers be identified with those whose hatred of Christ led them to exhibit him as an object of contempt on a hated Roman gibbet. The condemnation of these people is so strong that nothing but the gravest action on their part could account for it. It implies an attitude of unremitting hostility.

This passage has led to extensive debate and has resulted in much misunderstanding. The major problem is whether the writer is implying that a Christian may fall so far from grace as to be guilty of the worse possible offence against the Son of God. If the answer is yes, how do we account for those other passages in the New Testament which suggest the eternal security of believers? The following considerations may help us in seeking to understand the writer's mind at this point:

(i) Calvin, convinced as he was that God kept watch over his elect, could only suppose that the tasting mentioned here was merely a partial experience and that the people concerned did not respond to it.[1] The difficulty with such a hypothesis is that it does not do justice to the words of this epistle, which give no impression of incomplete enlightenment. Calvin speaks of some glimmerings of light. He makes a distinction between the grace received by reprobates and by the elect.[2]

(ii) On the other hand, can it be claimed that in view of the statements of this epistle the possibility remains for any believer to apostatize in the same way? This would make any assurance of faith less certain. It has even been suggested that the severity

---

[1] *Cf.* Calvin, *Comm.*, p. 76.  [2] Calvin, *Institutes*, III.ii.11.

of the warning here may link up with the unpardonable sin against the Holy Spirit. Some have been deeply troubled lest they have committed such a sin, but no-one with a state of mind so hardened as to hold up the Son of God to contempt would ever be concerned about a question like that. The concern itself is evidence that the Holy Spirit is still active.

(iii) It must be borne in mind that no indication is given in this passage that any of the readers had committed the kind of apostasy mentioned. The writer appears to be reflecting on a hypothetical case, although in the nature of the whole argument it must be supposed that it was a real possibility. The intention is clearly not to give a dissertation on the nature of grace, but to give a warning in the strongest possible terms. The whole passage is viewed from the side of man's responsibilities and must accordingly be regarded as limited. In other words the Godward side needs to be set over against this passage for a true balance to be obtained.

(iv) The passage, moreover, states the impossibility in terms of restoring the offenders again to a condition of repentance (verse 4). The question arises about the scope of repentance here. Does it refer to a man's initial act when he comes to God, in the sense in which it seems to be used in verse 1? If so, it is clearly impossible for such an initial act to be performed a second time, although it is surely possible to remind oneself of it. Since repentance is an act involving the self-humbling of the sinner before a holy God, it is evident why a man with a contemptuous attitude towards Christ has no possibility of repentance. The hardening process provides an impenetrable casing which removes all sensitivity to the pleadings of the Spirit. There comes a point of no return, when restoration is impossible. Although the writer is setting out an extreme case, he has confidence in his readers (verse 9). Nevertheless, he feels it necessary to return to severe warning in chapter 10.

**7–8.** What has just been said illustrates a principle which can be supported from nature. Neglect of proper cultivation of the *land* leads to worthless results, in a similar way that refusal to adhere to the provisions of God's grace leads to spiritual bankruptcy. The New Testament contains many examples of agricultural illustrations being used to commend spiritual truths. It is based partly on the view that natural laws are linked with spiritual laws because both have the same originator and for this reason natural phenomena may serve as spiritual analogies. No-one complains of thorns and thistles which are due to neglect, but every farmer expects that, given the right conditions of moisture, cultivated land will produce *vegetation*. Strangely the human agency is not mentioned, but the fruitfulness is judged by its usefulness to the cultivators and indeed to others. In the spiritual realm some kind of fruitfulness is essential for the fullest cultivation of spiritual experience. Those individuals or groups that produce nothing to share with others are barren (*cf*. 5:12 which suggests the readers face a temptation that way). It is worth noting that it is the *land*, not the people, which is said to *receive a blessing from God*, which presumably means that its own productivity is increased by God. Indeed, the biblical view of harvest is that God gives the increase.

The *thorns and thistles* are a direct reminder of Genesis 3:17–18, where the curse on the land was to take this form and man's toil was to be called out to keep them down and to cultivate the land. As all agriculturalists know a crop of weeds is good only to be burned. It is important to note that the words *near to being cursed* are less forceful than they would have been without the word 'near' (*engys*), but they nevertheless draw attention to the constant imminence of the end. The burning of the weeds would not be long delayed if the weeds persist.[1] The word translated 'worthless' (*adokimos*) occurs in 1 Corinthians 9:27 in the sense of disqualified and in 2 Corinthians 13:5 of failure to meet the test. It is no arbitrary rejection, but only as a result of due examination. In this case the land is proved to be worthless by the absence of effective fruit.

**9.** At this point the writer turns to encouragement. His stern warnings are for the moment finished and he almost hastens to assure the readers that he does not consider that they had reached the extreme position of which he has spoken. The words *yet in your case* (*peri hymōn*) mark a strong contrast with the supposed apostatizers, adding weight to the suggestion that

[1] Héring, p. 48, n. 16, cites the elder Pliny as evidence of the practice of burning the ground to destroy weeds. But Westcott, *Comm*., p. 153, sees here the image of the utter desolation caused by volcanic forces.

the latter were hypothetical. Indeed the writer suddenly addresses his readers as *beloved*, which he does nowhere else in this epistle, and this conveys a sense of particular warmth. It gathers strength by way of contrast with the previous warnings. There are similar uses of it in the Pauline epistles (*e.g.* 1 Cor. 10:14; 2 Cor. 12:19). Indeed Paul uses it in every letter except Galatians, 2 Thessalonians and Titus, and it occurs in most other New Testament books. It may be said, therefore, to be a favourite Christian term of affection. It is not without some significance that the Synoptic Gospels record occasions when Jesus was addressed by a heavenly voice as 'beloved'. In the present case its use shows the real concern of the writer for his readers.

*We feel sure* (*pepeismetha*) comes as the first word in the Greek text and therefore carries greater emphasis than the RSV suggests. In fact, the perfect tense shows that this is not some snap decision, but the abiding result of past consideration. This strong persuasion lay behind all the warnings just given. It seems to have been derived from the writer's personal knowledge of them. The reference to *better things* is in line with the characteristic use of the word 'better' in this epistle. In this case the contrast is with the apostatizers. The true Christian position is always on the side of the 'better' as compared with the 'worse'. The 'things' are specified as those *that belong to salvation*, which literally means those which 'hold on to' salvation. What the writer seems to be saying is that his convictions about them relate to the whole sphere of salvation and indeed this is made clear in the next verse.

**10.** As a basis for his firm persuasion, the writer cites two factors: (i) God's justice and (ii) the readers' works. His sense of God's justice, or rather, the conviction that God cannot be *unjust* (for it is expressed here as a double negative, *ou gar adikos*), is another integral part of the writer's theology. He can quote approvingly from Deuteronomy 4:24 that God is a consuming fire (12:29), but he does not regard him as a tyrant who pays no attention to justice. In 1:9 he quotes the Psalmist's parallel ascription to God of the love of righteousness and the hatred of lawlessness. God's word is a word of righteousness (5:13) and God's discipline is said to produce the peaceful fruit of righteousness (12:11). The writer cannot conceive that God could *overlook* work and love which in his opinion have proceeded from grace. This combination between *your work* and *the love which you showed* is important, for the work is expressed in terms of love and is not to be regarded as independent of it. It is taken for granted that those who show love by *serving the saints* are exhibiting the results of the 'better things'.

The additional words *for his sake* show that God regards deeds of kindness done to his people as done to himself. The force of the words in the Greek brings this out vividly, since the love is directed 'into his name' (*eis to onoma*), hence 'to him' (as NIV). There is no comparison or contrast with Jewish almsgiving here, although it might be noted that for the Jews love was not a notable constituent.[1] Christian love for the saints goes far beyond almsgiving, although the latter is not to be neglected. Service based on love is wholly different from service which is performed to accrue merit. It speaks much for those readers that they were so solicitous towards fellow Christians. It is the writer's conviction that these actions showed that God's grace is still active among them.

**11–12.** Although their love is commendable, there are other areas in which the same spirit could be exercised and the writer notes some of these. The verb *we desire* (*epithymoumen*) is a strong one, expressing more than a pious wish. Its plural form adds intensity, for the writer is expressing what he knows will be shared by Christians generally. The desire is towards *full assurance* (*plērophoria*), a word which comes again at the climax to the exposition (10:22), in which the possibility of such full assurance is unquestioned in the light of the sacrifice of Jesus. The writer's strong desire that the readers might have *full assurance of hope* suggests that at the moment it is lacking. Possibly the conflict over the pull of Judaism was robbing them of the joy of this assurance. It is possible for Christians to have great

[1] For the Jewish approach to almsgiving, *cf.* the articles on charity in the *Encyclopaedia Judaica* 5 (1972), pp. 338–354 and *The Jewish Encyclopaedia* 3, pp. 667ff. Charity was regarded as a duty and those who did not give to those poorer than themselves could be made to do so. At the same time every effort was made to avoid causing feelings of shame among the recipients. Love was not a dominant motive as in Christian charity, but Rabbi Akiba regarded charity as a means of making the world a household of love (see *The Jewish Encyclopaedia* 3, p. 668).

love for their brethren and yet lack assurance for themselves. If only the *earnestness* for the one overflowed to the other! It is a sad fact that many who are most active in Christian works are lacking in convictions. It may in many cases be because they are relying on works to contribute towards their salvation, an approach which could never lead to assurance, since they could never know whether their works were sufficient. Another interesting feature is that the author's strong desire is directed to *each one of you*, thus making both the earnestness and the assurance individual. Both are experiences which do not originate in groups.

*So that you may not be sluggish* gives the complement to earnestness. The word for 'sluggish' here (*nōthroi*) has already been used in 5:11 of the readers, who are there called 'dull of hearing'. Such dullness, if not checked, will develop into an inability to make any progress at all. Although he had just issued a serious warning, the writer does not now, as in 5:11, speak as if it is an accomplished fact. Instead he shows how such dullness may be avoided.

Another alternative target is a right kind of imitation. The New Testament has much to say about this subject of *imitators*. In the teaching of Jesus, his disciples are bidden to follow his example (*e.g.* Jn. 13:15). Paul on more than one occasion urged his converts to imitate him (1 Cor. 4:16; 11:1; 1 Thes. 1:6; 2:14), using the same word as here. Such imitation was of great practical value to those who had no New Testament scriptures to provide adequate standards. Men of God who had learned new moral and spiritual ideas became valuable guides to those less mature. In the present case the pattern was provided by *those who through faith and patience inherit the promises*. It has been suggested that the exhortation to imitate the faith of the inheritors of the promise refers to the men of the Old Testament and anticipates Hebrews 11. But there seems no reason why Christians may not also be included. The combination of faith and patience is suggestive for, although the fact of faith alone secures the inheritance, until it is actually possessed there is need for patience. The word used (*makrothymia*) means 'long-suffering' and occurs in Hebrews only here, but several times in Paul and a few times elsewhere. It is a god-like quality (*cf.* Rom.

9:22) which is not natural in man, but becomes characteristic of the followers of Jesus. It is among the fruit of the Spirit listed by Paul in Galatians 5:22. The heirs of the promise are mentioned again in verse 17.

13. At this point in the discussion the thought returns to *Abraham* who was last mentioned in 2:16. This section (verses 13–20) acts as a prelude to the exposition of the Melchizedek theme. What the writer is concerned to show is (i) the solemnity of God's promises, (ii) his unchangeable character, and therefore (iii) the absolute certainty of his word. This is really an explanation of the basis of the Christian's 'full assurance of hope'.

The *promise to Abraham* was confirmed by an oath. Many times the promise was made without mention of the oath, but the reference in Genesis 22:16 makes the specific claim, 'By myself, I have sworn'. This is clearly the basis of the present statement – *he swore by himself*. The writer elaborates on it, *since he had no one greater by whom to swear*, which is tantamount to saying that his own word was good enough. Philo (*Legum Allegoriae* 3.203) has a similar comment on Genesis 22:16.

14–15. The promise that Abraham would be blessed and multiplied has added significance when placed over against the command to Abraham to offer up Isaac. When Abraham's obedience was accepted in lieu of the act, it must have come with added force when God reinforced the promise with an oath. This is hinted at in verse 15. *Abraham, having patiently endured* clearly refers to the Isaac trial, as a result of which he *obtained the promise*. There is an echo back to verse 12. Abraham is an example *par excellence* of one who gained his inheritance by faith and patience. Even if the readers could think of no other example, Abraham would admirably illustrate the writer's meaning.

16. By appealing to human oaths the writer demonstrates that the divine promise is superior to man's word. The limitation of man's word lies in the fact that his word is not sufficient in itself. The very need for an oath to back up a statement reflects the character of the one who makes it. It should be remembered that Jesus was critical of men whose word was so unreliable that oaths were used to bolster their statements. He

urged his followers to 'let what you say be simply "Yes" or "No" ' (Mt. 5:37). There is therefore a difference between the Christian approach and the contemporary convention. The writer is here alluding to the contemporary view. His statement, *Men indeed swear by a greater than themselves*, reflects man's natural approach to the matter. Unless there is someone greater who is in a position to confirm the oath, the exercise would be valueless. Although the word 'greater' could be neuter and thus include things as well as persons, the context clearly shows that the masculine is intended.

Once an oath has been made there can be no change. In this sense it is *final for confirmation*. It affirms positively what it supports and effectively excludes what it denies. In any disputes (*antilogiai*) it is conclusive. This binding character of human oaths is used by the writer to transfer his thought *par excellence* to the inviolability of the divine word.

**17.** In explaining the reason for a divine oath, this writer shows it to be a concession to human convention. There was no need for God to confirm his word. It was inviolable. But if men were better persuaded through an oath, *So (en hō) . . . he interposed with an oath*. Presumably the interposing (*mesiteuein*, here only in the New Testament) was between God and Abraham. It is important to note that the oath was for the benefit of the *heirs of the promise*, although it was actually given to Abraham. What is true for Abraham is true also for his seed. The 'heirs' is a comprehensive term for the true children of Abraham and is not exclusively a reference to the people of Israel. Jesus, when addressing Jews who claimed to be Abraham's children, said 'If you were Abraham's children, you would do what Abraham did' (Jn. 8:39). The apostle Paul, in writing to the Romans, can refer to 'those who share the faith of Abraham, for he is the father of us all' (Rom. 4:16). The heirs of the promise are therefore distinct from the natural descendants.

In speaking of the divine intention the writer, in common with many New Testament writers, uses the stronger Greek word (*boulomenos*) rather than the weaker (*thelein*). God's intention is more than an inclination or wish; it is a definite resolve. It becomes even stronger when supported by the adverb *perissoteron* (*more convincingly*). In his gracious understanding of man's need for evidence that cannot be refuted, God makes it doubly convincing. The unchangeable character of the Creator has already been stressed in chapter 1 and now the focus falls on *the unchangeable character of his purpose*. This is a further development, concentrating particularly on the mind of God. The word 'unchangeable' (*ametathetos*) is used only here (and in verse 18) in the New Testament. There is evidence (according to MM) that it was used in a technical sense of the unchangeable character of a will. The unchangeable purpose of God sets him apart from the capricious contemporary pagan deities and makes all his promises utterly dependable. Indeed the Christian concept of God demands that what he has said he will honour. The oath, although adding nothing to this conviction, does nothing to detract from it. His word would still have been true without the oath.

**18.** The writer sees some significance, however, in the oath, for he sees a combination of *two unchangeable things* (*i.e.* God's nature and his oath, or the promise and the oath). Since neither can change, *it is impossible that God should prove false*. This is the sheet anchor of the Christian's conviction. He knows his assurance depends not on the stability or strength of his own faith, but on the absolute trustworthiness of God's word.

The heirs are now more specifically described as *we who have fled for refuge*, which not only makes the whole argument relevant to the readers, but also includes the writer. It is perhaps surprising that these people should be described as fugitives. The only other place where the same word is used is Acts 14:6 where it describes Paul's flight from his persecutors. But in the present context the flight is defined by the accompanying *encouragement to seize the hope*. It seems, therefore, to denote an urgent turning away from a state of discouragement and apathy. This may indicate a certain sense of urgency on their part, which would then need to be set against the strong warnings about apostasy. On the other hand the writer might be restricting the encouragement to that group of his readers who have fled from the dangerous position in which others have placed themselves.

There is no doubt in his mind about the character of the encouragement. It is a seizure of *the hope set before us*. The idea of seizure implies a taking hold of and grasping in a resolute manner, which again stresses the supreme importance of the action. Hope is of such a character that it needs tenacity to retain it. It does not simply happen. It is both set out as an objective reality to be seized and also as a subjective reality to be personally experienced. Our writer has mentioned hope twice before (see comment on 3:6 and cf. 6:11), and it occurs twice more, in 7:19 (a better hope) and 10:23 (the confession of our hope). It is another of his favourite themes.

**19.** Meditating on the theme of hope leads him to comment on certain striking characteristics of hope. The first is its immovability which is vividly illustrated by the figure of an *anchor*. Nowhere else in the New Testament is this used in a metaphorical way. It is a rich image. The job of the anchor is to remain fixed in the sea-bed whatever the conditions at sea. Indeed the rougher the weather the more important is the anchor for the stability and safety of the boat. It is an apt symbol of Christian hope. It was, in fact, used graphically as a symbol among early Christians, and was frequently linked with the fish symbol. It is surprising that no other New Testament writer makes use of it. Perhaps it is too fanciful to suggest that the writer had had experience at sea and had personally learned to value the anchor in times of danger. According to the RSV it is the anchor which is described as *sure and steadfast*, but the adjectives could refer to the hope. It makes little difference to the meaning. The first adjective means 'safe' (*asphalē*), incapable of being moved. The second (*bebaian*), secure in itself, is practically a synonym of the other. It is translated in 3:6 and 3:14 as 'confidence'. In New Testament thought generally, as here, confidence and hope are closely tied.

The strangest side to this metaphor is the anchor's entering *into the inner shrine behind the curtain* (*i.e.* the holy of holies). The writer has either purposely mixed his metaphors, or else he has rapidly transferred his thought about hope to a different scene in which an anchor seems incongruous. Some of the patristic commentators contrasted the natural anchor in the sea-bed with the spiritual in the heavenly place. But it seems best to suppose that the thought has switched from the sea to the tabernacle, as a means of introducing another and much firmer basis for hope, *i.e.* the high-priest theme. By this means the writer leads into his exposition of the order of Melchizedek.

**20.** The idea that *Jesus has gone* behind the curtain is highly suggestive. The curtain is the veil in the tabernacle (and Temple) which separated the holy of holies from the holy place. The allusion is to the fact that only the high priest could go behind the curtain and even then only once a year. We are reminded that the veil of the Temple was split from top to bottom when Jesus died (Mt. 27:51). But our writer is concerned with a deeper spiritual reality. It is a *fait accompli* that our high priest is 'behind the curtain', *i.e.* in the direct presence of God. The close connection between Christian hope and our exalted high priest is one of the major themes in this epistle. Hope is based on the finished and yet continuing work of Jesus as high priest.

He is first described as *forerunner* (*prodromos*), a word which occurs only here in the New Testament and which was used of an advanced reconnoitring part of an army. A forerunner, therefore, presupposes others to follow. It is a great inspiration to realize that what Jesus has done, he has done *on our behalf*, a statement which strongly brings out his representative character and may indeed imply a substitutionary role.

The concluding statement about *Melchizedek* links up with 5:10 and brings to a close the warning interlude. The one new factor is that Christ is *a high priest for ever*, a theme which is developed in the next section.

*(iv) The order of Melchizedek (7:1–28)*

**1.** Until now the writer has given no details about *Melchizedek*.[1] He almost assumes his readers will be familiar with him, although he now gives a few historical details which make him

---

[1] A Samaritan tradition held that Melchizedek was the first priest of Mt Gerizim. In the Qumran literature Melchizedek has no priestly function, but is both king and judge (*cf.* Theissen, p. 18; *cf.* also M. de Jonge & A. S. van der Woude, '11 Q Melchizedek and the New Testament', *NTS* 12 (1945–6), pp. 301–326; J. A. Fitzmyer, 'Further Light on Melchizedek from Qumran Cave 11', *JBL* 86 (1967), pp. 25–41. The latter finds some evidence for a priestly function, which the former deny). Philo expounds on the Melchizedek theme but his treatment shows few points of contact with Hebrews. There is little allegorization in this epistle, whereas Philo finds extensive opportunities for it. *Cf.* Spicq's treatment here. According to Windisch, pp. 61–63, the Melchizedek speculation in Hebrews was to supplant the Levitical priesthood. He sees it as akin to the Enoch type of apocalyptic. For a full treatment of this subject, *cf.* F. L. Horton, *The Melchizedek Tradition*, 1976.

come alive, but in a most mysterious way. He sees what details
he gives as possessing a spiritual significance which goes beyond the original historical context. He comes close to allegorizing, although he does not actually do so.

This first verse is a statement of facts in line with the account
in Genesis 14:17–20. It speaks of Melchizedek's position, as both
*king of Salem* and *priest of the Most High God*. This combination
between kingship and priesthood turns out to be significant for
the writer's purpose as the next verses show. It is immaterial
for him where Salem was located. There is a strong tradition
that it should be identified with Jerusalem. Bruce[1] cites the evidence for this tradition and shows that the connection of the
etymology of Jerusalem with *shalom* (peace) is well-founded.
The writer, however, is more interested in the symbolical significance of the name. The title here given to God is worth
noting, for it is found not only in Genesis 14:18, but also in
Deuteronomy 32:8 and various other places in the Old Testament, especially the Psalms. It draws attention to the exalted
character of God. Any priesthood is evaluated according to the
status of the deity who is served, which means that Melchizedek's must have been of a highly exalted kind.

The meeting of Melchizedek with *Abraham* is the feature
which brings the former into the biblical story. It comes at the
conclusion of Abraham's part in the conflict between two con-
federacies of kings. Abraham's remarkable victory, however, is
not what engages the interest of the author, but his being
blessed by Melchizedek, which at once placed the latter in a
position of superiority to Abraham. This in itself would be
regarded as a high dignity by Christian Jews as well as orthodox
non-Christian Jews, who held Abraham in the highest esteem
(see the development of this point in verse 4).

**2.** The further detail about Abraham giving Melchizedek a
tithe, taken from the Genesis narrative, reinforces the superiority of the latter. By doing this Abraham acknowledged the right
of Melchizedek to receive it. Having set out the historical facts
the writer next proceeds to give an exposition of them.

The first comment is based on the meaning of the name, *i.e.*

---

[1] Bruce, *Comm.*, p. 136, n. 16.

*king of righteousness.* This type of exegesis would possess special force for Jewish readers, for whom names were significant, because it was accepted that names denoted the nature as well as the identity of the person. The appropriateness of 'Melchizedek' as a description of the nature of Jesus as our high priest would immediately appeal to the writer. It would invest the order of Melchizedek with a special quality of righteousness. How Melchizedek acquired his name is not discussed, but the writer has clearly mentioned the Son's love of righteousness (1:9) and this for him is the crucial point in his present exposition.

He sees further significance in the name of the priest-king's city, *i.e. peace,* another symbolic deduction from what appears as a historical fact. It should be recognized that his exegesis runs backwards from the known characteristics of Christ to the Old Testament analogy. Although he has not previously linked 'peace' with Jesus Christ, his whole presentation of Christ's work implies it. There is undoubtedly some symbolic meaning in the order in which the characteristics are mentioned, since righteousness must be the basis of all true peace. In his letter to the Ephesians (2:14), Paul calls Jesus Christ 'our peace'.

**3.** It is when the writer bases his exposition on the silence of Scripture that his method of exegesis seems strangest to modern readers.[1] Because there is no mention of the origin or death of Melchizedek in the Genesis account, the writer deduces that *He is without father or mother or genealogy.* He has obviously drawn out from the narrative an interpretation which does not appear on the surface in the Genesis account. But his train of thought is clear. Unlike the Aaronic priests for whom Levitical descent was essential for eligibility to hold office, the order of Melchizedek is of a wholly different kind. There is no account of his father or of his children. He stands mysteriously apart from all need to establish his genealogy. For this reason he is again admirably suited to be compared with Jesus Christ.

When however the writer adds that Melchizedek *has neither*

---

[1] Some have considered that verse 3 is in hymnic form. *Cf.* O. Michel, *Comm.*, p. 259. He detects a similar form in verse 26. G. Schille, 'Erwägungen zur Hohepriesterlehre des Hebräerbriefes', *ZNW* 46 (1955), pp. 81–109, however, sees a hymn of three strophes contained in verses 1–3. Theissen, *op. cit.*, pp. 21f., is not partial to this view but makes his own attempt to reconstruct the underlying hymn (pp. 24f.).

*beginning of days nor end of life*, he pushes his argument from silence still further. Taken literally his exegesis would suggest that Melchizedek must have been a heavenly being,[1] in which case the historical account would be spiritualized since there is no suggestion in the Genesis narrative that Melchizedek was anything other than flesh and blood. The idea of basing exegesis on silence is familiar in Philo's writings and would not in itself have seemed strange to Jewish readers. But it is somewhat unexpected to find that Melchizedek is considered to be a priest for ever, just like the Son of God.

The real key to the writer's exegetical method is found in the phrase *resembling the Son of God*. The word translated *resembling* (*aphōmoiōmenos*) occurs only here in the New Testament. It is a suggestive word, used in the active of 'a facsimile copy or model' and in the passive of 'being made similar to'. It is because Jesus Christ is of the order of Melchizedek that the representative of the order is seen to be a model of the true. In other words, it is Christ's priesthood that is the standard, not that of Melchizedek. This passage comes close to being allegorical. Yet the important factor which the writer wishes to establish is the eternal priesthood of the Son of God rather than Melchizedek's, although the latter is implied. What makes Melchizedek's order perpetual is that Scripture says nothing about the succession. What makes Christ's perpetual is, however, his own nature. The fulfilment is more glorious than the type. The title *Son of God* takes the thought back to 4:14 where Jesus our high priest is given this title (*cf*. also 6:6 and 10:29, both warning passages).

4. The reason for the historical exposition is to provide a comparison between Abraham and Melchizedek. The statement in this verse sums up this point of view. *See how great he is!* This exhortation to special study of the greatness of Melchizedek is based on his superiority to the acknowledged greatness of Abraham. Both Jews and Christians recognized the greatness of Abraham. He stood out on the stage of history. Now another joins him to whom he offers a *tithe*, an action which shows his estimate of Melchizedek. Nevertheless the greatness has already

---

[1] On the pre-existence of Melchizedek, *cf*. G. R. Hamerton-Kelly, *Pre-existence, Wisdom and The Son of Man* (CUP, 1973), pp. 256ff.

been demonstrated in verses 1–3.

The position of the words in the Greek text heightens the contrast, for the words *the patriarch* come right at the end, as if to emphasize the dignity of the one who offered the tithes. The word occurs elsewhere in the New Testament only in Acts 2:29 where it is applied to David, and in Acts 7:8 to Jacob and his sons. It is especially appropriate as a title for Abraham since he was regarded not only as the father of Israel, but also of the whole family of the faithful (Rom. 4:11, 16).

**5.** The comparison which the writer intends to make is not between Abraham and Melchizedek, but between Aaron and Melchizedek. It is the two orders of priesthood that he has in mind. This explains the sudden reference to Levi. All the Aaronic priests had to be *descendants of Levi*, which at once contrasts with Melchizedek who had no descendants. The Levitical priests had a legal right, *a commandment in the law to take tithes from the people.* Numbers 18:26f. sets out these rights. Our author is concerned only with the priests, although special provision was also made for the non-priestly Levites (*cf.* Dt. 10:8f.). In the matter of rights Melchizedek differed from the Levitical priests in that he received tithes, not by command, but by the spontaneous action of Abraham. No attempt is made in this epistle to explain why Abraham tithed his spoils. The writer is content to leave this matter. What strikes him is Melchizedek's all-out superiority. Aaron's priests, moreover, exact tithes *from their brethren*, who like them *are descended from Abraham*. The contrast is now between Abraham's descendants and Abraham himself. The writer implies that Abraham's gifts must be greater than the gifts made by his descendants.

But is this a valid contrast? The basic principle seems to be that the status of the recipient determines the status of the giver, because the recipient is always superior to the giver (as verse 7 states).

**6–7.** Genealogy was an indispensable factor in the Jewish priestly system. The writer is obviously anxious to show that, although Melchizedek is without *genealogy*, he nevertheless *received tithes* and gave a blessing to no less a person than Abraham. Moreover, as Abraham had already received *the promises* from God, the blessing received through Melchizedek was an addition which would have been prized only had it been acknowledged as coming from an equivalent source. And so it was, for Melchizedek was priest of the Most High God, whose blessing he conveys. It is worth noting that the perfect tense is used for Melchizedek's receiving of tithes (*dedekatōken*) which draws attention, not only to the historic event, but also to its abiding significance. The writer is, as it were, transporting the event to the readers' own time to show the continuance of this order of priesthood. It continues in its perfect fulfilment in Christ. The writer underlines the superiority of Melchizedek to Abraham in verse 7. He calls it *beyond dispute* (*chōris pasēs antilogias*), expressed in the most comprehensive terms. He expects his readers to accept this position without question. It is an essential link in his argument for the superiority of Melchizedek over Aaron, as the following statements show.

**8.** The contrast between *here* and *there* is a reference to Aaron's line in contrast with Melchizedek's, with a further contrast between *mortal men* and *one of whom it is testified that he lives*. Although the Levitical order was arranged by God, the priests were, after all, mortal men. The most they could expect was a few years for serving God. On the other hand Melchizedek's order was entirely different, for the writer maintains his continual life. He does this by appealing to the precise text of Genesis, under the formula *of whom it is testified* (*martyroumenos*). The verb occurs seven times in this letter. In two other occurrences (7:17 and 10:15) it is used, as here, in reference to direct quotations from the Old Testament. Its use here is a delicate reminder that the writer is basing his statement on an authoritative source.

**9–10.** The argument takes on a different turn as the relationship between Levi and Abraham is expounded. For an orthodox Jew the order of Aaron would be the only authentic priestly order, for Abraham was not a priest. But the author suggests that since Levi was a descendant of Abraham he could be said to be already in Abraham's loins. He senses that this method is somewhat strange, hence his introductory formula: *One might even say* (*hōs epos eipein*), an expression found nowhere else in the New Testament. He seems to be preparing the readers for a turn of thought with which they may not be familiar. The idea is clearly that Abraham's descendants are identified in their forefather and that therefore the Levitical order was in effect acknowledging the superiority of Melchizedek. The force of this argument would come more strongly to minds familiar with the idea of solidarity, as the Hebrews were, than to those dominated by the idea of individuality. Neither the father nor the children could be independent of each other. Abraham's payment of tithes could be transferred to his descendant Levi and hence to the whole order of his priesthood. Indeed Levi's payment of tithes through Abraham looms as large as, if not larger than, his right to receive tithes from others. In this way a delicate balance is suggested between a man's indebtedness to the past and his responsibility for the present. Some aspects of the idea of solidarity are inescapable.

11. Now that he has demonstrated the superiority of Melchizedek to the Levitical order, the writer proceeds to show the need for a priest belonging to that superior order of priesthood. Melchizedek's personal superiority would not in itself establish him as superseding Aaron. Someone might at once object that Melchizedek's order was a flash in the pan, however mysterious, whereas Aaron's was a long established and respected line. The writer anticipates such an objection by pointing out the inadequacies of the Aaronic line and thus the need for a successor in Melchizedek. Admittedly the writer's standard is nothing short of *perfection*. The conditional sentence, *if perfection had been attainable . . . what further need . . .?*, depends on two assumptions. It assumes that 'perfection' is a desirable end, and it also assumes that the *Levitical priesthood* and with it *the law* could not produce such perfection.

The first assumption is part of the basic background of the epistle. Even the noblest in Israel's history (as chapter 11 shows) could not in themselves attain perfection (*cf.*11:40). All man's longings towards God are an expression of this deep desire for completeness. The Levitical system was a special provision by which the imperfect could approach God by means of vicarious offerings. It did not possess within it the power to effect perfection in the worshippers. Law had no mandate for such a positive aim. It has been suggested that divine legislation could have no other end than perfection (so Westcott). But Paul's arguments in Romans 7:7ff. are sufficient to show that in practice the law brought only frustration. The law could in fact do no more than reveal man's shortcomings. The need for a successor to Melchizedek thus rests on the inability of *the order of Aaron* to produce perfection. It may well be, as Bruce points out, that the linking of perfection to the Levitical order would have been intelligible only to Jewish readers, who might still be inclined after their conversion to Christianity to see some value in the old ritual.[1]

**12.** The close connection between the Aaronic priesthood and the Law is again stressed. In view of the sanctity of the Law in Jewish minds, there was a real difficulty in accepting any other priesthood than Aaron's, and this is the problem which the writer has in mind in maintaining that a different priesthood involves a different law. Only so could he support the order of Melchizedek. He thinks in a way similar to the argument used by Paul in Romans to the effect that the promise to Abraham preceded the giving of the law by some four hundred years. The writer is here arguing hypothetically, for the law itself cannot be changed. He has primarily in mind the law affecting the Aaronic priesthood.

**13.** *The one of whom these things are spoken* refers back to verse 11, where a successor to Melchizedek is in mind – a preparatory allusion to Jesus Christ who is introduced in the next verse as 'our Lord'. This rather roundabout method of argument was needed to justify identifying as a priest one who *belonged to another tribe*, *i.e.* the tribe of Judah. From this tribe no-one had ever performed the priestly office. Again the writer is anticipating objections to his main thesis of Jesus as a superior high priest to Aaron. The fact that he takes such trouble over each detail of his argument shows the importance he attached to the whole of his high-priest theme.

**14.** The words *For it is evident* imply that it was well known to which tribe *our Lord* was attached. And yet only here and in Revelation 5:5 is he said specifically to belong to this tribe, although it is assumed in Matthew's birth narrative (2:6). This suggests that the Lord's descent from *Judah* was an acknowl-

[1] *Cf.* Bruce, *Comm.*, p. 144.

edged part of tradition. The genealogies in Matthew and Luke would support this. Moreover, the fact that many times Jesus is named in the New Testament as Son of David is further testimony, since David was the most illustrious representative of the tribe of Judah. The word used here for descent (*anatetal-ken*) is sometimes used of a plant shooting up from its seed or of the rising of the sun. Whereas the previous verse appeals to the custom of the past as excluding Judah, this verse ends with an appeal to the silence of the Mosaic law regarding priests from Judah. To those for whom the testimony of Moses was conclusive, this was a considerable difficulty, but it is offset by the further appeal to the testimony of Psalm 110 (verse 17).

**15.** The writer returns to the thought of the order of Melchizedek. He does this because his mind is on *another priest* (*i.e.* Jesus Christ). The combination of descent from Judah and *likeness* to Melchizedek is regarded as a sufficient basis for a new kind of priesthood. In this verse the opening words, *This becomes even more evident*, show that the writer's thought moves backwards from the priesthood of Christ, which he regards as indisputable, to the existence of an earlier order which would accommodate it. It is important to bear this in mind throughout his exposition. Christ's right to the priestly office rests on totally different grounds from the Levitical priesthood. His is an inherent right which transcends tribal qualifications and finds a parallel in a fleeting mysterious figure from the partriarchal period. Indeed a change here from 'order' to *likeness* is significant, for it indicates that in some sense Melchizedek was considered in his person to foreshadow his successor in a way that Aaron never did. No doubt there is here an echo of his mysterious origin and destiny already mentioned in verse 3 and again specifically brought out in verse 16.

**16.** Whereas in the last verse another priest 'arises' (*anistatai*), here he is said to have 'become' (*gegonen*) a priest, referring to his historic taking up of the office. The priesthood of Christ is inextricably linked with his incarnation. As already pointed out in this letter he is eligible to be priest for his people only because he shares their nature (2:17-18).

A double contrast is seen here. *Legal requirement* is set against *power*, and *bodily descent* against *indestructible life*. The first contrast is between external restraint and inward dynamic which at once puts the new order of priesthood on a different footing. The requirement of the law concentrated on heredity rather than on personal quality. However good the priestly office was, it could not be guaranteed that Aaron's descendants would be worthy of it. The idea of inward personal power was lacking. But not so in the case of Jesus Christ. He was the embodiment of living power. The word rendered *bodily descent* (*sarkinēs*) literally means 'pertaining to or made of flesh', used in the New Testament in contrast to 'spiritual' (*pneumatikos*), as, *e.g.*, in 1 Corinthians 3:1. It is essentially mortal as contrasted with *indestructible* (*akatalytou*, literally incapable of being dissolved). This is simply a restatement, in different words, of the superiority of Christ over Aaron's priesthood, but with special emphasis on the continuity of the one compared with the constant succession caused by death of the other, which is expounded further in verses 23ff.

Although our high priest died, and his death was essentially a part of his priestly office, yet he can still be described as *indestructible*. Death could not hold him. His high-priestly office continues by virtue of his risen life. If for no other reason, this fact would set him immeasurably above all the priests of Aaron's line.

**17.** Once again the quotation from Psalm 110, which may be described as the signature tune of this part of the epistle, is repeated (*cf.* 5:6). Here it is introduced by the phrase *For it is witnessed of him*, closely paralleled in 7:8. As there, it adds a note of authority, drawn from the precise words of Scripture. The reason for the repetition of the quotation here is to draw attention to the words *for ever*, which directly support the claim to indestructible life made in the preceding verse.

**18–19.** In a sense verses 16–17 may be regarded as an interlude, for the next verses continue the theme from verse 15. There is a contrasting statement in two parts with a parenthetical comment between. *On the one hand* introduces the first part which is about the weakness of the law as far as the priesthood is concerned. The words rendered *a former commandment* refer not merely to a commandment which preceded in time, but which also prepared for a better. It therefore made the former no longer necessary. Three statements are made about the commandment: (i) it is weak; (ii) it is useless; (iii) it is set aside. Although the law performed a valuable function, its essential *weakness* was that it could not give life and vitality even to those who kept it, let alone to those who did not. In fact its function was not to provide strength, but to provide a standard by which man could measure his own moral status. A priesthood based on such a limited potential must necessarily share the same limitations. Its *uselessness* must not be regarded in the sense of being totally worthless, but in the sense of being ineffective in providing a constant means of approach to God based on a totally adequate sacrifice (a point to be elaborated later on). It is because of these two characteristics, weakness and uselessness, that the writer sees the commandment as *set aside* (*athetēsis*), a word which occurs again in 9:26 of the setting aside of sin. There is no doubt that the writer does not here mean that the law itself is annulled, but that it can be discounted as a means of gaining perfection. This is the reason for the parenthesis at the beginning of verse 19. It is characteristic of law – not merely the Mosaic law, but all law – that it has made nothing *perfect*. All it could do was to focus on imperfection. Indeed the Mosaic law went further and demonstrated in its application that perfection was impossible. Nevertheless the whole thrust of the argument in this epistle is that man must strive for perfection.

The contrasting part of the statement, *on the other hand* (*de*), fixes on the theme of *hope*, conspicuously absent from the legal approach. Moreover, the hope is described as better, a comparative already met with in 1:4; 6:9; 7:7 and linked here in verse 22 with a better covenant. The question arises in what sense the hope introduced by Christ is better. Does the statement mean that his hope is better than the hope brought by the commandment, or does it mean better than the commandment itself? This latter view would fit well into the context in which the *weakness and uselessness* of the commandment has already been stressed – not the kind of thing which offers much hope. The word *hope* is another characteristic of this epistle (see comments on 3:6; 6:11, 18 and 10:23; also the use of the verb in 11:1), although it occurs much more frequently in Paul (31 times). The

idea of hope as a means by which *we draw near to God* continues
from the thought of 6:19, which mentions the kind of hope
which even penetrates within the veil, *i.e.* in direct proximity
to God. It is worth noting that man's drawing near to God
occurs as the concluding exhortation of the doctrine part of the
epistle (10:22). In spite of an awesome view of God in 12:29,
there is still the encouragement to approach in worship. Only
a better system than the old could stimulate such
encouragement.

**20–21.** Another distinction between the Aaronic priests and
the order of Melchizedek is that for the latter an oath was
needed to establish who would exercise the same kind of
priesthood, whereas for the former no such oath was given.
The argument seems to depend on the fact that where God
adds an oath to his own word the matter becomes doubly
certain (*cf.* 6:18). Compared with this the Levitical order was
dependent only on the law. The writer is convinced that this
shows the superiority of Melchizedek, again because it is based
on Scripture. When he says *this one was addressed with an oath*,
he is referring back to the citation in verse 17, but he now cites
the first half of Psalm 110:4 which he had previously omitted.
The oath, in the psalm, is directly linked with the changelessness of God. Here the thought is repeated, in order to impress
on the readers the authority which lay behind this exposition
of the high-priest theme.

**22.** In a summary statement which gathers up the main point
of the preceding discussion, *Jesus* is again mentioned by name
(the last time was 6:20). Moreover in the Greek text the name
stands in the emphatic position at the end of the sentence. It is
clear that special significance must be attached to the use of the
human name here, since it is as perfect representative of man
that he becomes the *surety* (*engyos*). This word occurs nowhere
else in the New Testament. It is common in the papyri in legal
documents in the sense of a pledge or as a reference to bail.
When a father assents to the marriage of his daughter he gives
a surety of the marriage dowry (see MM). In the present case
the surety is related to the covenant and not directly to man.
Since the covenant in the biblical sense is an agreement initiated
by God, the surety (*i.e.* Jesus) guarantees that that covenant

will be honoured. In the next chapter the writer enlarges on the idea of the new covenant and clearly has this in mind when speaking of *a better covenant*. The old covenant was closely linked with the law and with the Levitical order. The new offers a better hope (verse 19) and without question has a better high priest.

**23–24.** The continuity of the high-priesthood of Jesus has already been stressed, but the writer cannot leave the subject without reiterating the contrast between the *former priests* (Aaron's line) and Jesus. The multiplicity of Aaron's line was unavoidable because each was *prevented by death from continuing in office*. It was the office that continued, not the person. By way of contrast, Jesus *holds his priesthood permanently*, *i.e.* it is inviolable. Some commentators have attempted to understand the word to mean 'non-transferable', but this is not the technical sense of the word. Although Jesus, our high priest, died, his priesthood did not cease, neither was it passed on to others, because his death was not a final act. It was eclipsed by his resurrection (*he continues for ever*), thus setting him apart from all other priests.

**25.** Here the result of the inviolate high-priesthood of Jesus is specifically stated to be his continuous ability to save. It would be wholly different if his priestly office had been only temporary. Indeed the whole force of argument in this epistle rests on the continuity of the office of Jesus. The ability of Jesus Christ has already come into focus before in this epistle, but nowhere as comprehensively as here. In 2:18 it was his ability to help, in 4:15 his ability to sympathize, but here his ability *to save*. Salvation has been mentioned before, but only here is the verb used applied to Jesus. This makes it more personal. But it is made even more comprehensive by the fact that his ability to save is said to be *for all time* (*eis to panteles*). The Greek generally means 'wholly', but a temporal meaning is justified by papyri parallels (MM). The meaning seems to be that as long as the high priest functions, he is able to save, a thought which is strengthened by the words *he always lives* (*pantote zōn*).

*Those who draw near to God through him* have already been referred to in verse 19, although a different verb is used here. There is a reciprocal connection between Jesus' ability to save and man's willingness to come. No provision is made for those who come any other way except through Jesus Christ. This writer shares with the other New Testament writers the conviction that salvation is inseparable from the work of Christ.

Already in this letter the intercessory work of Christ has been hinted at. His sympathy and help are in line with this, but it comes out more clearly in the present passage. The word for *intercession* (*entynchanein*) does not occur elsewhere in this epistle, but is used by Paul both of the Spirit's intercession (Rom. 8:27) and of Christ's intercession (Rom. 8:34). The function of our high priest is to plead our cause. Again he can do this more effectively than Aaron or any of his descendants ever could. This intercessory ministry of Christ shows his present activity for his people and is a direct continuation of his earthly ministry.

**26.** Here the writer proceeds to summarize some of those qualities which are particularly characteristic of an ideal high priest and which are perfectly seen in Jesus Christ.

Earlier in this epistle the writer has used the same formula – *it was fitting* (*eprepen*) as used here, *i.e.* in 2:10. In both cases it refers to the perfection of the activities of Jesus Christ. Here it implies that no other kind of high priest would meet the demands. This not only applies to the qualities about to be mentioned, but also to those already mentioned in verse 25, for the connecting word *for* (*gar*) gives both a backward and a forward look. It is assumed that the statement regarding the high priest is relevant only to Christians as the *we* (*hēmin*) implies. It does not appear fitting to everyone, but only to those who have a sense of coming to God through Christ (as in verse 25).

First of all three personal characteristics of the ideal high priest are mentioned, all closely linked with each other – *holy, blameless, unstained*. The first refers to personal holiness. It has a positive aspect, a perfect fulfilment of all that God is and all that he requires, a character which can never be charged with error or impurity. The other qualities relate to the impact of his character on others. No-one can accuse him of moral defection or corruption. The word *blameless* (*akakos*) means 'innocent' in the sense of guileless, while the word *unstained* (*amiantos*) means 'uncontaminated'. The three words combine to give a comprehensive picture of the purity of our high priest. He is not only inherently pure, but remains pure in all his contacts with sinful men.

Whereas earlier in the epistle the writer was at pains to stress the identification of Jesus Christ with his 'brethren', he here emphasizes that he was *separated from sinners*. This is true in two ways. His sinless character at once sets him apart from other men, all of whom are sinners. Moreover his office equally sets him apart, for only the high priest, even in the Levitical order, was permitted into the holy of holies, and then only after purging his own sin. It is a cardinal feature of New Testament teaching that Jesus Christ, in spite of his likeness to men, nevertheless stands unique above them. It is only when this uniqueness is recognized that the full glory of the ministry of Jesus on men's behalf can be appreciated.

The expression *exalted above the heavens* describes the present position of our high priest and recalls the statement in 1:3 about his being seated at the right hand of the Majesty on high. There are many New Testament passages which are parallels to this thought (*cf.* Eph. 4:10; Acts 1:10f.; 1 Pet. 3:22). The exaltation of Jesus is vividly brought out by Paul in Philippians 2:9. As contrasted with the limited glory of the Levitical priesthood, the glory of Christ is in his eternal exaltation. There is none other to bear comparison with him.

**27.** His superiority over Aaron's priests is further seen in the fact that no *daily* sacrifices are needed either for himself or for the people. A problem arises over the application of the word *daily* (*kath hēmeran*) to the Aaronic priests, for if the writer has the ritual of the Day of Atonement in mind this happened only once a year, not daily. Bruce[1] thinks the occasional sin-offering may have been in our author's mind when he used the expression 'daily'. On the other hand, Davidson[2] regards the Day of Atonement offering as summing up all the occasional offerings throughout the year. But the problem could be resolved by restricting the words to the ministry of Jesus, in which case the accompanying words *like those priests* would refer only to the

---

[1] Bruce, *Comm.*, p. 157.  [2] Davidson, *Comm.*, p. 144.

need for the priests to offer sacrifices. The whole sentence may then be rendered 'He has no need in his daily ministry to offer sacrifices for himself as those priests did . . .' This understanding of the word *daily* would be in agreement with the previous statements already made in verse 25 about the continuous character of the intercession of Christ. The fact that the Aaronic high priest needed an offering both for himself and his people shows a marked distinction from the action of Christ, who *offered up himself* once for all. The offering in his case was not for himself for he had no sin. Moreover the offering was *once for all*, needing no repetition. It is important to note that the reason for the difference is found wholly in the character of the high priest rather than in his office.

**28.** Here is a summary of the previous two verses. The contrast between the two orders being discussed is summed up as a contrast between *law* and *oath*. This is a drawing together of the argument since 6:13ff. Both are said to *appoint*, although the appointment clearly comes from him who constituted both law and oath. The difference is here explained by the difference of character in those appointed. *Men in their weakness* contrasts strongly with *a Son who has been made perfect for ever*, particularly because the human nature of the Son has already been brought out more than once in this epistle. The law could use only the kind of persons available for the office of high priest and whoever was chosen was afflicted by the weakness common to all men. This inevitably made the legal system of high priests correspondingly weak. The writer's purpose, however, is not to decry the ineffectiveness of Aaron's line, but to glorify the superiority of Christ's. The order of Melchizedek, being free from the encumbrances of human succession, was free from the weakness inherent in Aaron's system, and could be concentrated in a unique person.

The statement about *the word of the oath, which came later than the law* seems at first surprising in view of 6:13ff., which shows the oath to have been made to Abraham. This therefore antedates the law by several centuries. But what the writer evidently has in mind here is the appointment of Christ to the office of high priest, which historically places it centuries after the law. The writer may have been influenced by the reference to the oath in Psalm 110, already quoted in verses 20f. The major thought, however, is that of perfection, first introduced in the epistle in 2:10. With a perfect high priest, the office becomes permanent for there is nothing to render it invalid. The Christian may approach with confidence, seeing he has a high priest of such a character.

### (v) The minister of the new covenant (8:1–13)

**1.** As the writer has already discoursed at some length about Christ as high priest, it might be wondered what is still left to be expounded. But so far he has not explained how our high priest carries out his duties. This really forms the theme of the next two and a half chapters (to 10:18), but another important matter, the new covenant, is introduced in the course of the discussion. In the present chapter the ministry of Jesus and the need for a new covenant are linked together. The opening sentence draws out the main point of the preceding discussion (*Now the point (kephalaion) in what we are saying is this*). The word could mean 'summary', but the context shows that 'point' is better, because the focus falls on what the high priest has to offer and where he performs his ministry.

First, however, a brief statement is given of the particular characteristics of our high priest. (i) He *is seated at the right hand on the throne of the Majesty in heaven*. This point has already been made in 1:3 of the Son, but is now repeated with direct application to the high-priest theme. This shows how carefully the writer has worked out his thesis, constantly throwing out hints which are gems in themselves but which sparkle with new meaning when seen again against a different background. Indeed this idea of the seated Christ occurs again in 10:12 and 12:2. It signifies a work well and truly done. The idea is based on Psalm 110:1. Apart from the present statement and the parallel wording in 1:3, the only other place in the New Testament where the term *Majesty* is used is in Jude 25, where it occurs as an ascription to God, but not as a title. The fact that our high priest sits at God's right hand enhances his status compared with that of Aaron's line, whose priests could only stand in God's presence, their task never finally completed.

**2.** The second characteristic is that (ii) he is *a minister in the* *sanctuary and the true tent.* This seems strange at first, following as it does the sitting down. It draws attention, however, to the continuing work of Christ. The word for 'minister' (*leitourgos*) has occurred once before in this epistle in 1:7, referring to the angels in a quotation from Psalm 104:4. Paul uses the word of his own Christian ministry (Rom. 15:16) and of Epaphroditus' service (Phil. 2:25). He even uses it of the secular authorities in Romans 13:6. In the present context, however, the ministry in view is especially in holy things, as the context shows. The sanctuary (*tōn hagiōn*) might be particularly understood of the holy of holies, as in 9:3. The linking of this with the idea of the tent (tabernacle) is significant, for it shows that the basis of the writer's imagery is not the Temple but the tabernacle. The adjective *true* is intended to contrast with the earthly symbol. The place of Christ's ministry is real and spiritual, compared with the ministry of Aaron's line in a merely temporal tabernacle. Once again a contrast is brought out between the apparent and the real in that the former *is set up by man*, whereas the latter is set up by *the Lord*.

**3.** The main function of earthly high priests is now transferred specifically to our high priest. The writer wants to show that Christ fulfils the usual functions of the office, but in a much better way than Aaron's line fulfilled them. The statement, *For every high priest is appointed*, is a precise echo of 5:1, but whereas there the appointment is for a representative purpose, here it is more specifically *to offer gifts and sacrifices*, *i.e.* in the working out of the representative function. These sacrifices are a direct allusion to the Levitical offerings and possibly have mainly in view the ritual of the Day of Atonement. There is to be a fuller exposition of this in the next chapter. Here the immediate purpose is to comment on the spiritual offering which our high priest offered up. At this point the offering is not defined, but the writer has already shown in 7:27 that the offering was Christ himself and he further expands this later. He speaks of the necessity for our high priest to make an offering.[1] This is the

[1] Westcott, *Comm.*, *ad. loc.*, rightly rejects the view that Christ continues to offer sacrifices. Such a thought is alien to the author's view of Christ's offering as complete (once for all). Montefiore, *Comm.*, p. 134, shows that the idea of a blood offering in heaven was also alien to Hellenistic Judaism, which postulated offerings of a different kind. Only later in cabbalistic Judaism does the idea of an actual sacrifice in heaven arise.

only instance in the New Testament where the word here translated *necessary* (*anankaios*) is used of Christ. It is used of the
necessary work of any high priest, but it has a deeper meaning
when applied to Christ, for there was a divine necessity for him
to offer up himself. It should be noted, moreover, that the
principle of priestly offering is expressed in an impersonal form
– *something* (*ti*) – which becomes personal only when applied to
the offering of Christ himself.

**4.** It occurs to the writer that some confusion might arise in
his readers' minds over the co-existence of two orders of
priesthood. He proceeds, therefore, to show that the priesthood
of Jesus was not established *on earth*. The main point he is
making is the impossibility of Jesus fulfilling the conditions
either in the matter of genealogy, or in the precise nature of the
gifts, which are stipulated in the Mosaic Law. This leads into
his thesis that the superior priesthood is that which operates in
heaven, not on earth. This line of argument goes a long way
towards explaining why Jesus never performed any priestly
functions during his ministry. Yet it should be noted that
although his high-priestly work is in heaven, his offering up of
himself took place on earth. The earthly ministry must be regarded as the preparation for the heavenly work. The next verse
explains the basis of the connection between the Levitical cultus
and the work of Christ.

**5.** The thesis underlying this epistle is based on the existence
of some correspondence between the Levitical cultus and the
spiritual work of Christ, but the movement is always from the
lesser to the greater. The two words here used to express the
idea – *copy* (*hypodeigma*) and *shadow* (*skia*) – both imply a deeper
reality behind what is seen. A copy of a great master-work of
art is not the real thing but gives some idea of what the original
is like. The resemblance is incomplete and not until the original
is seen is the full glory recognized. Similarly a shadow cannot
in fact exist unless there is an object to cast it. There is some
correspondence, but the shadow is inevitably a distorted and
somewhat featureless picture of the real. The writer's purpose
is not to reduce the glory of the shadow, but to enhance the
glory of its substance. What is specially in mind is *the heavenly
sanctuary* (*epouraniōn*). Only the word 'heavenly' appears in the

Greek, however, and it is therefore best to treat it generally of heavenly things, the 'tabernacle' being implied from verse 2 and by the use of the word *tent* (*skēnē*), both there and here. It is particularly evident from the statement about *Moses* that it is the biblical background and not the background of Judaism, with its central Temple, which is in mind.

The writer's mind goes back to Exodus 25:40, where God's instruction to Moses is given. In Alexandrian Judaism the same Exodus passage was expounded according to Platonic principles, in which the tent that was constructed was regarded as only an imperfect copy of what already existed in heaven, which Moses himself saw. The tent on earth was only a shadow of the reality.[1] But why does the writer of this epistle quote the passage at this stage in his argument? It could perhaps be supposed that he thought his readers might be unfamiliar with the fact that God had given precise instructions about the details of the tabernacle, but this seems unlikely. It is more probable that he wanted to remind his readers that even the shadow was minutely ordered by God, so that he might demonstrate the greater excellency of the heavenly sanctuary. Moreover, if God ordained the details of *the pattern* (*typos*), their symbolic meaning is assured. All the meticulous detail in the Exodus account would have little purpose if some better antitype was not being foreshadowed by them. The word used for *instructed* (*kechrēmatistai*) in this verse is not widely used in the New Testament, but refers to a divine oracle, an authoritative word which must be obeyed. The Aaronic priesthood and the arrangements for it did not come about by accident, but by design.

**6.** Christ's ministry is here said to be *much more excellent* (*diaphorōteras*), a term which has already occurred in 1:4. It could be regarded as a kind of key word to express the superiority of Christ in this epistle, especially as in both its occurrences it is linked with the word *better*. In this context there is a parallel between the new and the old ministry and between the new and the old covenant. The writer intends to expound the superiority of the new *covenant*, but for the moment he is concerned to show that the ministry must be commensurate

[1] Montefiore, *Comm.*, pp. 136f.

with the covenant under which it is established. The minister is a mediator of the covenant. His ministry is seen in the context of the covenant, which accounts for the writer's sudden switch to the new covenant theme. The idea of mediating a covenant is also to be expounded more fully in the next chapter (9:15ff.). Since a covenant involves two contracting parties, the mediator is a go-between whose task is to keep the parties in fellowship with one another. In a case where God is one of the parties and man is the other, the covenant idea is inevitably one-sided. Defection is always on man's side and hence the mediator's task is mainly to act on man's behalf before God, although he has also to act for God before men.

The basis for the view that the new covenant is better than the old is that *it is enacted on better promises*. But in what sense is this to be taken? It implies that both were based on promises, but that there was a qualitative difference between the two in the nature of the promises. This view, however, is difficult, if all God's promises are equally inviolate. It is preferable, therefore, to take 'better' to refer to the higher spiritual purpose inherent in the new covenant, *e.g.* the idea of law written on the heart (verse 10). Promises which can do that must be better than promises which could only lead to the codification of the old law (*i.e.* the law of Moses).

7. It is the failure of the first covenant which provides the necessity for the second. When the writer implies that the *first covenant* was not *faultless*, he is not suggesting that the law was faulty, but only that man's experience under it was faulty. If indeed the law had been the complete answer to man's need, there would have been no need for a new covenant. This statement is the signal for the writer to quote an extended passage from Jeremiah to explain his approach to the new covenant.

8. The fault-finding function of the law is clearly brought out in this quotation from Jeremiah 31:31–34, which is introduced by the characteristic *he says* (*legei*). This, as noted before, indirectly makes the words of Scripture the word spoken by God. This writer is not interested in stating the name of the prophet, because for him the crucial factor is the divine authority behind the point he is making. The threefold *says the Lord* in this quotation reaffirms this. The context of the passage shows the

people of God at the stage of being restored after the trials of the captivity. The new situation demands a new approach in God's relationship with his people – in short *a new covenant*.

First there is in the quotation a statement of intention. *The days will come . . . when I will establish . . .* has a ring of authority which makes no provision for doubt. Such an action is as certain as God's word, although centuries were to pass before its fulfilment. Our writer has no doubt that the confident statement in this Old Testament prophecy applies to the Messianic age and has a direct bearing on the ministry of Jesus. He may well have had in his mind the reference to the new covenant in the institution of the Lord's supper (*cf.* Mt. 26:28).

Another feature of the covenant is its application to both *Israel* and *Judah*. Historically this involved the healing of the breach which had brought such disaster in the early history of the Jewish people. But even in this passage there is no hint of a new covenant which could extend to all people, Gentiles as well as Jews, as happened as a result of the gospel. Indeed it is worth noting that this universal aspect of the gospel finds no place in this epistle, but a sufficient explanation of this would be its restricted destination for a Jewish audience. The word for *new* (*kainē*) here points to something which is new in comparison with what has preceded it, whereas the alternative adjective (*neos*), applied to the same covenant in 12:24, points to its freshness, compared with something old and worn out. Both aspects are full of meaning.

**9.** The contrast of the new covenant with the old is seen in a specific reference to the historical circumstances in which the old covenant was made. Israelite thought constantly went back to the deliverance from Egypt, for that was the point in history from which the independent existence of Israel as a nation could be said to date. It is striking here that God himself made the covenant. He did not consult with men. Moreover, the expression *I took them by the hand* again stresses the divine initiative. Although the Greek speaks of 'my hand' and therefore heightens the anthropomorphism, it is nevertheless vividly expressive. It is a poetic way of making clear that the people were helpless until God, as it were, put his hand in theirs *to lead them out of the land of Egypt*, the place of their captivity.

A covenant normally involves the full co-operation of both parties. If one party defaults, the covenant becomes invalid. This is virtually what happened to the old covenant. The Israelites *did not continue in* the covenant, which means that they broke away from its conditions. The pronouns 'they' and 'I' in both cases are emphatic, again bringing emphasis on the divine prerogative. This is equally seen in the description of the covenant as *my covenant*. When God declares, *I paid no heed to them*, this is not to be taken as an arbitrary act of disinterestedness, but as the inevitable consequence of his people turning their backs on the covenant of grace which he had made for their benefit and blessing.

**10.** Now comes an exposition of the new covenant which is promised. It has several noteworthy features. It concerns *the house of Israel*, an expression ideally inclusive of the whole people of God, although in Jeremiah's context mainly of the Jewish people. It will become effective *after those days*, which connects up with 'these last days' mentioned in 1:2 and refers to the Christian era.

The Hebrew text of this verse has the singular 'law', which has been rendered for some reason in the Septuagint as a plural *laws*, as here. This is all the more significant because on no other occasion does the Septuagint render the Hebrew singular in this way. It may be that the translator wished to emphasize the separate parts of God's law to distinguish these parts from the law of Moses as a complete unity. The passage contains an implied contrast between law written on stone tablets and laws put into their minds. There can be no doubt that the latter is superior to the former, for what is in the mind cannot fail to affect the activity. The double statement *into their minds* and *on their hearts*, an example of Hebrew poetic parallelism, emphasizes the inward character of the new covenant. Of the two terms the more comprehensive in Hebrew usage is heart, which involved not only the will, but also the emotions. Both terms in this quotation are best regarded in a corporate sense, as if the writer has in view the corporate character of the other party in the covenant which God has made. There is a sense in which the new laws are impressed on the mind and heart of the *people* as a whole.

Although the old covenant had demonstrated that God was the God of Israel and that he would regard Israel as his people, there is a deeper sense in which this could be achieved in a fully spiritual sense only in the new covenant. There is a significant stress on the pronouns *their* (*autois*) and *my* (*moi*). The Greek expresses it cryptically – 'I will be to them as God, and they will be to me as people'. The relationship is to be intimate and mutual.

**11.** Another aspect of the new covenant is that knowledge of God can now come direct, without the need for intermediaries. Fellowship with God will be such that everyone will know him among his people. This rules out at once the idea of a privileged class of special initiates who alone could teach others, as existed for instance in the mystery religions and was certainly fostered to some extent in the scribal system of Judaism. Moreover in the new covenant community there would be no class distinctions due to age or rank, for the knowledge of God would be available over the whole range, *from the least of them to the greatest*. The true Christian community is intended to be a group in which all are on an equal footing through a common and personal experience of the Lord, *for all shall know me*.

**12.** The quotation ends with an explanation of the spiritual basis of the new covenant. God reveals his own character: *I will be merciful*. There is no suggestion that this is a new development in the divine character, for the old covenant was based on mercy. Man could never come to God at all were it not for his mercy. But in the new covenant the mercy of God comes most clearly into prominence. It provides a sure foundation for his people's approach to him. The second revelation, *I will remember their sins no more*, is reassuring because it means that forgiveness is complete. There will be no possibility of sins, once forgiven, being brought against the people of God. All the assurances to this effect before the Christian era were based on the efficacy of that perfect sacrifice yet to be offered, of which the Levitical offerings were but a shadow. Such a direct assurance of God's forgiveness must have been like the sound of music to an exiled people whose sacrificial offerings were no longer possible.

The parallel lines referring to *iniquities* (*adikiai*) and to *sins* (*hamartiai*) is another case of semitic poetic parallelism. The second word is more general and comprehensive than the first, but both complement each other in emphasizing the idea of complete forgiveness.

**13.** Having ended his quotation from Jeremiah, the writer now gives his comment on it and in doing so goes beyond the original purpose of the passage. He sees the exposition of the *new covenant* as implying that the old is *obsolete*. Looking at the passage from the threshold of the Christian era, he sees more in the words than it was possible for Jeremiah to see. The word translated *obsolete* (*pepalaiōken*) is in the perfect tense which suggests that the first covenant has already become obsolete, the result of which is still evident in the present. The same verb is used in the second sentence as a present participle, *becoming obsolete*, because the writer wants to point out that although theoretically the old has already become obsolete, in practice it is a gradual process. The combination of this thought with that of *growing old* brings out the inevitability of the process. As all people grow old and die, so illustrating their transient character, the old covenant is equally seen to be transient.

An interesting word is used to describe the end of the old covenant, *i.e. ready to vanish away* (*engys aphanismou*). The verbal form of the same word is used of the transience of human life in James 4:14, like a vapour which suddenly appears and as quickly vanishes. It is fundamental in Christian theology that the old has performed its function and has now given way to the new. Historically the continuation of the Temple ritual was made impossible by the destruction of that Temple by the Roman general, Titus, but in any case the days of the ritual were numbered.

*(vi) The greater glory of the new order (9:1–14)*
**1.** In case any of the readers should think that the writer was underestimating the old, he now outlines some of the glories of the old tabernacle. He is impressed by the orderliness of the arrangements within the Levitical cultus, and aims to present this in order to demonstrate the greater glory of the new. It may well be that he knows that some of his readers, who have been brought up in the atmosphere of glorifying the past, con-

sider that the Christian position has no substitute to offer for the dignity of the cultus. Yet while he himself is not unappreciative of the glories of the past, he wants to lead his readers to a truer appreciation of the superior glories of the Christian faith.

He is concerned first of all with *regulations for worship*. The word for regulations (*dikaiōma*) has many uses in the New Testament, as for instance 'the just requirement of the law', or 'the act which fulfils what is considered to be right'. What comes out most clearly in this passage is that regulations were laid down which were expected to be followed. But the main interest is in the place of worship. That was not to come until much later. The place of worship is here called an *earthly sanctuary* (*to hagion kosmikon*), strictly 'the' rather than 'an'. The distinction is not unimportant, for a particular sanctuary is in mind, the scene of priestly activity in the tabernacle. The word for *sanctuary* (*hagion*) stands for both the holy place (verse 2) and the holy of holies (verse 3). The only other New Testament occurrence of *kosmikon* (earthly, worldly) is in Titus 2:12, where it is applied to worldly passions. In the present case it is used without any moral connotation and denotes the earth in contrast to heaven as the sphere of activity (*cf.* 8:1–2).

**2.** No doubt the reason why reference is now made to the *tent* (*skēnē*) is so that no-one should suppose that the Temple is in mind. A comparison with the original tabernacle regulations is evidently regarded as more authoritative than the Temple for Jewish Christians. It may be, moreover, that these Christians were confused over what to do about the biblical cultus. The statement that the tent *was prepared* points back to the original erection. The tabernacle consisted of two parts. Mention is first made of *the outer one* (*prōtē*, literally 'first'), presumably called the first because it was nearer to the entrance from the outer courtyard. Three articles of furniture stood in this part, *the lampstand, the table* and *the bread of the Presence* (or shewbread). No explanation is given of the significance of these articles, for it is assumed that the readers will be acquainted with this. The precise details are found in Exodus 25, 37 and 40. The lampstand stood on one side of the holy place and the table on the other. In between stood the altar of incense which is not mentioned here, but is spoken of in the next verse as if it were beyond the dividing curtain (but see comment on verse 3).

**3.** The *second curtain* is clearly the veil separating the holy place from the holy of holies. This was the curtain which has already been mentioned in 6:19. This inner part is also called a tabernacle or *tent*, the writer using the same term to describe both inner and outer parts as if two tabernacles existed. Since the tabernacle was viewed as God's dwelling-place, the word was particularly appropriate for the inner shrine. The form of the expression *Holy of Holies* points to the special sanctity of the place and explains why normal access to it was barred.

**4.** A problem arises over the first item mentioned in the holy of holies. If *the golden altar of incense* is the correct understanding of the word used (*thymiatērion*), the placing of it in the inner shrine would depart from the Exodus account where it was placed in the holy place before the entrance to the inner place. It has been suggested that the word may be understood of the high priest's censer, but this is unlikely because the Exodus account does not regard it as golden. It must be conceded that the word *thymiatērion* primarily means 'censer' and is so used in the LXX. Nevertheless its derived meaning of 'altar of incense' is found in Philo and Josephus and this is clearly the sense intended in this context in Hebrews. It is inconceivable that no mention would be made here of the golden altar of incense. What then is the explanation of the placing of it in a different position?

First it may be observed that the writer does not say 'in which is the golden altar of incense' after the style of verse 2. He must have had good reason for making the difference. It has been suggested that the participle *having* (*echousa*) is intended in the sense of 'belonging to' rather than 'standing within', since the altar of incense, as it were, barred the entrance into the holy of holies and could in that sense be said to belong to it. This is supported by the fact that the altar was so placed that the smoke from the burning incense was supposed to penetrate the curtain and rise to God before the ark of the covenant. Nevertheless, since the same participle does service as well for the ark, which was quite definitely inside the holy of holies, the preceding explanation is not without some difficulty. Nevertheless it is the most reasonable. There is clearly a close link between the altar of incense and the holy of holies. We may also note that in 1 Kings 6:22 the incense altar is described as 'the whole altar' belonging to the inner sanctuary.

*The ark of the covenant* stood in the holy of holies in the tabernacle and in Solomon's temple, but not in the later Temple. Indeed in the latter the place was entirely empty except for a raised stone platform. When the writer says of the ark that it was *covered on all sides with gold*, he means both outside and inside (*cf.* Ex. 25:11). The cover over the ark was known as the mercy-seat and was adorned with the two golden cherubim (see verse 5). The focus of attention at the moment, however, is on the contents of the ark. Three items are mentioned. First is the *golden urn*. It is worth observing how three times in this description of the tabernacle furniture, the writer mentions gold. He is clearly impressed by the glittering character of the separate items. In the case of the urn the Hebrew text does not mention the precious material out of which it was made, but it comes in the Septuagint. The storage of *the manna* was to remind the Israelites of God's marvellous provision for them during the wilderness wanderings, and *Aaron's rod that budded* was to remind them of God's powerful intervention on their behalf. When the Temple was built, the ark of the covenant contained only *the tables of the covenant*, *i.e.* the tables of the Mosaic law. In the Christian faith there are spiritual counterparts, but the use of the symbolic objects here clearly meant much to both the writer and his readers. The writer's aim is to admit the glories of worship as set out in the tabernacle ritual in order to lead on to the specific ministry of Christ.

5. The expression *the cherubim of glory* is interesting because it does more than describe the cherubim as glorious. The glory (*doxa*) symbolized the presence of God. The cherubim, therefore, were reminders of God. Their position *overshadowing the mercy seat* shows them as guardians of the majesty of God. The word for *mercy seat* (*hilastērion*) means 'a propitiating thing', but came to have a further theological meaning in connection with the atonement, because it was this part of the ark which was sprinkled with blood on the Day of Atonement. This accounts for its use in Romans 3:25 in an applied sense relating to the

death of Christ. But the writer of this letter does not apply it in a spiritual or theological manner. At this juncture he is interested mainly in the glory of the old order. He could say more but refrains from doing so (*we cannot now speak in detail*), because he has other points to mention, especially its limitations.

**6-7.** In spite of all the splendour of the tabernacle furniture, worship under the Levitical order was severely limited. The Israelites could not approach directly; they had to come through their representatives, the priests. Even then only one could enter annually into the holy of holies. The way of approach was certainly not open as it came to be through Christ (*cf.* 10:19-20).

Within the tabernacle there was ceaseless activity as men approached God in his own appointed way. The whole scene witnesses to their desire to come to God, at the same time stressing the inadequacy of the old method. Certain *preparations* of a ritual kind were essential before the priests were allowed to enter, preparations which were intended to remind them of their own personal need and of God's provision which allowed them to enter. The present tense of the verb to *go into*, strengthened by the adverbial phrase *continually* (*dia pantos eisiasin*), brings out the repetitive character of the Mosaic order and this is again intended to contrast with the finality of the new way. Again as in verse 2 the holy place is identified as *the outer tent* (*i.e.* the first to be approached). The continuity was historically broken by the cessation of the tabernacle, but was resumed in the successive temples down to the writer's own day.

The *ritual duties* which were performed included the offering of incense and the trimming and lighting of the lamps. To anyone brought up in Judaism these performances would be regarded with a certain reverence and when such a person became a Christian he would not at once lose his respect for them. Particularly would this be true of the impressive events on the Day of Atonement *but once a year*. It is its infrequency which gives it greater point. As each annual event approached, the solemnity of the occasion would weigh upon the high priest's mind, especially as he prepared first to offer sacrificial *blood for himself* before providing it for his people. According to Leviticus 16:11ff., the high priest was required to sprinkle blood of the bullocks on the mercy-seat seven times and then to repeat the performance with the blood of a goat. Our writer is not, however, concerned to devote time and space to details of this sort. It is sufficient for him to give just enough information to lead into his theological application. It is noticeable that the annual offering is said to be *for the errors of the people* (literally 'ignorances', *agnoēmata*).

**8.** Since the details just given relate to the biblical cultus, the purpose of the Spirit in inspiring them to be recorded in the Old Testament next comes into focus. *The Holy Spirit indicates* the true meaning. This statement shows something of the writer's approach to inspiration, for the Spirit is continually demonstrating (present tense) how the cultus may now be applied. This explanatory ministry of the Spirit is in harmony with the promise of Jesus in John's Gospel (*cf.* Jn. 16:12ff.).

What is specifically said to be signified is that an obstacle bars the way into the holy of holies and thus into the presence of God. *The way into the sanctuary* must here be the inner sanctuary as compared with the outer tabernacle. The words *as long as the outer tent is still standing* seem to mean 'as long as approach is dependent on Levitical-type ceremonies' which barred all but the high priest from access to the presence of God, and even him for all but one day in the year. It is not without significance that the words 'is still standing' (*echousēs stasin*) could be more literally translated 'has standing', *i.e.* a place or status. Under the new covenant this status ceases.

**9.** The words in parenthesis (*which is symbolic for the present age*) give some indication of the writer's approach to the whole Levitical system. It was a figure (*parabolē*). It was therefore suggestive of deeper truths than it was itself able to fulfil. Moreover its symbolic purpose seems to be limited to the present age, by which the writer seems to be contrasting it with the future age (*cf.* 6:5). In the context of thought in this passage the 'present' age was that which prepared for the appearing of Christ (see verses 11f.), after which the symbol was fulfilled and therefore ceased to have any function.

The phrase, *according to this arrangement* (*kath' hēn*), presumably relates to all that precedes. Under the Levitical system *gifts and sacrifices* were regarded as temporarily effective in enabling men to come to God, but not to attain perfection. The true touchstone of the order of priesthood was whether it could make *perfect*. However glorious the trappings, any system was inadequate if this end could not be attained. The writer has once more in mind the clear superiority of Christ, which he later makes explicit (*cf*. 10:14). The main reason for the repetition of the ceremonial in the Levitical order was because imperfections remained. Another feature which is clearly brought out here is that worship is a matter of *conscience*. It is conscience which tells a person about himself and makes him aware of his accountability before God. It burdens a person with guilt. Where there is any hardening of conscience or where the conscience is overburdened with guilt, true worship is impossible. However incomplete the Levitical offerings were, their intention was to provide a means for *the worshipper* to cleanse his conscience. Again the superiority of the Christian way of approach is seen in 9:14 where purification is provided from dead works, and in the next chapter (10:22) where hearts can be cleansed from an evil conscience.

**10.** The limitation of the Levitical order is further seen in the fact that many of the regulations dealt only with external issues: matters of *food and drink and various ablutions*. Some difficulty arises from the fact that the Mosaic law laid down no regulations about any drink taboos, unless the Nazirite vow is taken into account (Nu. 6:3). These taboos and ritual cleansings were concerned with peripheral matters, although they were considered to be important. They are not to be identified with the gifts and sacrifices of the earlier verse, but they are accompaniments of them. Indeed they are here described as *regulations for the body*. There seems to be here, as in the next section (13–14) a contrast between conscience and flesh, between the inward and spiritual and the outward and physical. The minute regulations were moreover *imposed*, whereas in Christ a much more effective result is achieved by spiritual, not legal, means. No doubt many of the restrictions were beneficial to the body, but they did not bring liberty to the spirit. They were also only temporary, *until the time of reformation* (*diorthōseōs*). This unusual expression does not occur elsewhere in the Greek Bible, but is akin to expressions like 'regeneration' (*palingenesia*) in Matthew 19:28

and 'the time for establishing' (or restitution, *apokatastaseōs*) in Acts 3:21. For the writer of this epistle the time has come, identified in verse 11 as the time when Christ appeared as high priest.

11. At this point begins the explanation of Christ's special function under the new covenant. The writer transfers the main features of the old – the tabernacle and the atonement – into spiritual terms. In this way he shows their true value. They pointed to the greater reality behind the shadow.

First, mention is made of *Christ* having become *a high priest*. This is not a vision or a subject for discussion. It is a matter of fact (*appeared* is the aorist participle, *paragenomenos*). There is no need for further discussion, for it is assumed as a basic fact of the Christian faith. The special description of Christ as *a high priest of the good things that have come* shows another distinction between the old and the new. Whereas the old was a foreshadowing of better things to come, the new rests on an already accomplished fact. When Jesus Christ became high priest he at once dispensed many 'good things' as a result. Yet although they are perfectly realized in him, they are not yet so in us. These good things stand for all the spiritual blessings which are dispensed by our heavenly high priest. The alternative reading *tōn mellontōn* (*i.e.* good things to come) is well attested and may be original. It would fit the general idea of expectation in Hebrews, but the alternative suits the present context better.[1]

Next the focus falls on the place of Christ's ministry. Again the old symbolizes the new. The old tabernacle in the wilderness is now obsolete but it has its counterpart – what the writer calls *the greater and more perfect tent*. It is significant that the tent is described in definitive terms. The definite article points to a unique tabernacle which can be described as 'the greater'. There are no further possible comparisons with this spiritual tabernacle. It cannot be improved upon. The force of the word *through* (*dia*) should be noted since it affects our interpretation of the tent. It could mean 'through' (*i.e.* the high priesthood is by means of a tent); or 'by means of', giving the humanity of Jesus as the means; or 'by means of', understanding tent as the

---

[1] O. Michel, *Comm.*, p. 202, maintains that the expression with the future would have a precise meaning referring to the new age and therefore prefers this.

heavenly sanctuary.[1]

The words in parenthesis are to explain that the meaning intended was not literal but spiritual. Stephen had looked ahead to the Temple *not made with hands* (Acts 7:48), and would have understood this writer's transference of thought. Many patristic writers interpreted the better tabernacle as Christ's flesh, but it seems to mean more than that. The explanatory words, *not of this creation*, would indeed appear to exclude that view. It would seem, in fact, that the writer wants to deflect attention from the earthly symbol to lead into Christ's spiritual work without defining further what he means by the 'perfect tent'. When he proceeds in verse 12 to speak of the holy place he is presumably thinking of man's approach to God. It has been suggested that the 'tent' where Christ ministers is the spiritual community in the sense that his 'body' is a spiritual temple,[2] but this idea seems too remote from the context.

**12.** There is a marked finality about what Christ has done as compared with the continuous repetition of the Aaronic priesthood. This is brought out specially by the words *entered once for all*. The adverb has already occurred in 7:27 of Christ's offering for sin and is repeated again in 10:10 in the same sense. Our writer is clearly impressed by this sense of finality. Not only was the offering non-repeatable, but it was of a wholly different character from the old offerings, which consisted of *the blood of goats and calves*. The efficacy of the offerings rested in the shedding of blood and it is this feature on which the writer seizes in order to comment on the work of Christ. In no more dramatic way could the superiority be demonstrated than by comparing the self-giving of Jesus with the slaughter of animals. If blood was indispensable, no nobler blood than that of the high priest himself could be provided. It was no wonder that that sacrifice never needed to be repeated. Moreover, by taking as it were *his own blood* as the offering, our high priest was able to effect a permanent entry. No veil could keep him out of the holy of holies. Bruce[3] discusses the suggestion that it was not until Jesus ascended and carried with him the atoning blood that atonement was made. But he maintains that this is pressing the

---

[1] *Cf.* Montefiore's discussion here, *Comm.*, pp. 152f.
[2] *Cf.* Westcott, *Comm.*, pp. 256–258.   [3] Bruce, *Comm.*, pp. 200f.

analogy of the Day of Atonement too far.

The real effectiveness of the work of Christ is summed up in the words *thus securing an eternal redemption*. As here translated the participle 'securing' (*heuramenos*) is regarded as following from and subsequent to the entering. In this case the redemption is seen as the direct result of the offering. A possible alternative method of taking the participle is of an action accompanying the entering, but it seems better to understand it in the former sense. The word rendered 'redemption' (*lytrōsis*) occurs elsewhere in the New Testament only in Luke 1:68; 2:38, but it comes from the same root as 'ransom' (*lytron*, Mt. 20:28; Mk. 10:45) which is found in the most remarkable comment by Jesus on his own coming passion recorded in the Synoptic Gospels. There is no doubt that this idea made a deep impression, for the redeeming work of Christ finds strong mention in Paul's epistles where the compound noun (*apolytrōsis*, redemption) is used (*cf*. Rom. 3:24; 8:23; 1 Cor. 1:30; Eph. 1:7, 14; 4:30; Col. 1:14). Our writer employs the compound form in verse 15, but the idea of redemption is not as fully developed in this letter as in Paul's epistles. Whereas the idea of the compound form is of deliverance or release on payment of a price (*cf*. 11:35), that of the root form (*lytron*) is of an equivalent exchange price, particularly that paid for the freeing of slaves. The redemption is described as *eternal* because it is complete and therefore unrepeatable.

**13–14.** In the conditional clause which begins verse 13 the possibility of cleansing under the old law is taken for granted, for the writer wants again to bring out the superiority of Christ, this time in the evaluation of his offering. Two examples are chosen from the Levitical sacrifices to be representative of the general provisions of the Mosaic law to provide for purification from sin. The first – *the blood of goats and bulls* – is probably a reference to the offerings on the Day of Atonement (*cf*. Lv. 16), and the second – *the ashes of a heifer* – could refer to the occasional offering of a heifer (*cf*. Nu. 19). These were external provisions which offered ritual cleansing from the defilement *of the flesh*. It is important to note the contrast between 'flesh' and the 'spirit' in verse 14. One of the most important contrasts is between the external nature of the Levitical offerings and the essentially spiritual character of the offering of Christ. The Levitical offerings could and did provide ceremonial purity on a temporary basis, but the offering which Christ made could *purify your conscience, i.e.* it was an inner and spiritual cleansing. The writer does not offer any suggestion as to the way in which the Levitical procedures could cleanse from sin, even if only in a temporary manner.

It should be noted that the law made provision for *the sprinkling of defiled persons.* In 10:22 the same word is used of the Christian's conscience being sprinkled. Moreover sprinkling is actually applied to the book of the covenant in 9:19ff., as well as to the tent and the vessels (see comment later). Because all had been handled by men, they were ceremonially defiled until cleansed by the sprinkling.

Several important statements are made about the offering of Jesus. First of all it is summed up in the expression *the blood of Christ,* which occurs only here in this epistle, although the parallel phrase 'the blood of Jesus' is used in 10:19. It is intended to contrast with 'the blood of goats and bulls' in verse 13. In both cases the blood stands symbolically for the death of the victim, representing the yielding up of life on behalf of others.[1] The second fact about the offering of Christ, that it is *through the eternal Spirit,* at once places it in an altogether different category from the Levitical animal offerings. Christ made his offering with the full rational appreciation of what he was doing, whereas no animal ever could. But there is an even deeper significance here, for the expression *eternal Spirit* has no article in the Greek and must primarily refer to the spirit of Jesus as compared with his flesh. But undoubtedly the Holy Spirit is also in mind, since Jesus was working in conjunction with the Spirit (*cf.* the baptism). It is possible that the Isaianic servant of the Lord lies behind this concept, especially Isaiah 42:1, 'I have put my Spirit upon him'.[2] Only of Christ could it

---

[1] *Cf.* A. M. Stibbs, *The Meaning of the Word 'Blood' in Scripture* (London, 1947); L. Morris, *The Apostolic Preaching of the Cross* (London, 1955), pp. 117–124; J. Behm, *haima*, TDNT 1, pp. 172ff.

[2] Bruce, *Comm.,* p. 205. *Cf.* also H. L. Ellison, *The Servant of Jehovah* (London, 1953), pp. 29f. G. Vos, *The Teaching of the Epistle to the Hebrews* (1956), p. 114 (cited approvingly by Hughes), takes the expression here to mean 'through the heavenly aspect of his deity'.

be said that his spirit was *eternal*, a fact which even a sacrificial death could not affect. Since the redemption to be secured was eternal (verse 12), it was necessary for the offering to be made by one endowed with eternal spirit.

A further facet of Christ's offering is that he himself took the initiative – *he offered himself*. No other victim and certainly no other high priest had done this. It was both voluntary and premeditated. This means that it was in no sense an accident of circumstances. Moreover the offering is placed on the highest moral level, when the words *without blemish* are added to it. All Levitical offerings had to be chosen from animals without blemish, but the innocence could not be of a moral kind. The unblemished character of Jesus rested in his perfect fulfilment of God's will. He was obedient even unto death (Phil. 2:8). It is integral to the New Testament faith that Jesus lived and died without sin, for only so could he be a perfect sacrifice on behalf of his people.

With an offering so clearly superior, the results must be correspondingly greater. The purifying act is applied to the *conscience*, an idea already prepared for by 9:9, which showed the inadequacy of the old order in relation to conscience. Outward purification is useless if it does not effect some radical transformation of life. Man relies on *works*, but if these turn out to be *dead* in the sense of being invalid, because they are soiled with sin and self, the only hope is for the conscience to be purged from this awareness of failure. In 1 Peter 3:21 another statement is made which stresses the need for a clear conscience, as opposed to ritual cleansing. Indeed in Hebrews 13:18, almost as a parting statement, the writer, in urging prayer for himself and his associates, affirms that they have a clear conscience. It was part of the whole purpose of his argument to let his readers know the basis of his assurance.

When dead works are disposed of, the Christian is free *to serve the living God*. It is again basic to the Christian way that purity is not an end in itself. No man can divorce his religious status from his religious service. The word translated *serve (latreuō)* is especially used of service to God, and is found also in 9:9; 10:2; 12:28 and 13:10 in the sense of worship, which must be the main idea here. True worship necessarily involves whole-hearted commitment to God. It involves considerably more than mere ceremonial correctness.

## F. THE MEDIATOR (9:15 – 10:18)

Mention of the new covenant in the last section leads the writer to further reflection on Christ as a mediator. He shows the significance of Christ's death in his role as mediator between God and man and makes clear that he had entered a better sanctuary and offered a more complete offering, *i.e.* himself. This section concludes the main doctrinal argument.

### *(i) The significance of his death (9:15–22)*

**15.** What is about to be explained concerning the effectiveness of Christ's offering is directly dependent on the previous verses, as the word *Therefore* (*kai dia touto*) shows. It is in fact on the basis of his self-offering that Christ becomes a mediator (*cf.* comment on 8:6). The whole phrase *mediator of a new covenant* recurs in 12:24, almost as a title for Jesus, but with one difference. Here the word 'new' (*kainē*) means new in contrast to the old, whereas in 12:24 another word (*nea*) is used which calls attention to the fact that it is recent (*i.e.* as far as the readers are concerned). In the present phrase the emphasis falls on the word *covenant* (*diathēkē*) which is placed first in the Greek. Indeed it is the covenant rather than the mediator which is the main subject of the whole passage.

Nevertheless, the immediate switch in verse 16 from covenant to will shows the flexible way in which the writer approaches the idea of covenant (see comment on next verse). It may seem inappropriate to speak of a mediator of a will. Indeed Nairne[1] has maintained that the mediator of a will would not be the testator but the executor, but Bruce[2] argues that human analogies fail when applied to him who rose from the dead. 'He is testator and executor in one, surety and mediator alike.'

The purpose of the new covenant is said to be to provide *the promised eternal inheritance*. The idea of inheritance was central in the old covenant but it did not rise above the earthly level.

---

[1] Nairne, *The Epistle of Priesthood*, p. 365.   [2] Bruce, *Comm.*, p. 213.

Here it is eternal, hence clearly superior. This is the real fulfilment of the promise. In fact the order of words in the Greek
suggests that the phrase 'eternal inheritance' is an explanatory
afterthought to remind the readers of the precise content of the
promise. This inheritance is restricted not to a certain nation,
but to a certain class named as *those who are called* (*hoi keklēme-
noi*). This description is not found elsewhere in this epistle. The
idea of God's calling is familiar, however, elsewhere in the New
Testament (*cf.* Rom. 8:28; *cf.* also Rom. 1:1 where the calling,
*klētos*, is to a specific office). In the present context the expression refers to believers in general and is a reminder that God
has taken the initiative. The perfect participle, moreover, suggests the continual result of a past act, *i.e.* those who have been
called and are therefore presently conscious of that calling.

The concluding statement in this verse, *since a death has
occurred*, explains the basis of the effectiveness of the new
covenant. It is in the form of a genitive absolute which shows
it to be antecedent to the mediatorial office. The *death* is clearly
the death of Christ. It is said to be for a special purpose. The
association of death with covenant goes back to earliest times.[1]
The same principle is applied to the new covenant as applied
to the sequence of the old covenant. The translation *which re-
deems* does not bring this out as clearly as the Greek (*eis apoly-
trōsin*) which shows redemption to be the aim of the death.
The noun is a familiar Pauline word (*cf.* Rom. 3:24; 8:23; 1 Cor.
1:30; Eph. 1:7, 14; 4:30; Col. 1:14), and recurs in Hebrews 11:35
in a different sense (*i.e.* release from torture). Here, as in Paul,
it describes the deliverance effected by the death of Christ. His
death is the price of the sinner's release. It is specifically related
to *transgressions under the first covenant*, as if the redemption is
qualified by the thing from which deliverance is obtained. Once
before in the epistle the word *transgression* (*parabasis*) is used (in
2:2); apart from this it occurs only in Paul's epistles (Rom., Gal.,
1 Tim.). It has special point here since one of the main functions
of the law was to reveal transgressions by setting a straight path
and showing up all who stepped aside from it (*cf.* Rom. 4:15).
Under the old covenant no permanent help was given to those

---

[1] *Cf.* Hughes, *Comm.*, p. 366.

who transgressed, but Christ's redemptive death made deliverance possible. There is much of the Exodus imagery about this passage – the redemptive act and the covenant – which strongly reminds us of the background of the writer's thought.

**16.** The switch from covenant to *will* is more understandable in Greek than in English since the same word (*diathēkē*) does service for both ideas.[1] Indeed a 'will' is the more basic meaning of the word, although in the LXX it normally means covenant. A will comes into effect only on the death of the testator and the writer sees therefore a second application of the death of Christ within the covenant. It not only dealt with transgressions, but it also established the positive spiritual benefits of the covenant. There is a necessity for *the death* to be *established* (*pheresthai*), which could mean 'presented' or 'pleaded'. The will still stands whether the death has occurred or not, but it becomes active only when the testator dies. The thought of Christ as a testator is a continuation of the inheritance idea in the previous verse. This was the main legacy. The most essential feature is to be sure that the will (or covenant) is properly ratified, and this the writer proceeds to demonstrate.

**17.** This verse gives the same idea as the last verse, but in different words, and with an added explanation. It has been suggested by Westcott[2] that the imagery behind it is the ancient practice of ratifying covenants by a sacrificial victim, but this is in order to maintain that it is still a covenant and not a will which is in mind. If, however, the idea of *will* is uppermost here, the statement supposes that it becomes established in the sense of being unalterable after the testator has died. Until that time it is possible to add a codicil which might effectively change the character of the will. Nevertheless in the next passage the thought shifts again from will to covenant as the Mosaic order reappears in view.

**18.** The thought goes back to Exodus 24, which gives an account of the ratifying of the old covenant by the sprinkling of the blood of a sacrificial offering which has already been echoed in verse 13. The word translated *ratified* (*enkekainistai*) literally

---

[1] Westcott, *Comm.*, pp. 300ff., and Nairne, *Comm.*, p. 92, both maintain that *diathēkē* must mean covenant. But Bruce, *Comm.*, p. 211, strongly criticizes this.
[2] Westcott, *Comm.*, p. 258.

means renewed. It occurs again in 10:20 of the new and living way. In the present context it seems to mean to enter afresh into the conditions and provisions of the covenant. The sign and seal of this in the Mosaic covenant was the victim's blood. As he proceeds to enlarge on this theme, the writer leaves for the moment the better sacrifice of Christ which he returns to in verses 23ff.

**19.** The clause, *when every commandment of the law had been declared by Moses*, is a direct allusion to Exodus 24:3f. Moses is said not only to have told the people 'all the words of the LORD and all the ordinances', but also to have written them down. There was no question of the people entering into a covenant without knowing its terms. True, the people had no choice over the terms. These were essentially commandments which came with God's authority. The Exodus account does not mention that *goats* were slain; it refers only to oxen, and the sacrifices are described as burnt offerings and peace offerings. Moreover nowhere in the law were goats prescribed for either of these offerings, although they were for sin offerings (*cf.* Lv. 1:10). There may be an analogy here to the heifer and she-goat offered by Abraham as a ratification of God's covenant with him (Gn. 15:9).

Again the mention of *water and scarlet wool and hyssop* is not drawn from Exodus, but seems to be a combination of two allusions in the Mosaic law (*cf.* Lv. 14:4–5; Nu. 19:18). These additional items are incidental to the main point that is being made, *i.e.* that the old covenant was ratified with blood. The fact that both *the book itself and all the people* were sprinkled shows that the covenant involved the co-operation of the human partners, who needed a special cleansing to be made worthy to participate. In Exodus 24 there is no mention of the book being sprinkled, but the reading of it was central to the occasion. Perhaps some echo of this event is found also in 1 Peter 1:2, where Christians are spoken of as destined 'for sprinkling with his (*i.e.* Christ's) blood'.

**20.** Another difference from the Exodus account is in the report of the words spoken by Moses. Instead of *'This is the blood of the covenant which God commanded you'*, Exodus 24:8 has ' "Behold the blood of the covenant which the LORD has made with you in accordance with all these words." ' The different opening word (*touto*) is significant for in all probability it has been influenced by the words of institution of the last supper. The form of words must have been widely used in early Christianity. The change from LORD to God and the shortening of the rest are of less significance. There seems little doubt that the linking of the two events was intentional. As Hughes points out,[1] the shadow of Moses' blood-shedding gives way to the eternal reality.

**21.** More details are added here which are not only not in the Exodus account but do not appear at all in the Pentateuch, *i.e.* the sprinkling of *the tent and all the vessels*. The tabernacle had not been erected at the time of the ratification of the old covenant, but in any case was not said to have been sprinkled with blood, only anointed with oil (Lv. 8:10). The writer may be drawing on current belief, since Josephus says that the tabernacle was sprinkled with both blood and oil (*Antiquities* 3.8.6). In the present context the aim is clearly to focus attention on the importance of blood in the old order.[2]

**22.** The general conclusion on this theme is that, according to the law, *almost everything is purified with blood*. The word *almost* (*schedon*) qualifies the whole statement and has the meaning 'one might almost say', as if it was a general statement which applied in most cases. Some Jewish purificatory rites were through water or through fire, but the most significant were through sacrifices which involved the shedding of a victim's blood. It is worth noting that the words *with blood* (*en haimati*) could be rendered 'in blood', as the sphere in which the purification is made. *Everything* (*panta*), although neuter, is intended to include people as well as things, priests and congregation alike.

The concluding statement here – *without the shedding of blood there is no forgiveness of sins* – is based on the statement of Leviticus 17:11. It sums up the purpose of the blood sacrifices under law. The *shedding of blood* points to the death of the animal

[1] Hughes, *Comm.*, p. 376.
[2] J. H. Davies, *Comm.*, p. 90, refers to the writer's mistakes, but admits that these do not seriously violate the meaning.

and to the ceremonial outpouring of its blood.[1] It implies more than the giving of life. Its effectiveness rests in the application of the blood. In this way the writer is building up an explanation of the necessity of the death of Christ. It should be noted that Leviticus 5:11ff. makes an exception in the case of extreme poverty, in which case a tenth of an ephah of fine flour is accepted as a sin offering. But this is a concession and does not annul the principle which is still there in intention.[2]

Although the RSV reads *forgiveness of sins*, the Greek has only the unqualified word *forgiveness* (*aphesis*), which is remarkable since it is the only case of its kind in the New Testament (except in the quotation from the LXX in Lk. 4:18). The absolute use of the word makes its application more general. It becomes a reference to deliverance as well as forgiveness from specific sins. It was the aim of the sacrifices to bring some kind of remission of sin, but the word *aphesis* never fully came into its own until the New Testament age, where it at once became a feature of early Christian proclamation (*cf.* Acts 2:38). Compare also Matthew's account of the words of institution of the Lord's supper (Mt. 26:28).

*(ii) His entrance into a heavenly sanctuary (9:23–28)*

**23.** The last section (verses 15–22) was in the nature of a parenthesis and here the sequence of thought resumes the previous theme, although there are echoes of the purification theme as well in this verse. The writer is impressed with the fact that purification *was necessary* in the old order. He then proceeds to deduce from this that what is true for *the copies* (*hypodeigmata*) must be equally required for the realities, for otherwise it would make no sense to talk of the necessity of Christ's sacrificial works.[3] The readers have already been introduced to the idea of earthly realities being copies of heavenly realities in 8:5; this clearly plays an important part in the writer's

---

[1] T. C. G. Thornton, 'The Meaning of *haimatekchusia* in Heb. IX. 22', *JTS* 15 (1964), pp. 63–65, maintains that this word should be rendered 'pouring out of blood' rather than shedding of blood.

[2] *Cf.* Hughes, *Comm.*, p. 378.

[3] *Cf.* W. Manson, *The Epistle to the Hebrews* (London, 1951), pp. 140f., for an exposition of the purification of the copies in this passage. The new covenant and the new Israel have been consecrated by the blood of Christ.

whole argument and explains his constant emphasis on 'better' things. That the 'copies' had to be *purified with these rites* (Greek has only 'these', *toutois*) is because external things needed cleansing by external means (*i.e.* the shedding of blood).

The *heavenly things* of which the writer speaks are presumably the heavenly counterparts of the earthly sanctuary and its furniture. He is loath to lose sight of the glories of the Jewish heritage and imagines more glorious fulfilments of them in a spiritual sense. But it is clear from the fact that he equates the antitype of the sanctuary with heaven itself (verse 24) that he is not thinking in literal terms. All that the copies were intended to teach are to be seen in pristine clarity in the presence of God. When *better sacrifices* (plural) are mentioned, it is not to be supposed that more than one is in mind, for the single supreme sacrifice of Christ is seen in this letter to be entirely adequate. The plural is used in the sense that the one sacrifice stands as the complete fulfilment of all the different sacrifices in the old order. It may be said that the sacrifice of Christ is so many-sided that it required a whole range of sacrifices to serve as adequate copies.

**24.** The fact that Christ *entered* into the holy place has already been stated earlier in this chapter (*cf.* verse 12). The verb in the aorist tense (*eisēlthen*) points to a decisive act. A completed historic event is in mind and the sequence shows that the ascension, when Christ was received up into heaven, must be in view. Nevertheless the focus falls on the *sanctuary* which he entered. This is described both negatively and positively. It is not like the earthly tabernacle *made with hands*. This marks it out at once as a spiritual concept in contrast to a material creation. The statement is reminiscent of the climax of Stephen's speech in Acts 7:48, 'Yet the Most High does not dwell in houses made with hands', in which Stephen is defending the charge against him concerning the Temple (Acts 6:14). It was only by recognizing that a spiritual reality existed which transcended the glory of the earthly sanctuary that Jews who had become Christians would understand the absence from Christianity of any central place of worship. The Temple where our high priest officiates is in fact *heaven itself*, by which is meant, as this verse shows, the presence of God rather than a locality. The word *copy* (*antitypa*) which is used here differs from, but is closely linked with, that used in the previous verse. The antitype in this case is not the true thing, but a copy which foreshadows the true (*cf.* Acts 7:44). Sometimes the word is used in the opposite sense, in which case the antitype is the more perfect fulfilment of the type (*cf.* Acts 7:43, in a quotation from Amos 5:25–27).

The present mission of Christ which has been mentioned before is repeated again: *now to appear in the presence of God on our behalf*. This is Christ's intercessory work expressed in different terms. The main features which are worthy of note are: (i) The activity of Christ relates specifically to the present *now* (*nyn*). This compares with the finality of his high-priestly work at the time of the passion. However, the use here of the aorist infinitive (*emphanisthēnai*, to appear) states the appearance as an established fact. (ii) The activity of Christ is *in the presence of God*. There are no other intermediaries between Christ and God, contrary to what the later Gnostics maintained. Our high priest has direct access. This is much superior to the Aaronic high priests who were allowed only once into the holy of holies (see next verse). The word used here for *presence* (*prosōpon*, literally 'face') is highly suggestive, for the idea of 'the face' to express God's presence is paralleled only in Matthew 18:10 and Revelation 22:4; but *cf.* also Acts 2:28 (from Ps. 16:11) and 1 Peter 3:12 (from Ps. 34:15–16). 'Face' is more personal than 'presence' and contains the suggestion of communication. The high priest's office is representative – *on our behalf* (*hyper hēmōn*). As a perfect representative of man he gathers up in himself all humanity. But the word 'our' restricts his activity to those who commit themselves to him. He does for us what we could not do for ourselves.

**25.** In some senses the writer has combined our high priest's present mission with the grounds of his entry. If we recognize this, his statement in this verse becomes clearer. The Aaronic high priest in his annual entries into the holy place needed to repeat the sacrificial basis for his entry. Each time the blood had to accompany him. There was therefore no continuity. Fresh animals had to be sacrificed. But Christ's entry was different. He had no need to offer *repeatedly* and when he offered it was not *with blood not his own*. These ideas have already been hinted at, but it seems that the writer cannot say them too often. It is the finality of the voluntary self-offering of Jesus which he wants particularly to impress on his readers. The next few verses, 26–28, are a further explanation of this cardinal Christian position.

**26.** There was no difficulty for Jewish minds in a constant repetition of sacrifices since a constant supply of sacrificial animals was available. But the problem arose over the death of Christ, for in the nature of the case this could not be repeated. What the readers needed to know was that one sacrifice was adequate for continual access. The writer implies that if the offering had been *repeatedly* made it would have involved Christ in repeated suffering. He does not refer to repeated deaths, for this would be unintelligible, but he clearly implies it. By this means he shows that Christ is continually before the face of God, which shows the sacrifice to be sufficient. The effectiveness of that offering is always before the Father's eyes. But why does the writer suggest that suffering would be implied *since the foundation of the world*? It is implied, rather than explicitly stated, that the sacrifice of Christ, if repeatable, would have needed to begin from the dawn of human history and to continue throughout the ages. Since, however, the self-offering of Christ could happen only once in history, the timing of the event was attributable only to the perfect wisdom of God. The writer does not discuss why the event did not happen as soon as sin was committed. He is more concerned about the nature of the offering.

The words *But as it is* call the readers away from speculation to historical event. However intriguing it might be to consider why God chose one particular time in history rather than another, it is an established fact that he did. The writer dates the event *at the end of the age*, which is reminiscent of his opening phrase 'in these last days' in 1:2, although rather different from it. He evidently regards the atonement as the climax of the age just ended, since a new era has now begun on the strength of Christ's sacrifice. Several features about the atonement are here summarily presented. The first concerns the manifestation of Christ (*he has appeared, pephanerōtai*). This connecting of the sacrificial offering with the incarnation at once places the event in history, among men. The second facet is the finality of the offering – *once for all*, an echo of 7:27. This is the exact opposite of the 'repeatedly' of verse 25, which related to the offerings of the Aaronic high priests. The phrase stresses the complete adequacy of the sacrifice of Christ.

The third point is the effect of the sacrifice – *to put away sin*. There is a close connection between this statement and the idea of redemption from transgressions mentioned in verse 15. Here, however, the effect is even more comprehensive since the putting away (*athetēsis*) involves the annulment of sin, *i.e.* treating it as if it no longer existed. This cannot mean that sin is so treated for all men, for the epistle does not support the view that unrepented sin will now go unpunished. As in the Levitical system the effectiveness of the sacrifices for each worshipper depended on the attitude of the worshipper, so in the application of Christ's offering an attitude of repentance and faith is assumed. The fourth statement is a repetition of the fact that the offering that Christ made was *himself*. Again the writer is determined that his readers should not forget this. It is central to his whole argument.

**27–28.** It is somewhat unexpected for the writer to introduce at this stage the idea of judgment. But he has been dwelling on the necessity for Christ's death and this leads him to make a general statement about man's destiny. Death in itself is unavoidable: *it is appointed for men to die once*. No-one is exempt from this experience. The difference between Christ's death and all others is that his was voluntary whereas for all others it is appointed (*apokeitai*), *i.e.* stored up for them. The expectation that some will escape death (*cf.* 1 Thes. 4:15ff.) is an exception to the general rule stated, occasioned by the special event of the coming of Christ.[1] It is not therefore in conflict with this statement in Hebrews.

The words *and after that comes judgment* are not intended to imply that judgment follows immediately after death, but rather that judgment is to be expected subsequent to death. Furthermore this does not mean that no act of judgment ever happens

---

[1] Hughes, *Comm.*, p. 387.

before death. The *judgment* (*krisis*) alluded to is the final assessment.

In making the comparison between everyman and Christ, the writer begins with a common factor: he died *once*, a point repeated yet again. What is most significant about this statement is that the death is now stated in the passive, *having been offered*, instead of the active as in verse 14. No hint is here given about who made the offering. Taken in conjunction with verse 14, it may be said that both active and passive aspects are necessary for a complete understanding of the offering. While it was voluntary, it was also imposed by external circumstances: historically by the malice of the Jewish murderers and theologically by the definite plan of God (*cf.* Acts 2:23).

The purpose of the offering is again stated in similar though slightly different terms from verse 26. Here the phrase *to bear the sins of many* (*pollōn anenenkein hamartias*) is precisely paralleled in the Septuagint of Isaiah 53:12. The same idea occurs in 1 Peter 2:24 where the bearing of sins is said to have been 'in his body on the tree'. Similarly John the Baptist's announcement that the Lamb of God would bear away the sin of the world echoes the same thought. The 'many' contrasts with the one offering.

The Christ who has dealt with sin at his first coming *will appear a second time* for a different purpose. Had the parallel with judgment been pressed, some aspect of Christ's coming to judge might have been introduced. But the second coming is said to be for salvation. The second coming is in fact the divine seal on the complete acceptance of the sacrifice offered previously. The emphasis falls on the effect that the second coming of Christ will have on *those who are eagerly waiting for him* (*i.e.* Christians). Nothing is said about unbelievers as would have been natural after the mention of judgment. But it is Christ's work of salvation which engages the writer's attention. There might here be some analogy to the expectations of the worshippers as they wait to greet the high priest on his return from the holy of holies on the Day of Atonement. But the words *not to deal with sin* (*chōris hamartias*) quickly put a different complexion on the analogy. Sin needs no further atonement. All that is necessary is the appropriation of the salvation which Christ's self-offering has secured. The verb translated *eagerly waiting* (*apekdechomenois*) occurs in 1 Corinthians 1:7, Philippians 3:20 and Romans 8:19, 23, 25, in each case of the great expectancy of believers waiting for the glories to come.

*(iii) His offering of himself for others (10:1–18)*

**1.** It might be thought that the writer has sufficiently proved his point to dispense with any further comment on Christ's unique sacrifice, but he wants to press home the general ineffectiveness of the whole Levitical cultus. Inevitably in this section there is some overlap with the preceding sections, but there are nevertheless some fresh insights to engage our attention. First there is a succinct statement of the inadequacies of the old order (verses 1–4).

The contrast between *shadow* (*skian*) and *true form* (*eikona*) corresponds to the contrast between the old and new covenants, the old and the new approach to God. Yet there is a similar basic connection between them as an object bears resemblance to its shadow. A shadow can never claim to be a complete revelation of its object. At best it can give only the barest outline of the reality. Moreover, once the true form has been seen, the shadow becomes irrelevant. This observation is used by the writer to stress once again the inadequacies of the old shadowy procedures. *The good things to come* are clearly the gospel with its spiritual high-priesthood. Some patristic writers identified them as the Christian sacraments.[1] But the interpretation here seems to be more general in the sense of all good things of which the law provided only the adumbration. This throws us back on the list of 'better' things already mentioned in the epistle. It is worth noting that the law is said to 'have' the shadow rather than to 'be', which suggests that the law is not itself the shadow, but only that it possesses the shadow, *i.e.* the ceremonial cultus. There is also enshrined in the law what is more permanent, *i.e.* the moral demands.

In spite of the impressiveness of a ceremonial which must be repeated *year after year*, it could not achieve what was necessary. The repetition of the offering on each succeeding Day of Atone-

---

[1] For details, *cf.* Westcott, *Comm.*, p. 304.

ment and the continual daily offerings were testimony to a temporary character. We have previously seen that the author is much concerned with the pursuit of perfection (the verb *teleioō, make perfect,* occurring 9 times and the noun *teleiōsis* once), and recognizes that the Levitical system could not provide it. The impossibility is emphatically stated (*never, oudepote*). It had had a long period in which to demonstrate this. The description of those who hoped to benefit as *those who draw near* is paralleled to the description of those who come through Christ (*cf.* 7:25; 10:22). To draw near to God is man's highest exercise.

**2.** The deduction made from the repetition of the offerings is their inadequacy. If perfection had been achieved the offerings would have stopped, which they did not under the old system. What the offerings did was to offer cleansing for sins committed since the last offering, but they could do nothing about sin, the root cause. All *worshippers* under the old system knew they had not been finally cleansed (*kekatharismenous*). Again the emphasis here falls on *once* in contrast to *continually* in verse 1. It is the finality of Christ's atoning work for the perfection of his people which is in mind by way of contrast. *Consciousness* (*syneidēsin*) of sin is brought about by the constant reminder of man's need in the repeated sacrifices, the exact opposite of the effect of Christ's offering, which leads to the blotting out of sin (*cf.* 9:26).

**3.** This function of the Levitical offerings as *a reminder of sin year after year* vividly demonstrated their inadequacy to effect a permanent removal of sin and its consequences. Every offering that was made testified to the inadequacy of the previous offering and reminded the worshipper that another similar offering must follow. The sense of responsibility for sin was thus kept alive. The same word is found in the institution of the last supper in describing it as a memorial to the death of Christ, a reminder of the complete release from sin through that death. The superiority of this Christian reminder over the Levitical sacrifices is vivid. The latter sacrifices, which were ordained by God, were thus intended to prepare the way for that perfect offering which could effectively deal with the consequences of sin on a permanent basis.

**4.** The impossibility referred to in this verse is a moral one.

Animal sacrifices, because irrational, could have no permanent effects in achieving the removal of sin. Although they formed a part of the divine ordinance under the law, their intention was temporary, foreshadowing the perfect self-offering of a moral being. The long sequence of shedding *the blood of bulls and goats* was aimed at an impossible goal, if that goal was perfection. Those Jewish Christians who had come from a background of Temple worship would need to learn on reflection the ultimate futility of the system from which they had turned. The author's aim was to set out the immeasurable superiority of Christ, and to show that the Old Testament sacrificial system had validity only because it foreshadowed the supreme and final sacrifice of Christ. Worshippers in the Old Testament age were provided with a means of grace, but that means was never able to achieve a complete removal of sins, which could be voluntarily accomplished only by a perfect human, in contrast to an animal, sacrifice.

**5–6.** In view of the inadequacy of animal sacrifice, the need for a more effective approach is demonstrated and the writer proceeds to give the answer. He sees a foreshadowing of it in Psalm 40:6–8 which he first quotes and then expounds. He has no difficulty in ascribing the words of the psalmist to Christ himself as if Christ were speaking through the psalmist. Certainly the words did not find their perfect fulfilment until they applied to Christ.

The word *consequently* (*dio*) links immediately with the inadequacy of the Levitical offerings mentioned in verse 4. The qualifying clause, *when Christ came into the world*, shows that the setting of the psalm is transferred to the time of Christ and is seen to be most applicable then. It is as if the writer conceives of Christ, following his incarnation, taking the words of this psalm upon his lips as the expression of his mission. The reference is not exclusively, therefore, to the event of the incarnation, but to the continuous awareness of Jesus that he was doing his Father's will. It should be noted that the Greek text does not mention the name of Christ in this verse, but merely uses the third person. The writer assumes that everyone will at once identify him who *came into the world*. The title *Christ* is carried over from 9:28. There is no question that the author is convinced about the reality of the pre-existence of Christ.

In the Old Testament quotation four words are used for the Levitical offerings: *sacrifices* (*thysia*), *offerings* (*prosphora*), *burnt offerings* (*holokautōmata*) and *sin offerings* (*peri hamartias*). The first pair are general, the second representative. Together they fairly sum up the whole Levitical system. In the first statement the contrast is made between God's supposed desire for sacrifice and his actual provision of a *body* for the sacrificial work of his son. The words *a body hast thou prepared for me* follow the Septuagint text which differs from the Hebrew; the latter has 'ears hast thou opened for me'. The change is striking and the Septuagint must be regarded as an interpretation and extension of the Hebrew. The provision of ears shows the demand for hearing and implicitly the expectation of obedience. The *body* would, of course, include the facility of hearing, but goes beyond it. The statement refers to the perfect functioning of the human body, which was fulfilled only in Christ. As applied here the citation suggests that what Christ did had to be done in the 'body', *i.e.* as a human being. It was as man that he was to demonstrate his perfect fulfilment of God's will. Although the tense of the verb in the quotation is past, it cannot in this case refer to a completed act as the fulfilment is still future. It expresses rather what is timeless in the mind of God. It may be wondered in what sense a body could be *prepared* (*kataritizō*) as if its separate parts had to be brought together to form a completed whole? But the verb is probably chosen only to suggest the perfect character of the provision.

The parallel statement in verse 6, which shows that God has no more pleasure in the specific sacrifices than in the general, serves to add emphasis to what has already been said, according to the style of Hebrew poetry. Although the sacrifices were commanded by God, it was the attitude of the worshippers which was his concern. The history of Israel had shown the tendency for the sacrificial system to be regarded as an end in itself, becoming a mere formality. The need for fulfilling of the will of God had been neglected, hence the pointedness of the psalmist's words.

**7.** As the quotation is continued the obedience required to the will of God becomes more explicit. *Then I said* seems to refer to the time when the body was fully prepared, in which case the words were fulfilled at the incarnation and relate to Christ's approach to his whole ministry.

The words *I have come* express an accomplished fact, not a prediction, translating the psalmist's words into the very life and ministry of Jesus. His consciousness of his mission is clearly brought out in the Gospels, especially in John's Gospel. He was sent from God and had come to fulfil a divine mission. *To do thy will, O God* is the aim of the perfect man. It has only partially been fulfilled by even the most pious of men, except by Jesus. What was seen as the most desirable aim by the psalmist, becomes an expression of fact on the lips of Jesus. He actually did the will of God, even to the extent of becoming obedient to the point of death.

Some dispute exists over the word translated *roll* (*kephalis*), because of obscurity of its derivation with this meaning. Nevertheless it is found elsewhere in the Septuagint (*cf.* Ezk. 2:9). The phrase *roll of the book* apparently refers to some authoritative instructions which governed the behaviour and activities of the psalmist-king. It seems clear that for Jesus the book embraces all the written revelations of God's purposes and therefore provides the perfect pattern for the divine will. When applied to Jesus Christ therefore there is the obvious allusion to all that God has made known in prediction about the coming Messiah. In the New Testament there are many quotations from the Old Testament introduced with the formula *it is written* (*gegraptai*), which therefore take on an authoritative character. This is well brought out in Luther's understanding of the word as 'it stands written'. What stands written possesses an inviolable character.

**8–9.** The repetition here of the main ideas already found in verses 5–7 again emphasizes the contrast between the old and the new means of coming to God. Of special note is the recurrence of the words *Lo, I have come to do thy will* as an expression of the perfect obedience of Christ. The general comment on the whole quotation is *He abolishes the first in order to establish the second.* An unusual word is employed for the abolition of the first, for the verb which is translated 'abolishes' (*anairei*) generally has the sense of kill. There is a finality about the passing of the old. If there had not been, the second could never have been established. It is the difference between the total failure of irrational offerings to effect a final solution and the total adequacy of a rational obedience to establish a new way once for all.

10. *By that will* refers to the will of God which has just been mentioned in the quotation. Its only complete fulfilment is seen in the perfect obedience of Christ. The immediate effect is that *we have been sanctified*. The idea seems to be that those in Christ have been so identified with him that in him they too have fulfilled the will of God. This sense of solidarity with Christ is not as frequent in this epistle as in the epistles of Paul, but it is all the more striking in this context. The sanctification process is one which has never been completed except in Christ. Were it not for that the verb could not have been expressed as it is in the perfect tense. Since Christ is perfectly sanctified through his perfect obedience to the will of God, it may be said that his sanctification is shared by all who believe. It is noticeable, however, that the writer does not define the beneficiaries any further – the *we* must be interpreted in the light of the previous chapter (*cf.* 9:28).

The addition of the words *through the offering of the body of Jesus Christ* clarifies the means by which Christ's obedience can be effective for us. It is important to notice that it was the body of Christ which was offered, for this draws attention to the centrality of the cross. What he did, he did in the body, in the sphere of human life, the same kind of human life which we possess. In his self-offering he gathered up mankind. Of course, what the writer is saying is not that believers have no further need of obedience because Christ has accomplished it, but that God received us on the basis of Christ's perfect fulfilment of his will. The finality of it (*once for all*, *ephapax*) has already been mentioned in 7:27 and 9:12.

11. The next section (verses 11–14) concentrates on the present glory of Christ in order to complement the statement in verse 10 about the offering of the body. Although its finality is emphasized, it was not the end. In this epistle as in other parts of the New Testament the death is linked with the exaltation.

The endless continuity of inadequate sacrifices under the old order is in marked contrast to the new. The main points of interest in the present verse are (i) the position of the priests (*every priest stands*), (ii) the continuity of the sacrifices (*offering repeatedly*) and (iii) their ineffectiveness to achieve their purpose (*i.e.* to *take away sins*). The first is strikingly contrasted in the next verse with the sitting position of Christ. These priests could never sit because their work was never done. In the second place, the *repeatedly* (*pollakis*) is in direct contrast to *once for all* (*ephapax*). And in the third place, the inability of the old offerings to remove sins is contrasted in verse 12 with Christ's single offering for sins. Once again the weakness of the old order becomes the background for demonstrating the greater glory of the new.

The last clause draws attention to the quality of the sacrifices, as the relative *which* (*haitines*, 'which are of such a kind as') shows. It was inherent in their very nature that they lacked the power to *take away* (*perielein*) *sins*. The word literally means 'to take away what surrounds', like peeling off an unwanted cloak. It is more suggestive than the parallel word used in verse 4 (*aphairein*). The word found here is used in 2 Corinthians 3:16 of the removal of the veil from a man's mind when he turns to the Lord. It is further worth noting that, whereas in 10:4 the tense is present, here it is past (aorist), to correspond with the completed action of Christ's offering in verse 12.

**12.** There is a contrast here between every priest and 'this one' (which RSV identifies as *Christ*). He stands out against them as a priest of an entirely different kind. The construction in the Greek could permit the words translated *for all time* (*eis to diēnekes*) to be attached to the concluding part of the sentence, *i.e.* to show the finality of Christ's enthronement. But the RSV rendering brings out the idea which is basic to this epistle, *i.e.* the uniqueness and completeness of Christ's sacrifice, and this seems preferable.[1] The constant re-iteration of this central Christian idea may suggest that the writer knew that some of his readers were shaky about it and were perhaps wondering whether there was still the same inadequacy as with the old sacrifices. The conclusive character of Christ's sacrifice is seen not only in his single sacrifice but also in his enthronement: *he*

---

[1] *Cf.* Bruce, *Comm.*, p. 237, n. 57.

*sat down at the right hand of God*. This has been mentioned twice before (1:3; 8:1) and recurs again at 12:2, showing it to be one of the dominant characteristics of the letter, a good general title for which might well be 'Christ enthroned'.

**13.** The waiting period between the enthronement of Christ and his final triumph over his enemies is identical with the present era. There is no doubt about the ultimate outcome. In discussing the reason for the delay in subjugating the enemies if the victory has already been won, Hughes comments, 'The delay should be seen rather, as the prolongation of the day of grace, and therefore as a token of the mercy and longsuffering of God'.[1] The subduing of the *enemies* is another echo from Psalm 110 (verse 1), already much quoted in this epistle. Indeed it was in the writer's mind when he began to write (*cf.* 1:13). This idea is drawn rather from the enthronement imagery, than from the high-priestly office. It is at this point that the order of Melchizedek is clearly applicable, since our high priest has also taken on the office of king. It is as king that he will not permit his enemies to triumph. The same idea is expounded at some length by Paul in 1 Corinthians 15:23ff., where it is not, however, linked at all to the high-priestly theme.

**14.** The thought returns to the high priest and his *single offering* in order to draw attention to the result achieved by it, that is the attainment of perfection for believers. The linking of the offering with the act of purification has already been made in verse 10 and so the emphasis here must fall on the verb, *he has perfected* (*teteleiōken*). This regards the action as already completed, although presumably only in an anticipatory sense, as the words *for all time* imply. In himself Christ gathered up all those whom he represents to share with them his perfection. The phrase *those who are sanctified* (*tous hagiazomenous*) is in the present continuous tense and might be rendered 'those who are constantly being sanctified', *i.e.* the continual succession of people who come under the effective application of the single offering.

**15.** At this point the discussion turns again to the new covenant as the concluding section of the main doctrinal part of the

---

[1] Hughes, *Comm.*, p. 402.

epistle (verses 15–18). Again, as in 8:8ff. a passage from Jeremiah 31 is cited, although this time the extract is considerably shorter. There are indeed some significant differences, the first of which is the introductory formula. In 8:8ff. no formula is used, but here the definite witness of the Holy Spirit is seen in the passage (as in 3:7 in introducing Ps. 95). In this case it seems that the special function of the Holy Spirit is to draw attention to the combining of the idea of an inner law and the complete putting away of sin. Importance is clearly attached to the connection of the two ideas in the original passage (*for after saying . . . then he adds*), which shows the writer's view of inspiration which extended to the sequence of ideas. The expression *the Holy Spirit also bears witness to us* could be understood alternatively to mean witness in relation to us, rather than directed to us. But the main point is clear. What Jeremiah wrote has a direct relevance to both the writer and his readers.

**16.** In the first part of the quotation there is a change of wording in that *hearts* and *minds* have been interchanged compared with 8:10. It makes no difference to the sense.

**17.** In the second part there is an addition of the words *and their misdeeds*, which merely defines more specifically the nature of their sins, *i.e.* those acts which are contrary to God's law.

**18.** As a sort of parting shot, the writer again draws the conclusion that *there is no longer any offering for sin*. Since *forgiveness* is promised under the new covenant, the need for such an offering has ceased to exist. It cannot be doubted that since this main section of the epistle ends in this way, the perfection of the offering which Christ has made is intended finally to dispose of the continuous performance of the old cultus. A new era has dawned. A new covenant is in force which makes the Leviticus sacrifices obsolete. Whatever message they were intended to convey is more perfectly fulfilled in Christ.

## II. EXHORTATIONS (10:19 – 13:25)

Although various appeals to the readers have been made during the main doctrinal section, the concluding chapters contain Christian advice about various issues of practical life. There are extended passages on faith and discipline.

### A. THE BELIEVER'S PRESENT POSITION (10:19–39)

The writer sets out the privileges and responsibilities of the Christian life. This leads into another solemn warning passage and a reminder of the value of past Christian experience.

*(i) The new and living way (10:19–25)*

**19.** That the application of the preceding doctrinal discussion begins here is clear from the opening *Therefore*, which is best taken as referring to the whole preceding demonstration. It is on the strength of all that has been said about the high priest and his effective offering that the statement in the present verse can be made. *Since we have confidence* is stated as a fact. In view of what Christ has done and now is, there is no reason why all believers should not approach with confidence. During the course of his high-priestly exposition the writer has previously reminded the readers of their confidence in Christ (3:6; 4:16). The word here translated *confidence* (*parrēsia*) is the word for 'boldness' which in the New Testament generally relates to man's freedom because of his new relationship to God.[1] This

[1] *Cf.* W. C. van Unnik, 'The Christian's freedom of speech in the New Testament', *BJRL* 44 (1961–2), pp. 466f.

confidence is here specifically related to approach to God, to the entry into *the sanctuary* or holy place, understood symbolically of the presence of God. The picture is of all believers now having an open invitation to come into the holy place, which is no longer reserved for the priesthood.

The means of approach is said to be by *the blood of Jesus*, which here sums up all that Jesus did for us in the offering up of himself. The holy place is no longer sealed off for the continual performance of sacrifices. It is wide open on the strength of the perfect offering already made. However it should be noted that access is available only to those who are classified as *brethren*, those who, according to 3:1, 'share in a heavenly call'. It is important to note that those who discover a new approach to God through Jesus Christ also discover a new relationship to each other.

**20.** In describing the access as a *new (prosphaton) and living way*, the writer uses a word which occurs only here in the New Testament. It originally meant 'freshly slain', but its derived meaning is 'fresh' or 'recent'. It is meant to contrast with the old order and so calls attention to its recentness, which at once links it with the work of Christ. The idea of the *way* is also suggestive not only because this was the title by which the early Christians were known, but also because of a word play in the Greek between this word and the word used in verse 19 for entrance (*hodos* and *eisodos*). Indeed the whole phrase used here would be an apt description of this writer's view of Christianity. The idea of the *way* has already been introduced in 9:8 and seems to have been a kind of technical term for access to God. There is no word corresponding to *by* in the Greek, which makes the *way* the object of the verb *opened* and links it with the idea of entrance in verse 19. The construction is difficult in the Greek, but it seems clear that the words do not identify Jesus as the way. The way of access is, in fact, the result of his atoning work.

The following words, *through the curtain, that is, through his flesh*, have occasioned a great deal of debate. The first problem relates to the *curtain*. Since this is an allusion to the veil which sealed off the holy of holies, it seems most natural to regard the curtain as an obstacle which has to be overcome before

211

access can be gained. But it is difficult to tie this up with 'his flesh', for in this case it implies that the human life of Jesus was that which cut him off from God and which had to be penetrated before fellowship could be restored. Admittedly the human life of Jesus placed restrictions upon him and in that strictly limited sense could be said to be a 'curtain' through which he had to pass. But again it must not be supposed that in doing so he discarded his true humanity when he entered.

These difficulties would disappear if the words *through (dia) his flesh* are an explanation of the *way*, in which case the meaning is 'by a new and living way, *i.e.* his flesh'. This would amount to saying that the new way to God had been opened up by Jesus as a human being, and this would agree with the discussion in chapter 2 about the necessity for the incarnation. It is possible on the other hand to regard the curtain as symbolic of the means of approach rather than as a hindrance to such an approach, in which case there would be less difficulty in connecting the 'flesh' with the 'curtain'. As far as the high priest on the Day of Atonement was concerned, the curtain ceased momentarily to be an obstacle and became instead the way in. Since the great priest is mentioned in the next verse, it is highly probable that this idea was uppermost in the writer's train of thought.

There is some debate whether the writer is here alluding in any sense to the rending of the veil of the Temple at the time of the death of Jesus. Whatever view is adopted about this, it is clear that he regards the holy of holies as wide open through Jesus Christ.[1]

**21.** Already in 4:14 Jesus is described as 'a great high priest', and the present statement is an echo of that. The greatness consisted in the unique effectiveness of Christ's work in opening up a new and living way. The expression *over the house of God* is a recollection of the statements in 3:1–6, where the superiority of Jesus over Moses is seen in relation to God's house.

---

[1] *Cf.* Bruce, *Comm.*, p. 246, who cites C. H. Dodd, *The Apostolic Preaching and its Developments* (London, 1944), p. 51, and C. Lindeskog, *Coniectanea Neotestamentica* 11 (1947), pp. 132ff., on the symbolic meaning of the veil. J. Moffatt (*ICC*), p. 143, regards the statement here as an allegorizing of the veil as the flesh of Christ, which had to be rent before the blood could be shed.

Here the words are comprehensive including both the church on earth and the church in heaven, but the main emphasis is on the earthly community as the sequel shows.

**22.** It is here that we come to the main exhortation in the epistle. It is expressed in three stages: *let us draw near* (verse 22), *let us hold fast* (verse 23) and *let us consider how to stir up one another to love and good works* (verse 24). The first refers to personal devotion, the second to consistency and the third to social obligations. This is not the first time that the readers have been exhorted to *draw near*, for a similar statement is made in 4:16 before the discussion on the high-priestly work of Jesus has got under way. The repetition here of the same idea is by way of emphasis. In view of all that has been said, in the intervening passage, there is all the more reason to exhort the worshippers to draw near. Four conditions of approach are laid down in this verse:

(i) *With a true heart*. If the adjective is understood in the same sense as in 8:2 it refers to what is real as opposed to what is only apparent. There can be no pretence of a devotion which is not true. The expression would seem to refer to the genuineness of the worshipper's approach to God.

(ii) *In (en) full assurance of faith*. Already some emphasis has been placed on faith in this epistle and more is to follow in chapter 11. This fullness of assurance is important, for there is no longer any reason to doubt that access will be gained. The writer is not only clear about the possibility of full assurance, but assumes it to be present in all worshippers who take advantage of the 'new way'. The use of the preposition (*en*) in fact suggests that this faith-assurance is the sphere or environment in which approach is to be made.

(iii) *With our hearts sprinkled clean from an evil conscience*. Undoubtedly the metaphor of sprinkling is derived from the Levitical cultus, where blood sprinkling of people is spoken of at the ratifying of the old covenant (Ex. 24:8) and at the consecration of Aaron and his sons (Ex. 29:21). There is no specific mention there as here of cleansing the conscience. But the altogether more effective means of cleansing, which Christian worshippers have, relates directly to the conscience. It is more than a ritual act; it is a moral condition.

(iv) *And our bodies washed with pure water.* This appears to be an allusion to Christian baptism, although this view is not without its difficulties. If correct, it would require some initiatory rite of a public nature before anyone could draw near. But since the other conditions are not external it seems strange that the fourth should be so. The cleansing of the body might find some explanation from Ephesians 5:26 where Christ is said to have cleansed the church 'by the washing of water with the word', which is most intelligibly interpreted in a spiritual sense.[1] The use of the adjective 'pure' would also seem to suggest a symbolic meaning. The difference between (iii) and (iv) would then be between purity of inner attitudes and overt acts.

**23.** The second exhortation – *let us hold fast* – uses a verb (*katechō*) which has already been used in 3:6, 14, of holding on to our confidence (*parrēsia*) or our first confidence (*tēn archēn tēs hypostaseōs*). Here however it is another word that is used, *i.e. the confession* (*homologian*). Yet there is not much distinction in the main idea of these different words, for they both refer to the basic truth of the Christian position. Clearly an exhortation 'to hold fast' is never inappropriate in a world where values are continually shifting, but where Christian standards are constant.

The full expression, *the confession of our hope,* is surprising for we should have expected 'faith' rather than 'hope'. But hope is more comprehensive since it includes specific promises regarding the future. There is a more definite connection between faith and hope in the next chapter (*cf.* 11:1). It is moreover worth noting that in 3:6 there is a link between confidence and hope as things worth holding on to. For other references to hope, *cf.* 6:11, 18, 19; 7:19. Certainly this epistle is forward-looking and offers glories to come which outshine the glories of the old order. Nevertheless the writer is aware that some of his readers might be in danger of relaxing their hold on this hope since he urges them to hold on *without wavering* (*aklinē*). The

---

[1] It has been suggested by Riggenbach that spiritual cleansing must include the whole physical life (*Comm., ad loc.*). But Spicq considers that the idea here is of the spiritual effect on the physical life (*Comm., ad loc.*). 1 Pet. 3:21 makes clear that baptism was not intended to deal with physical impurities. Montefiore, *Comm.,* p. 175, suggests that if Apollos was the author this statement might be a slipping back to the kind of baptism administered by John the Baptist, who according to Josephus regarded baptism as a cleansing of the body.

Greek word translated in this way is used only here in the New Testament and is based on the idea of an upright object not inclining at all from the true perpendicular. There is no place in Christian experience for a hope that is firm at one time and shaky at another.

The maintaining of this assurance is not unjustified, since it does not depend on oneself, but on the faithfulness of the one *who promised*. Some facets of the promises of God are to be illustrated in the next chapter, which is in fact a running commentary on the statement made here. It not only records the faith of men, but also the faithfulness of God. Other specific statements in the epistle which call attention to faithfulness are 2:17 and 3:2, referring to our faithful high priest, and 11:11 where Sarah is said to have acknowledged the faithfulness of God.

**24.** The third exhortation focuses on social responsibility. It is significant that the word *consider* (*katanoōmen*) is used here, for what the writer is urging evidently demands concentrated thought. The target set out is *to stir up one another to love and good works*. Some thought is clearly necessary to decide how this can best be done. Something more than individual effort is needed if love and good works are to be fostered. Christians must be alert to the needs of their fellows. Corporate action is indispensable. The word for *stirring up* (*eis paroxysmon*) is a striking term meaning 'incitement' and is either used, as here, in a good sense or, as in Acts 15:39, in a bad sense (*i.e.* contention). It seems to suggest that loving one another will not just happen. It needs to be worked at, even provoked, in the same way as good works. This combination of love and good works is remarkable in emphasizing that love must have a practical outcome. The adjective for *good* (*kalos*) used here marks out the works as good in appearance, as having an attractive quality about them. It suggests that the works must be so self-evidently good that no doubt can exist about their true value.

**25.** Another requirement of a social kind, which has a direct bearing on the last statement, is the need for corporate fellowship. It stands to reason that no provocation to love is possible unless suitable opportunities occur for the stirring process to take effect. The words, *not neglecting to meet together*, presumably refer to worship meetings, although this is not stated. It may purposely be left ambiguous so as to include other gatherings of a more informal kind, but the Greek word (*episynagōgē*) suggests some official assembly. Some had evidently been neglecting to meet with their Christian brethren and this is seen as a serious weakness. It may be that the readers had splintered off from the main group, which meant that their opportunities to provoke to love and good works were severely limited.

Christian assemblies are intended to have a positive and helpful outcome, *i.e. encouraging one another*. The word used here (*parakaleō*) could equally be rendered 'exhorting'. The basic idea is that Christians should strengthen and stimulate one another. There is no doubt that immeasurable influence for good can come from the powerful example of right-minded people in association with others. The New Testament lends no support to the idea of lone Christians. Close and regular fellowship with other believers is not just a nice idea, but an absolute necessity for the encouragement of Christian values.

It is at first surprising that the writer should add at this point the words, *and all the more as you see the Day drawing near*. Nothing has prepared the readers for the mention of the 'Day'. There are many references in other New Testament books to the day of the Lord (*e.g.* 1 Thes. 5:2; 2 Pet. 3:10) and it must be supposed that the readers of this epistle would have known at once to what it referred. In any case it is familiar from the Old Testament, but the writer is using it in a specifically Christian way implying a day of reckoning (*cf.* Lk. 17:26; Rom. 2:16; Rev. 6:17). It is certainly connected with the second coming of Christ, although this also is not mentioned here. All that is in view is the salutary effects of being reminded of the approach of the day. The expression 'drawing near' (*engizō*) is commonly used in the New Testament to describe the approach of the day (*cf.* Rom. 13:12; Phil. 4:5; Jas. 5:8; 1 Pet. 4:7). For a similar appeal to the approaching day as a basis for careful ethical behaviour, *cf.* 2 Peter 3:11. It is worth noting in the present context that the verb is indicative and records an accomplished reality – *you see* – and is not as the preceding verbs, in the form of an exhortation. The imminence of the day was considered to be plain. It is not to be regarded as secret. Christians were to live as if the dawning of the day was so near that its arrival was only just beyond the horizon. Even if centuries have since passed, the possible imminence of the day still supplies a powerful motivation towards high moral standards for many believers.

*(ii) Another warning (10:26–31)*

**26.** This verse introduces a new section (verses 26–31) which warns against the dangers of apostasy in much the same vein as the warnings in chapter 6. It is sparked off presumably by the mention of the day of reckoning in verse 25. The serious aspects of adverse judgment are vividly brought into focus. *If we sin deliberately* places the emphasis on responsible sin, the kind of sin into which people enter with their eyes open. The position of the word *deliberately* (*hekousiōs*) as the first word in the sentence adds weight to this. The Levitical cultus made provision for inadvertent sins, but not for wilful sins. At this point the writer's use of the first person plural (*we, hēmōn*), identifies himself with those who receive the warning.

*The knowledge of the truth* is spoken of as a thing received, which suggests that it has an acknowledged form. Indeed the article with the word *truth* (*tēs alētheias*) makes clear that a definable body of doctrine is in existence which all Christians will know. It amounts to the whole Christian revelation. The apostle Paul has much more to say on *knowledge* (*epignōsis*) than the author of this epistle. In fact this is the only place in this letter where the word is used. It highlights the deliberateness of the sin if an intelligent understanding of 'the truth' had already been acquired.[1]

Such a deliberate sin, following a grasp of 'the truth', implies a rejection of the truth, the cardinal feature of which is the uniqueness of the sacrifice of Christ. If that is rejected, no other adequate sacrifice remains. In the Greek the order of words is again significant, since the stress falls on the words *for sins.* Sacrifice there might be, but none of any effectiveness for the

---

[1] H. Kosmala, *Hebräer-Essener-Christen* (Leiden, 1959), pp. 135ff., studies the phrase 'knowledge of the truth' in the Qumran literature. He wrongly suggests that in Hebrews the expression does not include faith in Christ. F. F. Bruce, ' "To the Hebrews" or "To the Essenes"?', *NTS* 9 (1962–63), pp. 217–232, discusses the connection between Hebrews and Qumran and does not think that the readers of the former can be identified with the Essenes.

removal of sins. This vividly brings out the serious consequences of deliberate sin.

**27.** Without an atoning sacrifice in which to trust, all that remains is *judgment* and *fury*. The alternative is strongly and vividly expressed. The first, *judgment*, is expressed in terms of man's fears (*a fearful prospect*), the second, *fury*, in terms of God's provision. They complement each other. *A fearful prospect of judgment* draws attention to the reaction which the prospect produces in those who fall into the category of deliberate sinners. The degree to which thoughts of judgment strike terror into offenders depends on the character of the judge, and as this passage proceeds it becomes clear that his judgment is not to be trifled with (*cf.* verse 31).

**28.** An example of capital punishment is quoted from the law of Moses as an instance of judgment under the old covenant so as to provide a parallel for similar judgment under the new covenant. The particular case cited is one in which a man *has violated (athetēsas) the law of Moses, i.e.* set it aside as of no consequence. This seems to imply a positive refusal to accept the authority of the Mosaic law. For such a man there was no *mercy* under the old covenant. All he could hope for was death.

Since the provision – *at the testimony of two or three witnesses* – comes from Deuteronomy 17:6, it is reasonable to suppose that the writer at this point has the whole passage 17:2-6 in mind. This deals with the specific sin of those who were within the old covenant but who had committed the sin of idolatry and as a result were condemned to death by stoning. The presence of witnesses was required to ensure that no-one was condemned on a false report. Nothing is specifically made of this when the parallels to the new covenant are suggested in this epistle.

**29.** The argument proceeds from the lesser to the greater, hence the words *how much worse* are applied to the most serious offence under the new covenant. The readers are exhorted to give special thought to this: *do you think?* (*dokeite*). Although the words are expressed in the form of a question, there is no doubt about the answer. The writer takes it for granted that the state of mind he is about to mention is worse even than the violation of the Mosaic law. It involves a greater punishment. When speaking of this *punishment* he uses a word (*timōria*) which occurs nowhere else in the New Testament and which describes it precisely in terms of what the offence deserves.

The particular offence, which is serious enough to warrant greater punishment, is expressed in a threefold way. (i) The first involved a spurning of *the Son of God*. The verb used here (*katapateō*) means to tread under foot or trample upon, a vivid expression when used of the Son of God. It must involve not only a rejection of the Christian position, but also the strongest antagonism against Jesus Christ. It is an extreme case of apostasy which is being envisaged. (ii) In the second place the offender has *profaned the blood of the covenant*. The Greek expression translated *profaned* (*koinon hēgēsamenos*) could be rendered 'common' in the sense of treating Christ's blood as no different from any other man's blood, but the more positive rendering of the words in the sense of 'regarding as unholy' is more probable. Since the blood was the means of ratifying a covenant (both old and new), to regard it as unholy was tantamount to destroying the whole basis of agreement. Anyone adopting such a view would in fact be utterly despising the work of Christ. In the qualifying phrase, *by which he was sanctified*, the contrast is brought out between the unholy attitude towards Christ's sacrifice and the holy results of that sacrifice for the believer. (iii) The third act is described as an outraging of *the Spirit of grace*. The verb is yet another word which occurs nowhere else in the New Testament (*enybrizein*), which means not only outrage, but insolence. It is an arrogant rejection of the Spirit through whose agency grace (God's free favour) has come to man. This is the sole instance in the New Testament where the Spirit is called the Spirit of grace, but here the writer's purpose is to sum up in a word the full benefits which the Spirit has brought.

All three of these aspects of apostasy place a man not only in a position of condemnation, but in a specifically anti-Christian position. Whether the writer has in mind any who had actually turned against Christianity after having been associated with it, or whether he is envisaging what would be the position of any who did, is impossible to tell. When this passage is taken in conjunction with chapter 6, it is clear that the writer has very much in mind the serious consequences for those who become antagonistic to Jesus Christ. Any who had already done so would not be swayed by the arguments throughout the epistle setting out the superiority of Christ. It seems best therefore to suppose that these strong warnings are set out to show the contrast between those who enter into the benefits of Christ's sacrifice and those who resolutely refuse to do so.

**30.** Lest some should think that he has overdrawn the prospect of judgment, the writer turns his readers' attention to the character of the judge, which is the guarantee that the judgment will be just. The words *For we know him* at once focuses attention on the person. Then follows a quotation or rather an adaptation of a quotation from Deuteronomy 32:35 (*cf.* also Rom. 12:19, where the same adaptation is found). The second quotation comes from the following verse in Deuteronomy 32. The passage concerned is that in which Moses gives his farewell discourse and reminds the people of Israel of God's dealings with them. The discourse also contains warnings, and it is from this section particularly that the citations are made. Both together stress the fact that vengeance and judgment belong to the Lord. Vindication of God's people goes hand in hand with the judgment of his enemies.

**31.** The fearfulness of the prospect mentioned in verse 27 is now strengthened by the use of the same word to describe the result of falling *into the hands of the living God.* The expression 'living God' has already occurred before in this epistle (3:12; 9:14) and occurs again in 12:22. It has a particular significance here in that it is linked with 'hands', symbolic of the activity of God. In so speaking of the 'hands' of God, the writer is using a well-known imagery for the implementing by God of his own judgments. Hence in this context 'the hands of God' are against those who through their actions or attitudes have placed themselves outside of his mercy. A different use of a similar expression, 'the mighty hand of God', is found in 1 Peter 5:6.

### (iii) The value of past experience (10:32–39)

**32.** The subject of the next section, verses 32–39, is endurance, which is first dealt with retrospectively and then as the subject of further exhortation. The process of recollection is sometimes a fruitful pursuit when it calls to mind former lessons, even if those lessons had been learnt in a hard school. The word *recall* (*anamimnēskō*) is used only here in this epistle, but occurs twice in Mark (11:21; 14:72) and three times in Paul (1 Cor. 4:17; 2 Cor. 7:15 and 2 Tim. 1:6). It denotes some effort in calling to mind. One would have thought that such effort would be unnecessary when the subject of recall is the believer's former sufferings, but it is surprising how most people's memories need to be prodded.

*The former days* implies that this group of believers have been Christians for some time. They can now look back on earlier days to the time of their enlightenment. This is an expressive way of referring to their conversion (*cf.* 6:4). It is reminiscent of the Pauline statement in 2 Corinthians 4:6, where the idea of spiritual illumination is prominent. These Christians are told *you endured a hard struggle*. The word *athlēsin* describing this is another word found nowhere else in the New Testament, meaning an athletic contest, and therefore applied metaphorically to a struggle. In this case the imagery seems to be an obstacle race with *sufferings* as the obstacles to be overcome.

**33.** Here details are given of the kind of suffering that the readers had endured. It is described as *being publicly exposed to abuse and affliction*. This shows how they had had a personal involvement in the sufferings of Christ. Of the two words used here to denote suffering, 'abuse' (*oneidismoi*) is found also in 11:26 in the description of the abuse which Moses endured as a result of his rejection of his exalted position in Egypt, and in 13:13 in the description of what is in store for those who go outside the camp with Christ. It is very much tied up with the reproach which Christ endured (*cf.* Rom. 15:3). The other word, *affliction* (*thlipsis*), is much more common in the New Testament, although it occurs only here in Hebrews. Perhaps the most striking instance of its use is in Colossians 1:24, in which Paul speaks of completing that which is lacking in Christ's afflictions. These Hebrews had had a part in a similar experience. The verb translated *being publicly exposed* (*theatrizomai*) occurs only here in the New Testament, but Paul uses the cognate noun in 1 Corinthians 4:9. Both the verb and noun derive their force from a theatrical spectacle, the idea being that the Christians had been made a public target for abuse. This again ties in with the abuse to which Christ himself was subjected.

In addition to their own personal sufferings, they sometimes suffered through association with others. A close-knit Christian community is bound to experience both kinds of suffering when persecution comes. What form this second kind took is not stated. It was enough for the writer's purpose to remind the readers that they were *partners* (*koinōnoi*), which recalls the familiar New Testament concept of fellowship or participation. The believers had found it a privilege to 'share' each other's sufferings. This is fellowship on the deepest level.

**34.** What is described generally in the last verse is described here more specifically by way of example, but in the reverse order. *Compassion on the prisoners* is an example of an active approach, while accepting *plundering* is an example of a passive approach. These Christians had experienced both. They had in fact shown sympathy, similar to that of our high priest (4:15), although on a lower level. As the Greek word (*synepathēsate*) shows, this Christian compassion consists in the ability to 'suffer with' those who suffer. They identified themselves in mind with the prisoners. No indication is given of the nature or cause of the imprisonment, but presumably it was on account of the Christian confession of the people concerned. We know from Paul's letters that he was imprisoned many times and we also know that several others were fellow-prisoners with him. It was fairly common in those early days for Christians to be imprisoned whenever their religious convictions were considered to be unpalatable to the civil authorities.

It is not clear under what circumstances these Christians had *joyfully* accepted the *plundering of* their *property*. This certainly showed a particularly mature approach, for their attitude was more positive than mere resignation. They had learnt to rejoice in loss. Their approach to their possessions was healthy since their spiritual position did not depend on material advantages. They had learnt the superior value of their *better possession*, which presumably refers to their advantages in Christ. This was what Jesus had called laying up treasure in heaven (Mt. 6:19). The further description of the possession as *an abiding one* adds another dimension to its superiority, because it is clearly placed beyond the possibility of loss.

**35.** Appeal to past experience is always valuable when it reminds of an earlier confidence, especially at times when that has since become shaky. Maturity of experience like that just mentioned could surely not be thrown away. The writer puts it as a direct personal challenge: *do not throw away (apobalēte) your confidence*. The word he uses means to cast or fling away as one throws out rubbish which is no further use. It would be tragic indeed, if their former confidence should be jettisoned in this way. Moreover, the writer speaks of having *a great reward* in the present tense (*echei*), in the sense that the believer who stands firm already begins to experience the reward, even if its fulfilment still lies in the future.

**36.** *Endurance* is a more specific aspect of confidence. It includes an element of perseverance, a persistence even when circumstances are contrary. The next chapter is to furnish many examples of the endurance of faith. The stress falls on the reader's need (*you have need*), which shows that the writer recognizes their lack of a spirit of endurance and this fits in well with the general background of the writer's fears for his readers.

The purpose of the endurance is precisely expressed in the words *so that you may do the will of God*. Already in this chapter the devotion of Jesus to the will of God has been mentioned (*cf.* verses 5ff.), and now the same goal is set before the readers. It is certain that any forsaking of former confidence would not be the will of God. It is also clear that the example of Jesus Christ included sufferings. It is one of the marks of a mature Christian that he has a view of God's will which makes provision for adverse happenings when they come. It is on the basis of doing God's will that the readers will *receive what is promised*. This is another way of referring to the reward mentioned in verse 35. The idea sums up the glorious inheritance of the believer, for the promises of God are utterly dependable.

**37–38.** In order to back up his point, the writer links two passages of Scripture: Isaiah 26:20 (LXX) and Habakkuk 2:3–4. The first phrase, *For yet a little while*, echoes the language of Isaiah 26:20 where the same words are followed by the clause 'until the indignation should be past', showing that in Isaiah's day Israel had to wait for God to act. It is quoted here to reassure any who imagined that lack of action showed failure on God's part to honour his promise.

The next part of the quotation comes from the Habakkuk passage, although there are modifications of the original. There is a different purpose, for the prophet was thinking of the threat from the Chaldeans.[1] Here the thought is of the certainty of God's intervention, which was particularly significant for the church in a time of persecution. The assurance that *the coming one* would not tarry shows that any delay should be regarded as temporary.

The first statement in verse 38 is quoted by Paul in Romans 1:17 to sum up the gist of his theological argument (*cf.* also Gal. 3:11). Here the main lesson to be learnt is the need for faith if the former confidence is to be maintained. The additional words *and if he shrinks back, my soul has no pleasure in him* give added importance to the need for faith. The possibility is expressed as a conditional clause and there is no indication that any had actually shrunk back. Indeed verse 39 suggests the reverse.

**39.** Here the writer identifies his readers with him in rejecting the very idea of shrinking back. The words translated *and are destroyed* (*eis apōleian*) are an interpretation of the passage just quoted, for the writer can only understand the outcome of God's displeasure in this way. Here it is contrasted with the result of faith, *i.e.* that writer and readers alike will *keep their souls*. This idea of preservation, the exact opposite of destruction, is characteristic of salvation. The same word is linked with salvation in 1 Thessalonians 5:9.

It is, however, the faith aspect which provides the link with the following chapter which describes some of the heroes of faith.

### B. FAITH (11:1–40)

The writer is well aware that the life of faith is not easy, but he calls to mind the exploits of many men and women of faith from the past. He produces a miniature picture-gallery of godly people who nevertheless, in spite of their achievements, did

---

[1] In Qumran exegesis Hab.; 2:4 is understood as a call to be faithful to the Teacher of Righteousness (1 *Qp. Hab; cf.* G. Vermes, *The Dead Sea Scrolls in English* (1962), p. 233).

not fully inherit the promises, since they had lived before the time of Christ.

### (i) Its nature (11:1-3)

1. There is no break between this verse and the previous one. The following survey of the effectiveness of faith in the history of the people of God is intended to provide an exposition based on 'those who have faith and keep their souls' (10:39). The writer wishes to illustrate the continuity between the Hebrew Christians and pious men of old.[1] Their exploits are seen as a fitting prelude to the Christian era (as 11:39-40 shows).

This account begins with some general statements about faith (verses 1-3). We need not suppose that the writer is attempting a precise definition of faith in his opening statement. He gives rather those important aspects which are illustrated so vividly in the past experiences of the people of God. The statement, *Now faith is the assurance of things hoped for*, introduces the word 'faith' (*pistis*) without the article, which shows that the writer is thinking of faith in general and not specifically Christian faith. It has certain qualities which apply to both the pre-Christian and Christian eras. The word translated 'assurance' (*hypostasis*) has already been used in 1:3 in the sense of 'nature' or 'essence' and in 3:14 in the sense of 'conviction'. These different uses could both apply in the present passage and it is a question for debate which meaning is best suited to the passage. If the former is right the statement would signify that faith gives reality to the things hoped for. If the second meaning is right (as RSV prefers), the sense is that faith consists of the conviction that what is hoped for will happen. The difference is that between a state and an activity. To decide which is preferable, the meaning of the further word *conviction* (*elenchos*) must be considered. This word basically means 'proof, test', which suggests that faith is seen as the proof of the reality of *things not seen*. If both parts of the sentence are to be regarded as parallel to each

---

[1] A recent German writer, E. Grässer, *Der Glaube im Hebräerbrief* (1965), makes an exposition of faith in this epistle the key to the understanding of the whole theme. He considers that faith has become academic rather than personal, as it is in Paul. To Grässer the background of Hebrews is a state of despair. But *cf.* the criticisms of this position in Excursus 2 of G. Hughes' *Hebrews and Hermeneutics* (1979), pp. 137-142.

other, it would be best to regard both the key words as pointing to the demonstrating function of faith. Nevertheless the difference between *things hoped for* and *things not seen* weakens the parallel and suggests that the two key words may be taken, one of a state and the other of an activity. Bruce[1] makes a comparison between physical eyesight which produces conviction about visible things and faith which does the same for the invisible order.

*Things hoped for* is quite general and focuses on *hope* rather than on any specific object of hope. It is not however hope in the abstract (*elpis*), but rather the result of the activity of hope. This close connection between faith and hope finds expression in Paul's epistles, as for instance, in 1 Corinthians 13:13 (*cf.* also Eph. 4:4–5). Faith is the act of commitment on the part of the believer, whereas hope is the state of mind which he possesses. On the other hand, *things not seen* describes generally all that is beyond man's normal knowledge or powers of comprehension. It includes, therefore, the whole range of spiritual experiences, although it is probably intended in a more restricted sense of those spiritual realities which relate to the future, in which case it approximates in some degree to hope. Faith provides a platform for hope and a perception into the reality of what would otherwise remain unseen. In the following discussion of men of faith, this pull of the unseen is particularly evident.

**2.** When the writer goes on to say, *For (gar) by it men of old received divine approval*, he is giving a judgment drawn from man's experience of God. It is a kind of summary of man's experience in the past, and especially of the men to be mentioned in the following catalogue. There is no disputing that these men received divine approval. Any readers who had been reared in orthodox Judaism would have learnt to revere these heroes of the past as people who gained special favour with God. Indeed the same would be true of Gentile readers who had taken over the Old Testament as Scripture and who would soon learn to recognize the divine stamp of approval on these men of the past. The word rendered *divine approval* (*emartyrēthēsan*) appears in the Greek without mention of God, but it is

---

[1] Bruce, *Comm.*, p. 279.

clear from the use of the same verb in verse 4 (*cf*. also verse 39) that God is considered to be the agent.

**3.** In contemplating the origin of the observable world of nature, the writer recognizes the need for a leap of faith. If the explanation were to be restricted to phenomena which can be tested, no faith would be needed. The unseen would automatically be excluded, since only what is seen would be regarded as valid data. But the words *By faith we understand* show that knowledge is not independent of faith. This statement has some bearing on the scientific view of the world. Science could not reject the idea *that the world was created by the word of God*, for this view does not rest upon a scientific evaluation of the 'seen' facts. The writer recognizes that acceptance of a special creative act of God is possible only to faith. But why does he introduce the subject at this stage in his discussion? What relevance has it for the catalogue of men of faith which follows? The answer lies in the fact that he cannot consider the world of men apart from their environment. Indeed God's interest in the faith of individuals is conditioned by his purpose in creation. If faith is exercised by men on earth, it must be concerned that everything that exists on earth is under God's control. The writer has already made clear in 1:2 that the Son was the agent through whom God created the world, although here he uses a more expressive verb (*katērtisthai*) for the act of creation. In this context it means 'to furnish completely or equip' and thus draws attention to the perfection of the total number of creative acts and sees the whole as a balanced and completed unity. It is the function of faith to discern this.

The result of faith is stated to be that *what is seen* came into being *out of things which do not appear*. This means that faith posits that an unseen power was the effective causation of the phenomenal world. This is a point of view fully in harmony with the creation narrative in Genesis. This idea of a creation *ex nihilo* was not favoured by the contemporary Greek world.

*(ii) Examples from the past (11:4-40)*

**4.** Now follow some comments on men of the age from creation to the flood (verses 4–8). Three men stand out to illustrate various aspects of faith. First to be mentioned is the sacrificial faith of *Abel*. The Genesis account does not in fact refer to the faith of Abel. It simply states that Abel brought of the firstlings of his flock and of their fat portions (Gn. 4:4). No indication is given of the reason why his offering proved more acceptable. The only hint is that Cain is told that if he did well he too would be accepted (Gn. 4:7), which suggests that it had much to do with Abel's attitude and manner of life. But the writer to the Hebrews gives his own interpretation and links Abel's *more acceptable sacrifice* with his faith. It is often supposed that Abel's sacrifice was superior because it was a blood sacrifice whereas Cain's was not. But there was no precedent to blood sacrifices and there is no evidence to suggest that God had instructed the brothers about what kind of offerings they should make. Nevertheless as the first one to offer animal sacrifices, Abel is of special interest to the writer.

No suggestion is made as to the method God used to signify acceptance of Abel's gift. The writer simply says *God bearing witness by accepting his gifts*, for the Genesis account is no more specific. Yet in some way both *Abel* and *Cain* knew God's judgment on their gifts. Acceptance of the gifts is clearly linked with *approval as righteous*, which in turn is linked with the more acceptable sacrifice. The righteousness spoken of seems to consist of a right attitude of mind which is pleasing to God.

It might seem that Abel received a poor reward for his acceptance by God when his brother killed him. But the writer is impressed with the timeless character of Abel's faith. It was through this that *he is still speaking*, the earliest demonstration that death, even violent death, cannot prevent the message of faith. This interpretation holds if the RSV is right in understanding *through* (*di' autēs*) to refer to faith, but the word *faith* does not occur in the text. It is possible to refer the pronoun (*autēs*) further back in the sentence and apply it to sacrifice, but the RSV rendering seems preferable since the theme of the whole passage is faith. The main thought is that the kind of faith which Abel exercised can communicate over the whole stretch of time. It still provides a source of inspiration in common with the other examples of faith. Where true faith in God is operative it is relevant in any age. If the pattern of faith in these early men of faith could speak to the Hebrews there is no reason why it should not be applicable to us.

**5.** It is natural in a catalogue of ancient men of faith to find a ready mention of *Enoch*. In the rather dull genealogies of Genesis 5, the brief comment on Enoch shines like a jewel and is hardly paralleled elsewhere in Scripture for concise effectiveness. 'Enoch walked with God; and he was not, for God took him' (Gn. 5:24). The Septuagint which has 'Enoch pleased God' and 'was not found' is followed here by the author. His comment on that statement highlights two features. (i) That Enoch's release from the experience of death was due to his faith. This is an interpretation of the statement *he was not found*. (ii) That *he was attested as having pleased God* before he was taken. Again this is an interpretive comment on the fact that he walked with God. The writer assumes that only a man of faith could enjoy close communion with God, and that anyone who communed with him like this must have pleased him. It was undoubtedly a right assumption. What is striking about Enoch is that he stood so much above the corruption of his age. Was it for this reason that God chose to remove him from the scene in an unusual way? Certainly his mysterious translation has deeply impressed our writer.[1]

**6.** The reference to Enoch's faith is justified by the comment *And without faith it is impossible to please him*. Man's relationship with God is built up on a mutual trust, and true communion cannot exist without this. The writer goes on, in fact, to point out something much more elementary, but which he clearly saw the need to mention. (i) *Whoever would draw near to God must believe that he exists*. It has already been seen how central to this epistle is the idea of drawing near to God (4:16; 7:25; 10:1, 22). The present statement must, therefore, be regarded as linking Enoch's experience with the whole purpose of the letter. It may seem strange that in an epistle which begins with an assertion of God (1:1), the writer should consider it necessary to point to the need for believing in his existence. But he is

---

[1] Another mention of Enoch in the New Testament is Jude 14, where a quotation from the book of Enoch is given. This reminds us that Enoch was a familiar choice among the apocalyptists. He is mentioned in the book of Jubilees 4:17; Ben Sira 44:16; 1 Enoch 71:14; in all of which cases his example is cited approvingly. *Cf.* also Philo, *On Abraham* 17f.; *On Rewards and Punishments* 17.

arguing from man's experience of communion with God to the fact that his faith in God's existence must be real. (ii) Such worshippers must also believe *that he rewards those who seek him*. This statement is intended to reassure those who are questioning whether the quest for God is always successful. It needs faith to accept this, but the conviction that God rewards the serious seeker is fully in harmony with the nature of God as he has made himself known throughout his revelations to men. There is no fear that any seeker may not find him if he acts in faith.

7. The next notable person in the early period is undoubtedly *Noah*, and again his achievements are attributed to faith. His faith developed in response to a specific warning from God (*being warned by God, chrēmatistheis*). The verb has already been used in 8:5 of God's instruction to Moses, with the force of an authoritative command. The subject of the warning here is said to be *events as yet unseen*, which is an indirect allusion to the flood, a symbol of divine judgment. The nature of Noah's faith is seen in his response to the warning (*took heed and constructed, eulabētheis kateskeuasen*). The former of these two verbs, which occurs only here in the New Testament, has the sense of reverential awe. Such godly fear formed an important element in Noah's faith. It was linked with immediate obedience to God's specific commands regarding the *ark*. Noah's faith, moreover, was not only effective on his own behalf but also on behalf of *his household*. This corporate aspect of faith shows a more extensive application than the faith of either Abel or Enoch.

It seems probable that the words *by this* (*di' hēs*) are intended to refer to the ark, although they could grammatically refer to Noah's faith. The ark was in any case a visible evidence of his faith to his unbelieving and scoffing contemporaries. The sight of the ark being constructed was a challenge to those contemporaries and forced on them their own condemnation. They were in fact rejecting the divine warning by their unbelief. It is a solemn thought that Noah's faith, because of its nature, was identified as the act by which he *condemned the world*. Where faith is resisted or rejected it leads to condemnation.

The expression *an heir of the righteousness which comes by faith* is interesting because of its linking righteousness (*dikaiosynē*) and faith (*pistis*) in a manner reminiscent of Paul (*cf.* Rom. 4:11; 10:6 and Phil. 3:9 for various formulae used). Here righteousness is said to be 'according to (*kata*) faith', but RSV, *which comes by faith*, is probably right in seeing faith as the channel through which it comes. The idea of 'an heir' has twice before occurred in this epistle, once of the Son (1:2) and once of the heirs of the promise (6:17). In the case of Noah, the righteousness was not something in the future but in the present. Indeed, he is the first man specifically described as righteous in the Old Testament (Gn. 6:9).

**8.** It is not surprising that the writer's comments on *Abraham* occupy more space than is devoted to any other ancient worthy (verses 8–19). His exploits captured the interest of Jews and Christians alike. He was *par excellence* a man of faith. The first aspect of his faith which is noted is his personal obedience. He *obeyed when he was called to go out*, a direct reference to Genesis 12:1–3. The construction in the Greek shows that the obedience accompanied the calling. It was, in fact, spontaneous, which was all the more remarkable because he did not know where he was going. His faith was of a different kind from Noah's, because the latter's directions were more detailed. It speaks highly for Abraham's faith that he accepted *an inheritance* on trust without even knowing where it was to be. It was because he left behind the 'seen' world of his former days and launched into a project involving an unseen inheritance that he has become an example of daring faith and merits the title, 'the father of the faithful'.

What is particularly significant about Abraham's act of faith is that it began the emergence of the theocratic community. Abraham acted as an individual, but even then many of his family followed him.

**9.** The development and extension of Abraham's faith is seen by the fact that *Isaac and Jacob* are linked as *heirs with him of the same promise* (*cf.* 6:17). Abraham's faith consisted of more than his initial act of leaving the city of Ur. It extended to his experience in the land of promise. The word used for *sojourned* (*parōkēsen*) has the meaning to dwell as a stranger in a locality, a sense strengthened by the words *as in a foreign land*. Although he dwelt in *the land of promise*, it was not as a rightful possessor, but as an alien. This fact is heightened by the nomadic character of his existence (*living in tents*). It speaks highly of Abraham's faith that it was so tenacious in such tenuous circumstances. Faith made a reality of what was not even apparent.

**10.** There is certainly a striking contrast between the tents in Canaan and *the city which has foundations* to which the faith of Abraham looked forward. There is something particularly attractive about a quality of faith which sees stability in other than material things. Abraham might have felt that the least that God could do was to allow him to build a city in the promised land for himself and his descendants, particularly in view of the considerable number of his attendants. But he had altogether different standards of value – a city whose foundations are utterly unshakeable. The writer thinks in spiritual terms of the city which God is building. We may compare this idea with the vision of the new Jerusalem which is described in Revelation 21 and 22, where again the spiritual aspects are without question the most important. Abraham had a wide and noble horizon which could look behind the immediate environment. Of the two words describing God's part in the city, the first, *builder* (*technitēs*), conveys the idea of 'architect', the planner of each part and integrator of these separate parts into a whole. The second word, *maker* (*dēmiourgos*) focuses more especially on the execution of the plans. It occurs here only in the New Testament.[1]

**11.** It is perhaps surprising to find Sarah spoken of as an example of faith, for according to Genesis she was more conspicuous as an example of doubt. But since the birth of the theocratic community is in mind, Sarah's part was as important as Abraham's. In view of her advancing years she needed some *power* (*dynamis*) beyond herself if she was to conceive and bring forth a child. An alternative text attributes to Abraham the receiving of power to conceive, which is more natural than attributing it to Sarah. The change in the text, however, looks like an attempt to avoid an apparent difficulty. In spite of the fact that Sarah laughed when first hearing that she was to have a child, her mockery must have turned to faith long before Isaac

---

[1] Both these words are linked in reference to God's creative work in Philo, *cf*. Williamson, *Philo and the Epistle to the Hebrews*, pp. 46ff.

was born. It needed a woman of faith to be wife of a believer as outstanding as Abraham. She too had to come to the same conviction as her husband that the God who had promised would honour his word (*she considered him faithful who had promised*). In all spiritual encounters it is easier to doubt than to believe, and Sarah must be commended for her willingness to change her approach and to make way for the development of her faith. The conviction that God is faithful is one of the cardinal aspects of biblical doctrine. It is as strong in the Old Testament as it is in the New Testament. It is the foundation stone of the faith of God's people.

**12.** The writer's thought now switches back to Abraham himself as the father of the people of God. There is a contrast here between the *one man* and the innumerable *descendants*. A similar contrast between the 'one' and the 'many' descended from him occurs in Paul's Adam theology in Romans 5:12ff. The imagery of the innumerable *stars* and *grains of sand* comes directly from the Genesis account (22:17; *cf*. 32:12). It is a vivid reminder of the magnitude of the promise of God, especially directed to the one who was *as good as dead*. Teeming life was to come from apparent death, a superb example of God's ways differing from man's estimate of what is possible (consider Rom. 4:19 where the same example occurs). It is worth observing that the *therefore* (*dio*) at the beginning of this verse shows the importance of Sarah's faith in the fulfilment of the promise to Abraham.

**13.** At this point a general summary of patriarchal piety is introduced (verses 13–16). The words, *These all died in faith*, imply that faith was their dominant characteristic to the end of their days. The words *in faith* (*kata pistin*) could more literally be translated 'according to faith', which shows faith to be the rule by which they lived and died. In spite of not having received the promise, they had in a measure experienced it: (i) They had *seen it . . . from afar*, as men who saw the objective on the horizon, but never actually reached it in this life. This is a remarkable example of the statement in verse 1 that 'faith is the conviction of things not seen', except that the conviction has now become so strong that the 'not seen' has become seen. (ii) They had *greeted it*. This makes it more personal, as if the fulfilment of the promise in the multitudes of descendants had become so real that those descendants could continually greet it. The words 'greeted it from afar' echo the text of Deuteronomy 3:25–27, a description of Moses catching a glimpse of the promised land.[1]

The patriarchs had *acknowledged* (*homologēsantes*) their true status as *strangers and exiles*. Abraham used the same description of himself in Genesis 23:4. In 1 Peter 1:1; 2:11 a similar description is applied to Christians. In Hebrews the idea fits in with the earlier allusion to the Israelites' wanderings in the wilderness (chapter 3) and the writer's aim is clearly to use this as a pattern. It is all of a piece with the underlying principle of the epistle that it is the heavenly and not the earthly things which are most important.

**14.** This idea of strangers and exiles is expounded in the next three verses, the main idea of which is the better country (verse 16). The Old Testament record of the patriarchs demonstrates that they never obtained a true *homeland* (*patris*). The word used is significant for it is rare in both the Septuagint and the New Testament. It means more than a place of habitation. It means a fatherland where the nation can find its roots. This was the desire of the patriarchs, and was a continuing motif for the people of Israel throughout their history, although the writer of this epistle is thinking of it in spiritual rather than national terms.

**15.** The *land* they were *thinking of* was clearly not Mesopotamia from which Abraham had set out. In spite of the ease with which he might have returned, neither he nor his immediate descendants desired to do so. This is all the more remarkable when it is recognized that the land they left behind had reached a much more advanced stage of civilization than the land of Canaan to which they went. It may well be that the writer is appealing to the patriarch's example in refusing to turn back to exert pressure on those readers who were tempted to turn back from Christianity.

**16.** The *better country* is at once identified as *a heavenly one*. The identification of the two adjectives (*kreittonos, epouraniou*) is particularly characteristic of this epistle. It places the emphasis

[1] *Cf.* Héring, *Comm.*, p. 103.

on spiritual rather than material inheritance. It is perhaps surprising in view of this to discover that what God *has prepared for them* is described in terms of *a city*, a symbol of man's creative genius and especially of his social life. But even the city can have a spiritual connotation, as 12:22 shows. What has been prepared is in fact an ideal city, of which man's cities are the palest imitations. We have already noted how surprising it is that a group of nomads should seek so stable a thing as a city (see verse 10).

No greater commendation could be given to any men than that *God is not ashamed to be called their God*. The Old Testament does not hide the weaknesses of the patriarchs, but here the writer is looking back on history. He singles out their faith, which cannot be denied. Moreover, he knows that the title 'the God of Abraham, the God of Isaac, and the God of Jacob' was the name specially chosen by God in his introduction of himself to Moses at the time of the exodus (Ex. 3:6). It is certainly unusual to read of God being unashamed, since shame is a characteristic of man. Nevertheless, he was in a special sense *their God* as the history of the chosen people shows. He delighted to be known as the God of Israel.

**17.** After these general comments on the patriarchs the writer returns to the supreme example of Abraham's faith: *he offered up Isaac*. This event points to the paradox of faith – its willingness to surrender the fulfilment of what it has inherited in the form of *promises*. The testing of Abraham makes his faith stand out in greater relief. His quality of faith is seen in obedience. As Westcott aptly says, 'The specific command could be fulfilled only in one way: the promise might be fulfilled in more than one.'

Hence the act of offering is spoken of in the perfect tense (*prosenēnochen*) as if what was intended was regarded as a completed act with a continuous consequence. The second verb (*prospheren*) is translated *was ready to offer* in an attempt to bring out the distinction between this and the former verb and to indicate that the act was considered in intention rather than fulfilment. The pathos of Abraham's dilemma is vividly brought out by the use of the term *only son* (*monogenēs*), which must be understood in relation to the promise. Ishmael was also Abraham's son, but Isaac was the sole heir to the promises. It was this that constituted the real test to Abraham's faith. To be commanded to offer any of his sons would have been a shattering challenge, but doubly so the child of promise. The writer of this epistle does not discuss, any more than Paul in his Roman letter, the moral problem of God commanding a human sacrifice, for to him there was no question of God accepting such a sacrifice. The promise stood between. Indeed the promise made impossible the completion of the sacrifice.

**18.** While the words *of whom it was said* are a possible rendering the Greek (*pros hon elalēthē*) is better understood as 'to whom', *i.e.* to Abraham. The words quoted from Genesis 21:12 are intended to explain the nature of the promises mentioned in verse 17. There is obvious point both in the Genesis context and here in the specific reference to Isaac. God spoke the words *'Through Isaac shall your descendants be named'* to Abraham after Sarah had requested him to cast out Hagar's son. They draw attention to God's plan for Abraham's seed, in contrast to Abraham's own designs.

**19.** Reflecting on the nature of Abraham's faith, the writer conjectures on what must have taken place in the thought of Abraham. The conclusion to which he had come is expressed as a decisive and carefully reasoned act as the verb shows (*logisamenos, he considered*). God's ability *to raise men even from the dead* would not have been too readily accepted even by Abraham, but he had come to the view that this would be the only way that God could maintain his integrity if the offering of Isaac was to proceed. To argue like this speaks much for the maturity of Abraham's faith, for it would have been more natural to question his guidance in the offering of Isaac. But he seems to have had no doubts about this. The words could, of course, be taken in a different way to refer to Isaac's birth, which was as much a challenge to Abraham's faith. Indeed the quotation in verse 18 comes from the account of Isaac's birth. This would give added point to the 'only son', *i.e.* the son who was virtually raised from the deadness of Sarah's womb. This is the sense in which Paul considers Abraham's faith in Romans 4.

The Greek phrase translated *figuratively speaking* (*en parabolē*) has given rise to various interpretations. If the reference in the first part of the verse is to Isaac's being sacrificed and then saved from it, the parabolic or symbolic meaning may be found in the substitute ram that was offered in Isaac's place. On the other hand, if the allusion is to Isaac's birth the parabolic character of the action when Abraham received him back rested in the deeper significance of that event, *i.e.* the birth of the child of promise, *i.e.* Christ. Some understand *en parabolē* as referring to the general resurrection of the dead. But the reference is specifically to Isaac.

**20.** Isaac's position in the line of succession was different from Abraham's, for his twin sons were both in the line of succession. The blessings invoked upon them were recognized as being overruled, since God reversed the natural order and the heir of the promise became the second rather than the first of the twins. The problem of God's choice of Jacob rather than Esau is touched upon in Romans 9:13, the only other book in the New Testament which mentions Esau. The author of Hebrews, unlike Paul, does not quote the saying which comes in Malachi 1:2 ('Yet I have loved Jacob but I have hated Esau'). He describes him nevertheless as 'immoral or irreligious' in 12:16. In the present context he is concerned only with the faith which activated Isaac when he *invoked future blessings on Jacob and Esau.* No mention is made of Rebekah's deception, presumably because Isaac himself recognized that the blessing he had given to Jacob could not be reversed.

**21.** The blessing which passed from father to son was of great significance to the Hebrew mind. Our writer sees the act as an act of faith. In the case of *Jacob,* the farewell blessings on *each of the sons of Joseph* are mentioned as particular evidence of his faith (*cf.* Gn. 48:16ff.). And once again the natural order was by-passed, for Reuben was Jacob's eldest son, but Joseph was chosen as the recipient of the greater blessing. It is further worth noting that the writer here shows no interest in the importance of Jacob's other sons as representative heads of the tribes of Israel. They are not so much as mentioned. The faith of Jacob is parallel to that of Isaac in perceiving the hand of God in blessing the younger Ephraim before the elder Manasseh. God's ways are sovereign and his choice must be accepted in faith. Indeed, the writer sees all the dominant stages of Israel's history as a progression of acts of faith.

When Jacob is said to have blessed *bowing in worship over the head of his staff*, the words follow the Septuagint rather than the Massoretic text, which has 'bed' instead of staff. The detail is transferred from an earlier encounter between Jacob and Joseph in Genesis 47:31, but the writer evidently records it for its religious significance. In spite of Jacob's advanced age, the act of blessing is seen as an act of worship. Moreover, the staff was significant in Hebrew thought as a sign of God's favour and there may be hint of such a symbolic meaning here.

**22.** The faith attributed to *Joseph* was of a different kind, for in giving *directions concerning his burial* he had faith to believe that his descendants would one day leave Egypt for the promised land. He had cherished the promise to Abraham, Isaac and Jacob, and signified his own confidence (Gn. 50:24ff.). This was an act of considerable faith which proved to be fully justified. The *exodus of the Israelites* became one of the most significant events in the whole history of Israel. The word 'exodus' is not frequent in the New Testament, for it occurs elsewhere only in Luke 9:31 referring to the death of Christ and in 2 Peter 1:15 to the death of Peter. The dominant idea is of a triumphant deliverance.

**23.** It is not surprising that the faith of *Moses* is given more extensive treatment than that of Isaac, Jacob or Joseph. The exodus held a prominent place for every devout Jew in demonstrating God's action on behalf of his people, and Moses was consequently held in the highest esteem. Our writer sees two aspects of his faith: personal and national. The first evidence of faith was exercised by Moses' *parents* on his behalf. The hiding of the child *for three months* is described in Exodus 2, where Moses is said after that period to have been placed on the Nile in a wicker basket daubed with bitumen and pitch. In view of *the king's edict* which condemned the male Hebrew children to death, this faith was courageous. They trusted God to effect a deliverance.

The fact *that the child was beautiful* is also mentioned in Acts 7:20 in Stephen's speech and is derived directly from Exodus 2:2. In both New Testament occurrences the same Greek word (*asteios*) is used, which in the papyri is used of elegance in clothing. There was clearly something striking about the appearance of Moses to create such an impression on Pharaoh's daughter.

**24.** *When he was grown up* points to a new development in Moses' story, for now he is in a position to exercise faith on his own behalf and he does this by refusing *to be called the son of Pharaoh's daughter.* The tense of the verb *refused* (*ērnēsato*) points to a specific act of choice. It illustrates faith acting in a crisis, although it need not imply the absence of considerable premeditation. What the writer carefully notes is the quality of faith which could make a decision of this kind. In his speech Stephen makes no reference to Moses' faith, but stresses his disappointment that the Israelites did not share his conviction that God would use him to deliver them. Faith in this case presupposes a firm conviction in Moses of God's call to a most difficult task.

**25.** The contrast between the alternatives facing Moses is vividly set out – *ill-treatment* or *the fleeting pleasures of sin.* That his faith chose the former instead of the latter shows its self-effacing character. Moses had much to lose that was attractive, although the pleasures are specifically attributed to sin. Faith and sinful pleasure do not belong together. The word for *ill-treatment* (*synkakoucheisthai*) occurs only here in the New Testament and serves to link the sufferers closely together. There was a solidarity between Moses and the people of God when he had once thrown in his lot with them, a solidarity in suffering. In the contrast which is made there is no comparable time restriction in the former as compared with the latter (*proskairon,* for a season, *fleeting*). The most that sin can provide is temporary pleasure, but the ill-treatment meted out to the people of God has no such temporary character. Those who identify with God's people at once become the targets of God's enemies.

**26.** The writer next comments on the reason why Moses made the choice he did. He expresses it in another contrast – the superiority of abuse for Christ over *the treasures of Egypt.* This is a strange and irrational superiority, which seems ludicrous in a materialistic age. But part of the greatness of Moses was that he recognized that there were more valuable things in life than material treasures. It is surprising that the *abuse* is said to be *suffered for the Christ*, for this seems like a reading back of Christian conditions into the time of Moses. It is not, however, entirely inappropriate for a writer who has many times in this epistle invested the Old Testament allusions with Christian significance to do the same here. He implies that all the sufferings of God's people are in some way linked with sufferings on behalf of the Messiah, the perfect representative of God. All that Moses suffered was in the cause of God's plan of salvation for his people, culminating in the abuse which was heaped on *the Christ* himself, of which the writer is acutely conscious throughout this epistle.

The words *for he looked to the reward* mean that Moses focused his gaze on a nobler target. The verb (*apeblepen*) means 'to look away' implying a deliberate turning from one thing to another. It has already been noted that the idea of reward and particularly the word used here (*misthapodosian*, recompense) is characteristic of this epistle. The word occurs elsewhere in 2:2 and 10:35. In none of the occurrences is the recompense defined. In the context of Moses' life it must be interpreted of the spiritual treasures which he knew would be his, in view of the fact that he was not permitted to enter the promised land. Spiritual rewards, unlike material advantages, have an enduring quality which infinitely enhances their value.

**27.** The historical consequences of Moses' choice are now given in brief compass – *he left Egypt* and subsequently kept the Passover (verse 28), and led the consequent exodus of Israel from Egypt. The many steps leading to the exodus are passed over because again it is the powerful activity of faith which concerns the writer. Faith is seen to override the king's *anger*, a remarkable achievement when it is remembered that the king had despotic powers. Since anger of that kind can be tyrannical, it takes a brave man to defy it, but faith can supply the courage to do so. In view of this statement, there may at first sight appear to be a contradiction with Exodus 2:14f. which states that Moses was afraid and fled from Pharaoh. The explanation may be that Moses feared that God's purposes would be thwarted if he did not escape, but this is to be distinguished from personal fear.

A spiritual explanation is given for Moses' courage: *for he endured as seeing him who is invisible.* The eye of faith can see what is invisible to the eyes of others. Moses, in all the wanderings in the wilderness, was conscious of God's presence in a remarkable way (*cf.* Ex. 33; Nu. 12:7–8). The writer traces the secret of his endurance to a source beyond himself, which his opponents never even knew existed. In Colossians 1:15 Paul speaks of God as invisible, although he recognizes that he has shown his image in Christ. There is undoubtedly a paradox in the seeing of the unseeable, but this is of the very essence of faith (*cf.* 11:1).

**28.** *The Passover* occupied a place of considerable significance for the Jewish mind and came to have an even greater meaning for Christians because it was so closely linked with the passion of Jesus (*cf.* 1 Cor. 5:7). It was naturally an event of historic importance when the original passover was instituted. It centred in the faith of Moses, according to this writer. It was essentially performed in faith because the sprinkling of blood did not appear as a logical means of warding off the angel of death. In the expression *sprinkled the blood,* the Greek has a noun (*proschysin,* sprinkling), rather than the verb, which more vividly places both the passover feast and the sprinkling in close proximity as objects of the same verb, but they are nevertheless viewed as separate actions. In the Hebrew text of Exodus 12:23, it is the Lord who will execute judgment, but here there is simply a reference to the *Destroyer.* The allusion is to the angel of death who passed over the houses where the sacrificial blood had been sprinkled on the doorposts and lintels, which ensured that the *first-born* might be saved.

**29.** The thought now moves away from individual faith to national faith, although the people's faith was still inspired by the faith of Moses. Clearly the movement of the Israelites out of the bondage of Egypt was a co-operative effort. At no time was faith needed more urgently than when the Israelites faced the formidable obstacle of *the Red Sea* which barred their advance with *the Egyptians* hot on their rear. The way they *crossed as if on dry land,* while the Egyptians *were drowned,* was to become a national saga of God's deliverance. It is now considered to have come about by faith. It is well to remember that corporate faith of this kind is but the sum total of the faith of each individual.

Such faith must, however, be set against the development of unbelief during the subsequent wilderness wanderings. On this the writer has already commented in chapters 3 and 4, and here he contents himself with the more positive aspects of faith.

**30.** The next dramatic event which comes to the writer's mind is the conquest of Jericho, not only because of the miraculous manner in which it was accomplished, but also because it set a seal upon the coming conquest of Canaan. The encircling of Jericho for *seven days* demanded a high quality of corporate faith, for it appeared to be so utterly futile to the pagan onlookers who had no concept of what God in his power could do. Moreover, the extraordinary confidence and unusual methods must have struck terror in the minds of other Canaanite cities. Faith often requires the conviction that God can do the seemingly impossible.

**31.** The position of the woman *Rahab*, who gave protection to the spies in Jericho (Jos. 2:1ff.), caught the imagination of our writer, who, in spite of the fact that she was a pagan and a *harlot*, mentions her among the heroes of faith. The fact that faith could be exercised by such a person was evidence of its universal character. Another New Testament writer, James (2:25), was also impressed by Rahab's act. The distinction between Rahab and the other inhabitants of Jericho is marked by the description of them as *those who were disobedient*. This implies that the people of Jericho, having heard of the exploits of God on behalf of his people, should have acknowledged these acts instead of resisting God's people. Certainly Rahab must have been prompted by such reports of God's dealings to lead her to give *friendly welcome to the spies*. She does not regard them as enemies, but as agents of God, and this perception is attributed to her faith.

**32.** The entry of the Israelites into the promised land was only the beginning and many exploits of faith followed in the chequered history of God's people. The writer realizes that it is out of the question to speak of further individual acts of faith, and he therefore contents himself with giving a kind of inventory of different exploits. He first gives a list of names which are assumed to be so well known that there is no need to mention their doings.

The rhetorical question, *And what more shall I say?* almost suggests that he does not consider there is much point in mentioning more examples. Those already given are sufficiently impressive. Moreover, lack of space prevents him from continuing with the same detail. The six mentioned by name are major representatives of the period of the judges and of the early monarchy. To these are added as a group *the prophets*. All these together span the biblical history of Israel. It is worth noting that the judges are not mentioned in order of time, but in order of importance. For *Gideon, cf.* Judges 6-8; for *Barak*, Judges 4-5; for *Samson*, Judges 13-14; and *Jephthah*, Judges 11-12. The space devoted to the story of *Samuel* and *David* in the Old Testament is a measure of their greater significance in Israel's history. The special mention of them here may be because Samuel serves as the link between the judges and the monarchy, while David is the most outstanding representative of the latter.

**33-34.** In these verses nine statements are made describing the achievements of faith. These are arranged in three groups of three. In each group there is a common feature to link them together. The first group marks attainments – the conquering of *kingdoms*, the establishment of *justice*, the inheriting of spiritual *promises*. This was true to a marked degree in the time of David, but all three attainments can be illustrated from various times in Israel's history. The books of Judges and Samuel are full of accounts in which *faith conquered kingdoms*, in the sense that weaker forces, empowered by God in response to faith, overcame the enemies of Israel. They *enforced justice* (*ērgasanto dikaiosynēn*) in the sense of making it the working principle of the society. This idea of righteousness differs from, but is akin to, the righteousness of which the apostle Paul speaks in a theological sense. It stresses the practice of righteousness, rather than a state of righteousness. Men of faith choose justice and hate injustice, because God himself does the same. Already in this epistle the example of Abraham has been mentioned as one who *received promises* (the same Greek words, *epetuchen epangelias*, are used in 6:15). Abraham was the supreme example, and yet he was the first in a long line of spiritual heirs.

The second triplet is concerned with specific kinds of endurance and deliverance. They *stopped the mouths of lions*, a clear allusion to Daniel's exploits (Dn. 6) and perhaps also to those of Samson (Jdg. 14:6) and David (1 Sa. 17:34f.). In the case of Daniel it was God who stopped their mouths, but Daniel's own faith is prominent in the story. The slaying of lions by both Samson and David are examples of courage, which was fortified by faith. The reference in the next statement – they *quenched raging fire* – is presumably a reference to the ordeal of the three Hebrews in Daniel 3. Again what God was instrumental in doing is attributed to the faith of the men who were miraculously delivered. The third hazard from which deliverance came is described as *the edge of the sword*, which sums up a wide range of violent action. The phrase is a familiar one in the Old Testament.

The third triplet turns away from marvellous deliverances to mention more positive achievements. They *won strength out of weakness*. This at first sounds paradoxical but some instances can be recalled, as for example the case of Hezekiah (Is. 38), or perhaps more vividly the tragic case of Samson. His last desperate act was viewed as an act of faith. A New Testament example may be seen in the revelation to the apostle Paul that his strength matures in weakness (2 Cor. 12:9). Paradoxically, the next feature is that they *became mighty in war*. The idea of *strength* here is an extension of the idea of strength gained from weakness, but in the specific area of battle. Again this feature is vividly illustrated from David's time. An extension of this is seen in the statement that they *put foreign armies to flight*. Clearly in looking back on Israel's past history, the writer of this epistle sees its military exploits as an integral part of its faith in God, although the Old Testament does not always concern itself with this element of faith. To him all the heroes of the past illustrate in some way dependence upon God, and this is interpreted in terms of faith.

**35.** There follows in the next three verses a series of examples of remarkable feats of endurance. The first statement, however, stands on its own – *Women received their dead by resurrection* – as perhaps the most outstanding evidence of the power of faith. Two such instances are recorded in the Old Testament. Elijah raised the widow's son (1 Ki. 17:17ff.) and Elisha raised the Shunammite's son (2 Ki. 4:18ff.). In neither case, however, was the faith exercised by the women but by the prophets. It is worth noting that women were in some way implicated in all the New Testament cases of raisings from the dead (the widow's son at Nain, the daughter of Jairus and Lazarus the brother of Mary and Martha of Bethany). The words *by resurrection* (*ex anastaseōs*) mean literally 'out of resurrection', as if resurrection was the sphere from which the dead emerged to life.

The catalogue of feats of endurance points to the indomitable character of the human spirit faced with incredible odds. It requires an inner source of strength which comes only to men of faith. First, *Some were tortured*, which draws vivid attention to man's inhumanity to man. It is not yet outdated, for torture as a means of pressurizing people into a common mould is still relished in totalitarian political systems. The primary reference here is generally held to be the slaughter of the seven brethren in the Maccabean period (2 Macc. 6:18ff.). There is some dispute about the precise meaning of the verb *were tortured* (*etympanisthēsan*). It may have denoted beatings with clubs or scourgings.[1] The extreme sufferings of many Jews in the intertestamental period were presumably well known to the readers of this epistle. In the case of the Maccabean martyrs they refused *to accept release*, although they were given the opportunity on the condition that they were prepared to forgo their principles. These martyrs pinned their hopes on bodily resurrection and declared that their persecutors had put themselves outside such a hope (2 Macc. 7:9ff.). The *better life* which they chose was regarded as better in contrast to a continued earthly existence which denied them the right to their convictions.

**36.** The sufferings of others who became models of endurance are now brought into focus. *Mocking, scourging, chains* and *imprisonment* are characteristic of the hardships to which many have been subjected both in the times of Israel's history and during the development of the Christian church. Jeremiah may be cited from the Old Testament and Paul from the New Testament. The readers of this epistle would no doubt have known some of their own contemporaries about whom the description

---

[1] The Greek verb *tympanizō* used here means to beat as a drum and it is probable that the reference is to the torture inflicted on Eleazar who was probably stretched on a drum to be beaten to death (2 Macc. 6:18–30). *Cf.* F. Rendall, *Comm.*, p. 118.

would be relevant. But the writer is confining himself at this point to Israel's history.

**37.** Another list of hardships of an even more acute kind is next enumerated. Death by stoning was a well-established method of execution (*cf.* the case of Achan in early Jewish history). The words *they were sawn in two* are considered to be an allusion to the tradition of Isaiah's death as recorded by both Justin and Origen. The apocryphal book *The Ascension of Isaiah* relates the death of Isaiah in this way. Death at the edge of *the sword* was also common in those times (*cf.* 1 Ki. 19:10). Some texts insert between the first and second statements another, 'they were tempted' (*epeirasthēsan*), but this seems so unexpected in the context that it is best omitted. It looks like a modified duplication of the preceding verb 'they were sawn in two' (*epristhēsan*).

In addition to violent death, there were cases of prolonged hardship of which four samples are given. They were outcasts of society, living a primitive existence with only *skins* for clothing, *destitute*, deprived even of the necessities of life, *afflicted* and *ill-treated*. The skin clothing recalls the dress of Elijah who undoubtedly acted as a model for John the Baptist's similar attire.

**38.** The exclamation *of whom the world was not worthy* is an interjection at this point, as if the writer was suddenly conscious of the spiritual stature of the men being described. By comparison the men of the world, in spite of their possessions and status, are so inferior that the men of faith are not worthy to be compared with them. It has always been true that the world has failed to appreciate the value of some of its noblest sons. But there has been some dispute over the meaning of the word translated *worthy* (*axios*). It has been argued that if it is understood as 'worthy', the statement is almost a truism, and that it is better to understand it as meaning hospitable.[1] But the idea that the world offered no hospitality to the formidable list of persecuted people is as much a truism as the alternative.

*Deserts, mountains, dens* and *caves* are all places of solitude, as if the attitude of society was to banish these men of faith. The

---

[1] Héring, pp. 108f., favours the suggestion that *axios* is an inaccurate rendering of the Aramaic *zākāh*, which means 'hospitable' or 'worthy'.

denial of fellowship with others can often be a hardship difficult to bear. For illustrations of these hardships, we may note the reference to a hundred prophets hidden in a cave (1 Ki. 18:4), and to the prophet Elijah hidden in a cave (1 Ki. 19:9).

**39-40.** The account of the triumphs and trials of faith is now drawn to a conclusion by a statement that there were better things to follow. The promise was not yet fulfilled, because fulfilment was not possible until the coming of Christ. Indeed the promise was synonymous with that coming. Even so the writer does not want to leave these heroes of the past without again testifying to their faith. He comments that they were *well attested by their faith.*

In explaining the relation between the Old Testament saints and the Christian church, the writer goes back to the plan of God. He uses the word which is translated *foreseen* (*problepsamenou*), which draws attention to God's overall view of his mission for man's salvation. The thought reaches ahead to the time of consummation when the sum total of God's people will be complete. It is for this reason that the Old Testament worthies could not as yet receive the promise. *Something better for us* undoubtedly refers to the superiority of the Christian revelation which provides for the development of a faith to match its object. The *better* theme has occurred so many times in the epistle that its presence here is only to be expected. It may be that the writer has in mind some who had exalted the heroes of Jewish history to such an extent that they had forgotten their imperfections and their need to be complemented by believers in Christ.

The key is to be found in the word *made perfect* (*teleiōthōsin*), another familiar idea in this epistle. Here however it is used in a corporate sense with the idea of completeness. No part of the true Christian community can be complete without the rest. There is a strong element of solidarity behind this idea (*cf.* the reference to the 'assembly of the first-born' in 12:23), which is also evident in some of the New Testament metaphors for the church, like body or building.

The first two verses of chapter 12 proceed to give an ethical exhortation on the basis of the heroes of the past, which then leads into a section of a more practical nature to conclude the epistle, with nonetheless many theological asides.

## C. DISCIPLINE AND ITS BENEFITS (12:1–29)

Next the readers are exhorted to look to the example of Christ and this leads straight into a discussion on discipline. The writer shows that this is essential for the Christian life and he puts in a strong plea to his readers to avoid moral inconsistency, appealing to the case of Esau to illustrate the point. He again stresses the great advantage of the New Covenant over the Old.

### (i) The need for discipline (12:1–11)

**1.** Although the first two verses are a continuation of the preceding chapter, they bring out in a more direct way the difference between the old order and the new. The heroes of the past are now viewed as spectators, whereas the Christians are in the arena. The focus shifts to the present, but the value of the examples of the past is incorporated into the total picture.

We note that the writer identifies himself with those in the arena, which clearly shows that he is describing the position of Christians generally. When he says *we are surrounded by so great a cloud of witnesses*, he assumes that Christians are aware of the presence of these spectators. The word used here for witness (*martys*) does not usually denote 'spectator', and yet the use of the imagery here presupposes such a meaning.[1] Nevertheless the word which the writer has chosen tells us something about the character of the spectators. They are to be distinguished from the fickle approach of those whose only desire is to be entertained.

These witnesses who watch from the stands are those well qualified to inspire – they bear witness to the faithfulness of God in sustaining them. They are there as encouragers to the present contestants. It may be wondered why the writer chooses the figure of a *cloud*. It is intended to convey the idea of a massive body of people, and may have been suggested by the idea of the verb *surrounded* (*perikeimenon*), which perhaps conjured up the picture of people being enwrapped in a cloud.

---

[1] *Cf.* T. W. Manson's article, 'Martyrs and Martyrdom', *BJRL* 39 (1956–57), pp. 463ff., for the connection in OT days between witness and martyrdom.

Nevertheless it must be admitted that the idea seems somewhat foreign to the arena imagery, unless the view (suggested for instance by Chrysostom) be held that the cloud would offer protection to the contestants from the intense heat. But this is perhaps straining the analogy too far. Since a 'cloud' of witnesses is a good classical locution for a 'host', the metaphor should not be pressed.[1]

The writer next turns his attention to the preparation necessary before the contestants begin the race. The imagery is drawn from the rigorous approach of Greek athletes to training. Nothing which adds weight is retained; all but the bare essentials must be laid aside. As the writer goes on to give a spiritual interpretation of possible encumbrances by referring to *sin which clings so closely*, there can be no doubt that the *weight* (*onkon*, found only here in the New Testament) is also intended to be applied metaphorically of any affairs which would impede a Christian convert in his new faith. The nature of the clinging sin is not defined, so as to have the widest possible application. The word translated *clings* (*euperistaton*) occurs here only in the New Testament and is of uncertain meaning. Moulton[2] lists four possibilities: (i) easily avoided, (ii) admired, (iii) easily surrounding, *i.e.* besetting, (iv) dangerous (from the sense, 'having easy distress'). The RSV approximates to the third. Whatever the precise meaning it is evident that the writer regards sin as a major impediment in the spiritual race. It must not be supposed that any particular sin – a besetting sin – is in mind. It is rather sin itself which is the hindrance.

The exhortation *let us run with perseverance* is the positive side to the shedding of unnecessary burdens. It is this positive side which carries the emphasis in the Greek. It is an action which requires effort. No athlete can expect to win without determination. The word used implies the idea of endurance, a pressing on to the end in spite of the difficulties. The same Greek word is used in 10:36. The idea recurs again in the present chapter in verse 3 and in the whole concept of submitting to discipline. Moreover, the word for *race* used here (*agōna*) is a word which denotes 'conflict'. It is used several times by Paul. In Philippians

[1] *Cf.* Bruce, *Comm.*, p. 346.
[2] J. H. Moulton, *Grammar of New Testament Greek* 2, p. 282.

1:30 it refers to his suffering; in Colossians 2:1 to his strivings on behalf of the Colossians; in 1 Thessalonians 2:2 to the opposition he encountered in the preaching of the gospel and in 1 Timothy 6:12 and 2 Timothy 4:7 to the fight of faith. It will be seen, therefore, that the race involved here was a stern test of endurance. It must be noted too that contestants cannot choose their own race, for the race is *set before us*, *i.e.* by God himself. It is on his programme.

2. Another unusual word is the verb translated *looking to Jesus* (*aphorōntes eis*) which implies a definite looking away from others and directing one's gaze towards Jesus. It suggests the impossibility of looking in two directions at once. In any contest a single eye for the finishing-post is essential and the writer turns this thought into a means of focusing on Jesus himself. Indeed the ethical injunction merges into a doctrinal statement. It is not without point that the name chosen here is *Jesus*, thus emphasizing his humanity (as in chapter 2). A target must be knowable and the writer is exhorting his readers to fix their gaze on the most perfect example of manhood.

The further descriptions, *pioneer* (*archēgon*) and *finisher* (*teleiōtēn*), are highly suggestive. Together they span the whole range of the activities of Jesus in relation to our faith. While the word *archēgos* can have the meaning 'founder' (so MM) in the sense of 'author', it may also have the sense of 'leader' (*cf*. the comment on 2:10). It may be thought that Jesus was not the pioneer of faith for those mentioned in chapter 11 since he was historically after them. But the writer seems to regard Jesus as the one who supplied the inspiration for all the saints of old. The second word occurs in the New Testament only in this passage and does not occur in the Septuagint. It portrays the same thought as in other parts of the epistle where the cognate verb occurs (*teleioō*, used 9 times). The object of these activities of Jesus is described as the *faith* (*tēs pisteōs*), which is an expression used apparently to sum up the whole Christian position. The word 'our', added in the RSV, does not belong to the Greek text, but is a fair interpretation.

The linking of *joy* with suffering in this verse echoes a constant New Testament theme. Indeed on the eve of his passion Jesus spoke of his joy and of his desire that his disciples should share it (Jn. 15:11; 17:13). It is highly probable that the disciples remembered this remarkable fact when they later reflected on the passion of Jesus. The writer here does not consider it necessary to enlarge on the theme of joy, but he attaches some importance to the fact that it was *set before him* which suggests that it took precedence over everything else. There is some correlation between the race set before us and the joy set before Jesus. In both cases the processes of salvation are in the hands of God.

The suffering is focused on the *cross*. The idea of endurance has already been introduced in verse 1, but here we have the supreme example of it. It is reinforced by the accompanying clause, *despising the shame*, an attitude which does not ignore the shame, but holds it to be of no consequence in view of the joy.

The seating of Jesus *at the right hand of the throne of God* echoes the idea expressed in 1:3 and 8:1. The passion is seen as part of the path to the throne. As so often in the New Testament the cross is at once linked with exaltation. It is never seen as an end in itself, for in that case it would suggest a tragedy instead of a triumph.

**3.** A word occurring only here in the New Testament and absent from the Septuagint is used in the opening exhortation in this verse: it is translated *consider him* (*analogisasthe*). In the papyri this word is used in the mathematical sense of 'reckon up' (MM) and clearly implies a careful assessment. The readers are exhorted to weigh up carefully the endurance of Christ when contemplating their own hardships. If the mathematical sense is still present, the idea must be of considering each aspect of the hostility which Christ had to endure against him until a complete picture is obtained. Both here and in verse 2 the readers are turned away from themselves to focus their gaze on Christ.

This writer is fond of using the perfect tense when referring to the achievements of Christ as he does here in the verb *endured* (*hypomemenēkota*). What he has done has an abiding significance. The word for *hostility* (*antilogia*) has the prime sense of hostility in words, which in the case of the enemies of Christ led further to the hostility in action which reached its climax in the shame of the cross.

The purpose of fixing attention on Jesus Christ is *so that you may not grow weary or faint-hearted*. Evidently the writer knew that there was a tendency for his readers to lose heart, not in a single moment but over a period of time, with a gradual slackening of resolve. A corrective for this tendency is an ever deepening attention to the glorious object of Christian faith, Jesus himself.

**4.** Christians have a *struggle against sin*. This does not exclude the constant inner conflicts, but the emphasis is clearly on those antagonistic to the Christian faith. Those responsible for such sin are personified as sin itself. Although the struggle has already been intense (the verb is *antagōnizō*), yet the resistance has not yet been *to the point of shedding your blood*. The Greek here is not so specific (*mechris haimatos*), for the words could refer to martyrdom or could be understood metaphorically in the sense of 'uttermost'. The former seems preferable here, since the statement seems to contrast with verse 3, where the hostility which Christ endured had been 'unto blood'. Probably the thought of the writer is still influenced by his arena imagery in verse 1.

**5.** At this point another rhetorical question is introduced, *have you forgotten?* He seems to have feared that some of his readers had forgotten the point of the scripture which he proceeds to quote from Proverbs 3:11–12, for after quoting it he gives a full discussion of its main theme. In describing the scripture as *exhortation* (*paraklēsis*) he may have intended to suggest that scripture can also be an encouragement, for the word used has both meanings. The scripture itself is personified as if it could personally address the readers. The 'son' of Proverbs is automatically applied to the Christians (*you as sons*) who will receive the letter. It is one of the remarkable characteristics of Scripture that it is timeless in its application.

The exhortation not to treat discipline lightly is constantly needed since men have an inborn dislike of discipline and never more so than today. It is all too easy to regard it *lightly* (*oligōrei*, to belittle or treat as insignificant). This is all the more evident when it is *the discipline of the Lord*. To many the concept is a contradiction, since they have so poor an understanding of the character of God. This whole chapter is bent on rectifying this.

It is because men do not naturally recognize the need for discipline that they *lose courage* when *punished*. They cannot see the long-term benefits, nor the concern of God over them.

**6.** The linking of discipline with love is difficult to grasp, but is basic to a right understanding of the Lord's dealings with his people. Chastisement that springs from love cannot be vindictive, but must always be beneficial. Especially is this so in true father-son relationships. The Old Testament passage is setting out a profound view of love, a love which does not hesitate to correct. The expression *every son whom he receives* shows how basic the idea of chastisement is for the development of the best relationships. Indeed chastisement becomes synonymous with sonship, as the next verse shows.

**7.** The writer seizes on the word *discipline* from the Old Testament text in order to apply it specifically to the readers. Moreover he uses the verb to *endure* (*hypomenō*) which he has already applied to Christ in verse 3. The same patient acceptance is expected of all the *sons* as is seen in the Son *par excellence*. Such acceptance is possible only where an understanding of the motive behind the discipline is fully grasped. The principle laid down here is that the relationship determines the purpose of the discipline. A *father* who neglects to discipline a *son* is deficient in his capacity as father, and a son who escapes all discipline is losing out on his sonship. This is a principle which would not be recognized by all schools of thought in this modern age where permissiveness has such powerful influence. The authority of parents has been so eroded that discipline rarely if ever comes into play. It has generally ceased to be a part of sonship. It is small wonder that those brought up in such an atmosphere find genuine difficulty in understanding the discipline of God. There would have been less difficulty in appreciating the point among the first readers of this epistle.

**8.** The same point is even more strongly driven home in this verse, for it is assumed that all true sons submit to discipline and those who do not *ipso facto* have no claim to be called sons. They are in fact *illegitimate*. There could be no more vivid contrast with the true sons. The father does not give the illegitimate son the same rights and privileges, neither does he bother to discipline him. The absence of discipline, therefore, reflects on the status of the person. True sonship involves responsibilities, for which each person must be prepared by discipline.

**9.** At this point the writer makes a comparison between earthly and heavenly discipline. He is introducing a further point (as seen in the words *besides this, eita*), which centres on the respect which earthly fathers gain from their sons when they discipline them. It is an important point. Sons have greater regard for fathers who use their authority in a right way to guide and train them. They despise those who are so spineless that they never cross them. There is no doubt that the secret for recovering respect for authority is to be found in the home. Parental authority is indeed a microcosm of authority in society and where one breaks down the other must suffer. The writer uses the analogy to illustrate a higher spiritual principle.

The title *Father of spirits* is intended to contrast with the human analogy. This unusual title (here only in the New Testament) is more expressive than 'heavenly' as against earthly, for in drawing attention to the spiritual nature of God the author shows how it affects our view of discipline. As our earthly existence was mediated through an earthly father, so our spiritual existence is through the agency of a spiritual father (*i.e.* God). He is the father of our spiritual life. When elevated to a spiritual plane, discipline becomes an essential feature of true life. We begin to *live* only when we accept the fact that, in a spiritual sense, God is our Father. This thought is expressed in the epistle, as a rhetorical question, which assumes that the answer is axiomatic. Indeed all scripture bears testimony to the disciplinary activity of God. This is a classic case of an argument from the lesser to the greater.

**10.** Another contrast is made between the different kinds of discipline exerted by human fathers and by God. The former kind is brief in duration (*for a short time*) and for an inferior motive (*at their pleasure*). However high the principles on which an earthly father acts he is not infallible. He is governed by his own pleasure which may at times be unwise or even against the best interests of the son. By contrast God's knowledge of us is perfect and what he does is *for our good*, for he understands what discipline is needed. He will never overdo it, nor will he neglect it. He wants to make his sons like himself. He has a specific aim that they *may share his holiness*. While the earthly father's action is essentially short-term, the heavenly father is concerned with our eternal welfare. Sharing his holiness is the antithesis of a short-term benefit. Incidentally, the only other occurrence of the word *holiness* (*hagiotēs*) in the New Testament is in 2 Corinthians 1:12, where Paul uses it of the behaviour of himself and his companions.

**11.** All would agree to the painful character of discipline. It is axiomatic. At least, that is how it appears *for the moment*. It is difficult to appreciate the purpose of disciplinary action at the point of impact. The idea of being *pleasant* seems utterly alien. But *later* things fall into place. The real purpose becomes clearer. What seemed painful is still recognized as such, but is tempered by the effectiveness of the result. The imagery is drawn from the field of horticulture where an accepted principle is that the discipline of pruning produces greater fruitfulness. In applying the metaphor the writer thinks of *the peaceful fruit of righteousness*. The combination of peace and righteousness is natural, for no true peace can exist without righteousness. It comes out of it. When a man gets right with God his heart has peace. A similar idea occurs in Romans 5:1 where peace follows from justification by faith. Undoubtedly *righteousness* (*dikaiosynē*) as used here must be interpreted in the light of the 'holiness' referred to in verse 10. The genitive can be understood either in the sense of 'consisting of righteousness', in which case the righteousness becomes identified as the fruit; or in the sense of 'belonging to' righteousness, in which case the fruit results from the righteousness. The latter seems to fit the context better. It is noticeable that by putting the word *righteousness* at the end of the sentence the writer intends to place considerable emphasis upon it.

*Those who have been trained by it* are those who have submitted to discipline. Since the verb used here (*gymnazō*) is one frequently used for athletic training, there is probably an overtone from the metaphor of the arena with which the chapter begins. It is not, however, entirely out of place here to speak of training in connection with the horticultural metaphor, since the pruning of plants may be described as a 'training' process. Nevertheless the writer brings his imagery to more personal terms, since this is the context in which he speaks of discipline.

*(ii) The avoidance of moral inconsistency (12:12–17)*

**12.** In view of the general statements regarding discipline which have just been made, the writer addresses a direct exhortation to his readers. The introductory *therefore* (*dio*) shows the dependence of this exhortation on the previous discussion. It is couched in Old Testament language, the first part coming from Isaiah 35:3 and the second part (verse 13) from the Septuagint of Proverbs 4:26. It is probable that this section continues the athletic figure of speech.[1] The words here are vivid with encouragement. *Drooping hands* and *weak knees* are typical of low spirits. They portray persons who have become incapable of action through sheer exhaustion. The RSV takes the exhortation as addressed to the readers to *lift* their own hands and *strengthen* their own knees, but the Greek text could be understood in the sense that others were encouraged to help strengthen their brethren. While the latter is possible, no-one who does not exert effort to revive himself has any hope of reviving others.

**13.** The idea of *straight paths* introduces a different thought. It is no use the weak knees being strengthened to walk on devious paths. The straightness links with the righteousness idea of verse 11. Since natural paths are mostly winding, avoiding rather than confronting the difficulties, a straight path is a path which has been specially prepared with some effort (*cf.* the imagery of Isaiah 40:3ff.). Boulders and stumbling-blocks must be resolutely removed. A straight clear road is a blessing for those who are lame, no less in the spiritual sense than in the physical. The idea seems to be that the readers must accept the beneficial effects of any discipline they may at present be enduring and therefore pull themselves together and see to it that they make progress. Those in a weak state should concentrate on healing and not dislocation (*ektrapē*). The picture of a *lame* man putting his disabled leg completely *out of joint* because of the unnecessary roughness of the path vividly brings home the seriousness of ignoring spiritual and moral weakness. The aim must be healing rather than injury.

**14.** Some indication of what the writer means by 'straight paths' is now given. First, Christians must strive for *peace with*

[1] *Cf.* Bruce, *Comm.*, p. 363.

*all men*. There is a direct parallel in Romans 12:18 which is equally comprehensive. But that this does not mean peace at any price is clear from its close link with the pursuit of holiness. Peace with all men is possible only within the limits of what is right. There are in fact times when standing for just causes brings intense antagonism and peace is inevitably shattered. But the meaning must be that every effort must be made to maintain peace if at all possible. The word *strive* (*diōkete*) is a strong word, expressing something of the eagerness of pursuit. The idea of tracking down peace is echoed from Psalm 34:14, where it is linked with a conscious departing from evil.

The second object of pursuit, *holiness*, is taken up from verse 10, but the qualifying clause – *without which no one will see the Lord* – explains why this essentially spiritual quest is indispensable. This is really a fuller statement of the reason why God desires us to share his holiness. It amounts to raising us to the same level as himself. Absolute purity cannot but abhor impurity. The 'seeing' of God could be understood in a spiritual sense of communicating with him, but there is the further sense in which a fuller prospect is in mind than is now possible (*cf.* 1 Jn. 3:2 which points to the coming again of Christ). The future tense (*opsetai*) looks forward to an event as yet unfulfilled.

**15.** The word translated *see to it* (*episkopeō*) is common in the papyri in the closing greetings in letters (MM). It literally means 'to exercise oversight', and may be used in some kind of official capacity. Some of the readers should have been in a position to exercise such a function as 5:12 implies. The matter to be attended to is of utmost spiritual importance: to see that *no one fail to obtain the grace of God*. It is noticeable that it is the present tense which is here used (*hysterōn* has the force, 'continuing to fail'). *The grace of God* stands here for all the benefits which God in his grace has provided. Much failure among Christians is due to a lack of appropriation of those benefits. A specific example is here quoted – as when a *root of bitterness* causes trouble. The words are taken from Deuteronomy 29:17f., but are here applied in a general sense of anyone or anything which results in bitterness, as the root of a plant affects the fruits which the plant produces. The springing up of the root picturesquely describes the development and therefore multiplication of bitterness. The writer links bitterness with defilement here (*and by it the many become defiled*), since bitterness, wherever it exists, extends its influence. Bitterness indeed always corrupts and spoils. The same word (*mianthōsin, become defiled*) is used in Titus 1:15 in describing unbelievers whose minds and consciences are said to be corrupt.

**16.** The bad effects of the kind of 'bitterness' which the writer has in mind are further defined as *immoral* (*pornos*) and *irreligious* (*bebēlos*). The words *like Esau* could refer to both of these expressions or only to the latter. There is no evidence from the Old Testament that Esau acted immorally (*cf.* Gn. 25:33f.), although he could be described as irreligious. The selling of the *birthright* was against his religious heritage, but cannot be described as immoral. Nevertheless Philo in commenting on Esau regarded him as a man of vice (*e.g. Legum Allegoriae* 3.2), such was the widely held opinion of him. Although omitted from the heroes of faith in chapter 11 Esau finds an unenviable mention here. His foolishness in exchanging his privilege as the eldest son *for a single meal* is so glaring that he has become a type of all who put material or sensual advantages before their spiritual heritage. The word for 'irreligious' (*bebēlos*) occurs also in the Pastoral Epistles (*cf.* 1 Tim. 1:9; 4:7; 6:20 and 2 Tim. 2:16), where godlessness is one of the characteristics of the false teachers.

**17.** The writer appeals to his readers' knowledge of the Esau story (*for you know*). It would be familiar to those with knowledge of the Old Testament that Esau could not reverse what he had done in frittering away his birthright. The reference to the *blessing* is an allusion to the account in Genesis 27 where Isaac was tricked into giving his patriarchal blessing to Jacob and yet recognized that it could not be reversed even when he discovered his mistake. What impressed the writer of this epistle is the sheer futility of Esau's *tears*. The words *he found no chance to repent* could more literally be rendered 'he did not find a place (*topos*) of repentance', which could bear the meaning that there was no opportunity for him to change his circumstances. In this sense no chance to repent remained, but it is a New Testament principle that an opportunity for spiritual repentance is possible wherever there is a spiritual desire. It is in this sense that the gospel can be said to be based on a call to repentance. It may be wondered what possessed the writer to bring in the tragic history of Esau at this point of his discussion and the answer must be that Esau was regarded as one of the most striking examples of those who failed to appropriate 'the grace of God'. The solemn note which this introduces is developed further in the next passage.

### (iii) The benefits of the new covenant (12:18–29)

**18.** The section 18–24 compares the awesomeness of the giving of the law with the majesty of the new covenant. Again a considerable knowledge of the Old Testament background is assumed. A reference to *what may be touched* conjures up the scene at the giving of the law (Ex. 19:12–22; 20:18–21). In fact the Israelites and even their animals were forbidden to touch the holy mount (*cf.* verse 20). The whole emphasis was on a sensual approach to majesty. The description is of the physical accompaniments: *fire, darkness, tempest, trumpet* sound. The giving of the law came in a way that could be appreciated through the senses of touch, sight and sound. The whole scene is dramatically called to mind without so much as a reference to Mount Sinai itself. The awesome nature of the event speaks for itself. The details come from Deuteronomy 4 and 5 and Exodus 19 and 20.

**19.** In the account of the giving of the law in Exodus 19, the *trumpet* sound increased in intensity as the presence of God became more recognized and the sense of awe correspondingly increased. The trumpet *sound* (*ēchō*) became a familiar feature of apocalyptic imagery (*cf.* Mt. 24:31; 1 Thes. 4:16 and the seven trumpets of the apocalypse of John). It is intended to convey an authoritative command which cannot be ignored. The *voice* of *words* (*phōnē rhēmatōn*) was equally terrifying. According to Exodus 19:19, God answered Moses in thunder. It was as if the importance of the whole act of communication had to be given the utmost impressiveness. There was no direct message from God to the people, except through Moses, but even those communications which were intelligible filled the hearts with dread. The request that *no further messages be spoken to them* is striking in view of the impressive revelation of God and his evident desire to make provision for them. There were, of course, conditions, the most striking of which was the need for a due sense of awe, and it was this that troubled the people, as the next verse shows.

**20.** The writer singles out the feature which must have impressed the Israelites the most, the exclusiveness of Moses' communication with God. It was a vivid reminder of their unworthiness that they were not allowed to go anywhere near the mount, nor were their beasts (*cf.* Ex. 19:12–13). The fact that *they could not endure the order that was given* suggests that they were totally overawed by the glory of the occasion. It is not surprising, since even Moses himself is said to have trembled. Throughout the era of law, separateness had been a feature of God's dealing with his people, as the holy of holies showed. This build-up of awesomeness was calculated to set out in greater relief the approachableness of God under the gospel, as verses 22–24 show.

**21.** It was not only the people, but Moses himself who was terrified. The special impact on Moses is described as *the sight* (*to phantazomenon*), a word comprehensive enough to include the special revelation to him which the people did not see. If the Israelites, kept at a distance even at the foot of the mountain, were overawed, it is no wonder that Moses trembled as he advanced in face of the awe-inspiring demonstrations of natural phenomena to the place of receiving the tablets of the law. There is no specific Old Testament record of Moses saying, *I tremble with fear* on the occasion of the giving of the law, but the occurrence of trembling in the circumstances is not difficult to imagine. The nearest statement is Deuteronomy 9:19, which records Moses' recollection of fear. Moreover, there is reference to his fear at the burning bush (Ex. 3:6), a fact which Stephen notes in Acts 7:32. This dread on the part of Moses abruptly ends the writer's comment on the old order. His interest is centred in the new order.

**22.** It is surprising that *the heavenly Jerusalem* should be set over against the giving of the law, but the intention seems to be to stress the superiority of the spiritual approach available to Christians. Gone is the sense of dread and separation. There is a poetic quality about the style in the following full statement of the Christian position. The Greek contains no articles until the last word in verse 24 (*Abel*). This gives the statement a remarkably concise quality. In fact there is an almost liturgical structure about the sequence of clauses.[1]

Whereas the mount where Moses met with God is not mentioned by name, the mount where Christians meet with him is specifically named as *Mount Zion*, which heightens the superiority of the latter over the former. Moreover, to prevent any misunderstanding, it is described as *the city of the living God* in addition to *the heavenly Jerusalem*. The absence of awe-inspiring demonstrations is heightened by the holding of a *festal gathering*. A stronger contrast is hardly conceivable. Like the peace after the storm is the calmer picture of the dwelling-place of God and of his people. The heavenly Jerusalem seems to foreshadow the idea of the new Jerusalem in Revelation 21 (*cf*. also 3:12), the perfect abode of the people of God. There may be significance in the linking of the *Mount* with *the city*, a not unfamiliar combination in ancient times, especially in the Greek environment, when the city centre (or 'agora') was dominated by the near-by mount (on which stood the acropolis). In the writer's mind both are spiritually conceived. Mount Zion became symbolic of the true worship of God and Jerusalem became symbolic of the true community.

The *innumerable angels* to whom reference is made populate the scene and show God surrounded by his servants. This is what impresses most in this scene. God is no longer non-approachable or awe-inspiring. He dwells among a worshipping society. The reference to angels is particularly relevant in view of the discussion in chapters 1 and 2 on their relationship to Christ. These angels are the 'ministering spirits' sent out to serve. There is some dispute whether the word for *festal gathering* (*panēgyris*) should be restricted to the angels (as in RSV), or whether it refers to a joint gathering of angels and believers. The former is the more probable and is perhaps intended to offset any thought that the angels were angels of judgment (as in the apocalypse). Another possibility is to regard the word *angels* as isolated and to link the festal gathering to the 'assem-

---

[1] P. Carrington, *The Primitive Christian Calendar* (Cambridge, 1952), p. 56, n. 5, suggests that this statement is reminiscent of the 'Shofaroth' of Tishri 1, which is the Day of Trumpets. He suggests the whole letter may have been a *megillah* for the Day of Atonement.

bly'. It seems best, however, to treat the two groups separately.

**23.** The word translated *assembly* (*ekklēsia*) is elsewhere rendered as 'church', and some association with this more normal meaning must be intended here. The only other use of the word in this epistle is in 2:12 where it occurs in an Old Testament (Septuagint) quotation and is rendered 'congregation'. First, the company in mind are described as *the first-born* (*prōtotokoi*). There is here a marked distinction between the church and the patriarchal age when the first-born was restricted to one for each household (*cf.* Esau in verse 16). In the Christian church all the heirs are placed on the same footing. Such a company is not only especially distinctive, but unparalleled. We should note that for Paul there is only one *prōtotokos*, *i.e.* Christ (Col. 1:15). There is some connection with the thought here, if the *prōtotokoi* are those reborn through Christ.[1] Their names are *enrolled in heaven*, showing them to be officially accepted members of the heavenly Jerusalem. The same idea of enrolment in the book of life is found in Luke 10:20 and in Revelation 21:27.

In the second part of the verse the focus switches to the theme of judgment and deals with it from the point of view of those already dead and of those still alive. The *judge* is identified as *God of all*, which highlights the fact that his judgment will be in conformity with that revelation of his nature, *i.e.* the one who knows all things, whose judgment is therefore universal. It should be noted that God is not to be regarded here exclusively as a judge who condemns but rather as one who examines and discriminates.

The use of the word *spirits* is suggestive because the writer has earlier in the chapter described God as the Father of spirits (verse 9). Moreover the angels are described as 'ministering spirits' in 1:7 (from Ps. 104:4). Clearly the expression is being used in the sense of spiritual beings. In the present case, however, they are distinguished from angels by the description *just men made perfect*. The phrase 'just men' describes what they have come to be and does not indicate the grounds of their perfection. They have become *just* by virtue of what Christ has done for them. The word *perfect* should be understood in the

[1] *Cf.* Héring, *Comm.*, p. 117, n. 15.

sense of completed; all that God designed for these people is now fulfilled. It has been suggested that the 'just men made perfect' are the pre-Christian saints mentioned in 11:40.[1] But there is no indication in this context that requires this interpretation. Another suggestion is that the 'enrolled' are the elect under the old covenant and the 'just made perfect' are the Christian martyrs (cf. Rev. 6:9). Nevertheless, Jesus spoke of his followers' names 'enrolled in heaven' (Lk. 10:20); so this reference seems to include all believers.[2] The one who carries out the perfecting of his people has already been identified as Jesus in verse 2.

**24.** The focus changes yet again; this time it concentrates on *Jesus* as *mediator*, since it is through him that the process of perfection has been possible. The writer in a few words here sums up his main message. He has already in chapter 8 and in 9:15 set out the mediatorship of Christ and has contrasted the old covenant with the new. Here only is the covenant described as *new* (*neas*) in the sense of 'recent' instead of new in the sense of character (*kainē*), as in 8:8, 13 (from LXX) and 9:15.

*The sprinkled blood* sums up the sacrificial act of Jesus. It recalls the sprinkled blood which ratified the old covenant (*cf.* 9:19), and at once establishes the superiority of Christ's offering. It has a voice, which speaks in totally different style from the voice at Sinai. The blood speaks of deeper things than itself, for it proclaims a new way of approach to God. The RSV describes the voice as speaking *more graciously* than Abel's blood, but the word used (*kreitton*) is the theme song of this epistle, *i.e.* 'better'. Already Abel's sacrifice has been mentioned in 11:4, where he is said to be still speaking through his faith. It may be noted that the phrase *the blood of Abel* is not represented in the Greek text, which simply has 'than Abel' (*para ton Abel*). It is more natural, however, to suppose that it is the 'blood' of Abel that is being compared with the blood of Jesus.

**25.** At this point the discussion leads into a concluding section which ends with an impressive statement about God (verse 29). A direct warning is given to the readers – *See that you do not refuse him who is speaking* – in terms which show that the writer

---

[1] *Cf.* Bruce, *Comm.*, p. 378.   [2] *Cf.* Héring, *Comm.*, p. 117.

has still in mind the attitude of the Israelites (*cf.* Ex. 20:19). The same verb here translated *refuse* (*paraitēsēsthe*) is translated in verse 19 as 'entreat' and must, therefore, be understood against the background of the giving of the law. The speaker referred to in this context is God, but there is an interesting point of parallel with the 'blood that speaks' in the previous verse.

There is a direct contrast between the voice *on earth* and the warning *from heaven*. Nevertheless, although the location is different it is the same voice. The difference lies in the greater responsibility which falls on those who receive the heavenly warning. The Israelites did not *escape*. The writer returns to the idea of escape which he has introduced earlier in the epistle (2:3). The consequences of lack of faith on the part of the readers would be no less than they were for the Israelites. The warning from heaven is linked with the whole Christian revelation centred in the mediatorial work of Christ. This is another instance of a powerful argument based on a transference of thought from the lesser to the greater. It throws considerable light on the relevance of historical example.

**26.** Remembering the physical accompaniments of the giving of the law, the writer dwells on the theme of the instability of the old and the stability of the new covenant. The shaking of the earth is thus applied metaphorically. The earthquake at Mount Sinai was an impressive reminder of the majesty of God and of the instability of the earth (*cf.* Ex. 19:18). It is not surprising, therefore, that earthquakes became a familiar feature of apocalyptic thought (*cf.* Mt. 24:29).

The words *but now* (*nyn de*) transfer the thought from the age of Sinai to the Christian age. The promise referred to is a quotation from Haggai 2:6. The prophet looks forward to a time when there will be another cataclysm accompanying a revelation of God. The introductory words – *yet once more* (*eti hapax*), which occur in the Septuagint – are seen as significant because they imply some finality in the coming revelation, as verse 27 shows. The inclusion of a heavenly as well as an earthly shaking in the coming disturbance (*I will shake not only the earth but also the heaven*) adds further weight to this sense of finality.

**27.** This verse gives an example of the writer's method of dealing with scriptural interpretation. He clearly attaches considerable importance to the actual words of the text and does not hesitate to draw a specific conclusion from an inference based on the words *yet once more*. The word *indicates* (*dēloi*) is used in 1 Peter 1:11 of the interpretation by the Spirit of the predictions of the sufferings of the Messiah. What has become clear in the understanding of Scripture has been made clear by the Spirit. The writer here assumes rather than specifically states this. By referring to the earth and heaven in the words *as of what has been made*, he wishes to draw attention to their transient quality.

He concludes from the Haggai passage that the promise assures *the removal of what is shaken*, that is to say the establishment of such stability that there will be no room for shakeable things. Clearly what is unshakeable must be eternal, for any possibility of change would lead to instability. It is not possible to be certain what the writer has here in mind, for he does not enlarge on these unshakeable conditions. What he is concerned to demonstrate is that the Christian position, unlike the era of the Mosaic law, leads to a state of absolute stability. There is an echo here of the theme of changelessness found in chapter 1. The imagery of physical changes is often used in Scripture to express spiritual truths and especially in this epistle things which are seen, with all their changeable qualities, are regarded as shadows of greater spiritual realities. The idea expressed here of the instability of the existing world contrasts vividly with the Platonic view of the eternity of the world.

**28-29.** Whatever the precise meaning of the shaking, the focus falls on the *kingdom*, which is to be the embodiment of stability (*that cannot be shaken*), in striking contrast to the transience of what the writer has been describing. The kingdom is here undefined, unlike the occurrences in the Gospels where it is always kingdom of God or kingdom of heaven. Here it is clearly a spiritual kingdom and must be understood in the same sense as Jesus used it. For the mention of it in Paul's epistles, *cf.* Romans 14:17; 1 Corinthians 4:20; 6:9; 15:24, 50; Galatians 5:21; Colossians 1:13; 4:11; 1 Thessalonians 2:12; 2 Thessalonians 1:5; 2 Timothy 4:1.

The writer speaks of the readers as receiving the kingdom. It is on the strength of this that two exhortations are addressed to them: *let us be grateful*[1] and *let us offer worship*. In fact they are inextricably connected for gratitude to God is an ingredient of true worship. The former exhortation could be understood to mean 'let us have grace' in the sense of possessing grace, but this does not fit the context so well. In view of the shakeable character of other things, there is good reason to be thankful when something unchangeable is placed within our grasp. Moreover it should lead us to worship.

There are certain features about worship which are worth noting in this context. First, it must be *acceptable*. Even although fully acceptable worship is difficult, if not impossible, to attain, the writer is convinced that the ideal must be set before his readers. Moreover, the worship must be *with reverence*, an attitude of mind which acknowledges the greatness of God. Linked with this is *awe* (*deous*), which is particularly appropriate in view of the idea of God as a *consuming fire*, echoing the words of Deuteronomy 4:24. This awe-inspiring view of God takes its colouring from the Sinai event. It is a reminder that even the believer in Christ must recognize that the character of God is righteous and that his character will not change. Even although the epistle ends on a softer note (*cf.* 13:20f.), this sense of the awesomeness of God cannot be dispensed with, but should inculcate a true sense of reverence.

## D. CONCLUDING ADVICE (13:1-25)

A series of apparently disconnected exhortations and other incidental teaching is found in this last chapter. The moral advice covers social, private and religious life. The final exhortation is to the readers to make a clear break with Judaism, which is mentioned under the term 'camp'. A magnificent doxology precedes the closing salutation.

---

[1] Since the literal meaning of this expression is 'let us have grace', which is difficult, it is generally supposed that *echōmen* should be taken in the sense 'let us give thanks'. It should be noted that some texts have *echomen* (indicative) which would lessen the problem, but this looks suspiciously like a scribal mistake. The subjunctive must here be the original reading.

*(i) Exhortations affecting social life (13:1–3)*

**1.** This chapter contains a number of somewhat disconnected exhortations, interspersed nevertheless with a few allusions to the main body of the epistle. Some have seen it as a kind of appendix to give the whole treatise something of the flavour of a letter, although even so it is somewhat general, except for verses 23 and 24.[1]

The first exhortation is a familiar New Testament theme. *Brotherly love (philadelphia)* expresses that special mutual regard for one another irrespective of race which is particularly characteristic of Christians. It is a combination of two basic ideas – the exercise of love and the adoption of a new relationship within the household of faith. The fact that the readers are urged to *continue* suggests that there might have been a tendency for them to neglect this basic requirement of mutual understanding. For other New Testament occurrences of the idea of brotherly love, *cf.* Romans 12:10; 1 Thessalonians 4:9; 1 Peter 1:22.

**2.** Another practical matter of considerable importance for Christians is hospitality. In the environment of the early church it was essential, since alternative facilities for travellers were such that Christians would not choose to make use of them. Wayfarers' hostels, where they existed, were notorious for immorality. But the New Testament concept of hospitality has a much wider application than this. In the Middle East, hospital-

---

[1] C. R. Williams, 'A word study of Heb. xiii', *JBL* (1911), pp. 128–136, regarded Heb. 1–12 as a homily, and chapter 13 as an addition by the same author. Many extend the homily idea to 13:21 and regard verses 22–25 as an addition to give the homily the appearance of a Pauline letter (*cf.* W. Wrede, *Das literarische Rätsel des Hebräerbriefs* (Göttingen, 1906), who considers the writer changed his mind and decided to turn the homily into a letter (pp. 39–64). He thought parts of chapter 13 were modelled on Philippians and Philemon. *Cf.* also H. Thyen, *Der Stil der Judisch-Hellenistischen Homilie* (Göttingen, 1955), pp. 16–18, who considers that Hebrews was a sample of Hellenistic synagogue preaching and that 13:22ff. was not original. In his monograph on Heb. 13 entitled *Yesterday* (London, 1967), pp. 16ff., Filson bases his approach to the whole epistle on the grounds that Heb. 13 is an integral part of the whole work. *Cf.* also R. V. G. Tasker, 'The integrity of the Epistle to the Hebrews', *ExT* 47 (1935–6), pp. 136–138, and C. Spicq, 'L'Authenticité de chapitre XIII de l'Épître aux Hébreux', *Coniectanea Neotestamentica* II (1947), pp. 226–236, for special studies which conclude for the unity of the epistle. *Cf.* also C. C. Torrey, 'The Authorship and character of the so-called Epistle to the Hebrews', *JBL* 30 (1911), pp. 137–156, who regards chapter 13 as a later addition. A. Vanhoye, *La Structure Littéraire de l'Épître aux Hébreux* (Paris, 1963), pp. 219–221, who treats the whole epistle as constructed on a chiastic pattern, cannot fit in 13:19 and 13:22–25 and regards these as later additions.

ity is a means of friendship. To invite a person to a meal is to extend fellowship to him. It is against this background that the exhortation, *Do not neglect to show hospitality to strangers (philoxenia)*, must be considered. The same idea occurs in Romans 12:13. It is one of the qualities required in aspirants for the bishop's office (1 Tim. 3:2; Tit. 1:8) and for widows wishing to be enrolled (1 Tim. 5:10). It is enjoined in 1 Peter 4:9. It is not clear from the word used here whether the hospitality was for Christian strangers or non-Christians. The reference to *angels* would favour the former, but the latter is not necessarily entirely excluded. It is clear that something more than the mere entertaining of friends and acquaintances is in mind. It is, in fact, a Christian social service which is envisaged. The readiness with which early Christians were prepared to do this became a source of amazement if not scorn to non-Christian observers.

The reference to some who have *entertained angels unawares* (found only here in the New Testament) seems to be an allusion to the incident recorded in Genesis 18 – 19, in which Abraham offered hospitality to the mysterious visitors, who turned out to be angels. The writer clearly assumes that his readers will know what he means. The principle is that it is better to assume that guests are angels and to act accordingly rather than risk treating worthy people unworthily. The Genesis story shows that Abraham reaped rich blessing through his hospitable act.

**3.** The thought switches to those in less fortunate circumstances – the imprisoned and the ill-treated. *Those who are in prison* are presumably Christians who have been persecuted for their faith. Some members of the community have been subjected to considerable pressure, as chapter 10 has already shown. But prisoners are out of sight and apt to be forgotten, hence the exhortation to *remember*. This is intended to mean more than simply to call to mind: it involves the idea of identification with them. This would require deep Christian understanding and sympathy; to sit as it were with those who are afflicted. The *ill-treated* are presumably again Christians who are suffering for the faith, although it may be meant in a wider sense. The words *since you also are in the body* are added to remind the readers that they too could be exposed to the same treatment. The words draw attention to the physical limitations to which all are subject. This is a more likely understanding of the text than to suppose that the body refers to the body of Christ.

*(ii) Exhortations affecting private life (13:4-6)*

**4.** Another practical matter of importance is *marriage*. In New Testament times even the Jews approached the matter with laxity if they followed Hillel's teaching, although the followers of Shammai were more strict. In pagan circles laxity and immorality were widespread. It was necessary for Christian teachers to give specific guidance on this theme. It has a strange relevance to our modern permissive society in which the institution of marriage is being increasingly challenged. The writer of this epistle has no compunction in stressing that marriage must be honoured. Moreover he makes no exception among Christians (*among all*). The contemporary world, then as now, has other standards. The defiling of *the marriage bed* is declared to be against Christian principles on the grounds that it is subject to God's judgment; *God will judge the immoral and adulterous*. Such sanctions carry weight only with those who acknowledge God's sovereignty over them. Nevertheless it is an integral part of the divine law that man was not made for immorality and adultery.

**5.** Yet another problem which is shared by both early and modern Christian society is the menace of materialism. *Love of money*, according to 1 Timothy 6:10, is the root of all evils. It is certainly a recurring problem which has not been avoided by many Christians especially in Western society. It is important to note that it is not money itself which is to be avoided, but love of it. The latter develops when money becomes an end in itself. Many who have discovered its snares would have saved themselves much misery had they heeded the advice given here. The further exhortation, *be content with what you have*, may be paralleled in Philippians 4:11. This is not an argument for an economic *status quo*. It refers rather to an attitude of mind. Contentment means more than passive acceptance of the inevitable. It involves a positive recognition that money is relative.

In support of this view, the writer quotes from the Old Testament: *I will never fail you nor forsake you*. The words appear to come from a mixture of sources (cf. Jos. 1:5; Dt. 31:6, 8). Moreover Philo has a similar quotation (*De Confusione Linguarum* 166). The writer's intention is to show that contentment should be based on the character of God, especially on his unfailing presence. As this promise had been a great support to the Israelites faced with the hardships which preceded their entry into the promised land, so the readers of this letter could take their stand on the same promise.

**6.** Having made an appeal to the Old Testament the writer now gives another, from Psalm 118, a famous Jewish thanksgiving psalm which was regularly used at festivals. It is taken for granted that Christians can appropriate Old Testament words as an expression of their own experience. Moreover, the words prompt us to do so *confidently* (*tharrountas*) in the belief that there is a sound basis for such application. The words are suitable because they affirm the changeless character of God as *helper* (*boēthos*). Although this is the only occasion in the New Testament where God is so described, it fits well into the character of God seen in other descriptions. There are several occasions when the corresponding verb (*boētheō*) is used, including Hebrews 2:18, where the help comes from Jesus the high priest. When God is the helper there is no surprise that the believer can say *I will not be afraid*. The children of God have many times proved the truth of the psalmist's words, *what can man do to me?*, for although expressed as a question it nevertheless implies a negative answer.

*(iii) Exhortations affecting religious life (13:7–9)*

**7.** The readers' attention is now drawn to the need to exercise respect towards *leaders* who have died, but whose memory is still fresh. It is reasonable to suppose that these former leaders were the founders of the church. It apparently required some effort for the Hebrews to respect their former leaders, for otherwise the exhortation would not have been necessary. The present tense, *Remember* (*mnēmoneuete*) is significant, for it stresses continuity, *i.e.* 'keep on remembering'. Although the writer is not urging the readers to dwell in the past, he is deeply conscious of the influence of the example of other men as chapter 11 shows. The same verb is used in 2 Timothy 2:8, where

Timothy is exhorted to remember Jesus Christ. In the present case the leaders were those who *spoke . . . the word of God* to them, and this is an expression which sums up the Christian revelation. There is value in remembering the human agencies through whom God speaks, even if the revelation itself is infinitely more important. The relative pronoun used here (*hoitines, who*) draws special attention to the fact that these leaders were the kind who spoke the message. This was their main characteristic. But another aspect also deserves consideration, *i.e. the outcome of their life*, which points to the practical effect of their manner of living or life-style. Evidently not only their words, but their behaviour was worthy of attention. The verb *consider* (*anatheōreō*) occurs only here and in Acts 17:23 in the New Testament and implies careful observation. The imitation which is urged upon the readers is no mechanical copying of the actions of others, but a call to emulate *their faith*.

**8.** It is at first surprising that a statement should be abruptly introduced at this point about the changeless character of Jesus Christ, *the same yesterday and today and for ever*. But the connection of thought may well be that since Christ is the same, the faith is equally the same. Past exponents of Christian faith may therefore serve as a pattern for succeeding generations. In introducing his statement the writer has given expression to a profound truth, which is in fact basic to the argument throughout the epistle. Only a changeless high priest could be spiritually acceptable. Moreover, it is fitting that the idea of divine changelessness which occurs at the beginning of the letter (1:12) should find a place at the end. It is here comprehensively expressed, for the phrase *and for ever* (*eis tous aiōnas*) includes the other two concepts, *yesterday* and *today*. This changelessness, in fact, embraces all aspects of time. It does not imply that God has no interest in time.

But we may enquire whether the idea of changelessness exhausts the meaning here. If *yesterday* refers to the immediate past of our high priest, the whole statement may, in fact, be referring to the sequence of his acts for men, a past sacrifice, a present intercession and a future consummation. In that case it would stress that Jesus Christ need never be replaced. Filson goes much further in his understanding of 'yesterday', taking it to refer to Christ's qualifying himself for the high-priestly office *yesterday* in order to be able to act on man's behalf *today* (30ff.). He denies any Platonic ideas here. He compares 5:8–9; 2:9; 2:17–18; 2:10; 9:11–14; 7:25 as evidence that Jesus had to become qualified.

**9.** By way of contrast to the stability of Jesus Christ are the *diverse and strange teachings* of men. There must have been a real danger that the readers would be misled by such teachings, connected, no doubt, with the general drift of their background as already mentioned in chapters 2, 6 and 10. Indeed, there are further hints of this later in the present chapter (*cf.* verse 13). Here the only indication given concerns *foods*, which suggests some kind of ritual observances. It is noticeable that even at this early stage in Christian history adverse teachings can not only be spoken of in the plural, but can be positively described as *diverse*. Their strangeness consisted in their alien character compared with the truth in Christ. Here the readers are warned not to be led away, which again suggests a deviation from an accepted standard.

A reason is given: dependence on God rests on *grace*, not on foods. There can be no doubt that the grace intended is the grace of God (*cf.* 2:9; 4:16), which sums up God's gracious dealings with man. This grace is contrasted with foods as a means of strengthening the persons concerned. It is not clear what is in mind, but the writer seems to imply that some were supposing that all that was needed was dependence on physical rather than spiritual sustenance. The word for *adherents* (*hoi peripatountes*, literally those that walk) of the food cult suggests that these people were regarding these foods as part of their way of life. It is an unusual idea, to connect walking with foods, but may be contrasted with the idea of walking in good works (Eph. 2:10), or of walking 'in newness of life' (Rom. 6:4). Such wrong walking is here described as unprofitable (*foods . . . have not benefited*), presumably because the spiritual side of man's nature has been neglected.

*(iv) About the Christian's new altar (13:10–16)*

**10.** The idea of the feasting of the deviators leads the writer to an affirmation of the Christians' unique privilege in having their own *altar*.[1] It seems certain that the background to the idea is the Christian passover. As in the Jewish festival the participants shared in the food of sacrifice at the passover feast, so Christians have an exclusive feast of their own. The *altar* seems to be used as a general term for the benefits of the whole system. According to Bruce, *altar* is here used by metonymy for 'sacrifice' and refers to the sacrifice of Christ, the benefits of which are eternally accessible.[2] The writer recognizes that Jews who have become Christians have forfeited the right to continue at the Jewish altar, but he assures them that Christians have an altar, at which Jews who are not Christians have no right to eat. There is no justification for seeing here a reference to a sacrificial interpretation of the Christian communion service. For Christians there is no longer any need for an altar of sacrifice. The Christian altar is to be understood generally of the full benefits which come to those who serve Christ. On the contrary Jews who are not Christians are picturesquely described as *those who serve the tent* (*skēnē*), a remarkable contrast to those who serve Christ. The material and spiritual aspects of the two approaches are vividly brought out. The food from the Jewish altar is material food, but from the Christian altar it is Christ himself, a difference which has clearly deeply impressed the writer. The question of *right* (*exousia*) is inextricably bound up with the exposition of faith earlier in the epistle. Faith brings a right through God's grace to which unbelief has no access.

**11.** The thought is further pursued by illustration from the Jewish sacrificial system. The central idea is of the presentation of the *blood* to God and the destruction of the bodies of the victims outside the camp, a procedure followed on the Day of Atonement. The body played no part in the offering for sin. The offering is made *by* (*dia*) *the high priest*, which recalls the noblest and most awe-inspiring action of the old order. The writer is setting this out in order to contrast the superior gain that Jewish Christians have received. The burning *outside the camp* is seen as significant, for the phrase is repeated in a Christian symbolic sense in verse 13.

---

[1] *But cf.* W. H. Spencer, 'Hebrews 13:10', *ExT* 50 (1938–39), p. 284, for the view that the 'we' here are Hebrews, not Christians.

[2] *Cf.* Bruce, *Comm.*, pp. 399ff.

**12.** The writer draws a parallel with *Jesus*, although it is by no means an exact parallel. The bodies outside the camp cannot be exactly equated with the fact that *Jesus suffered outside the gate* of Jerusalem. Some mental adjustment is needed. The comparison is clearly not intended to be precise. The major point is that both the shedding of blood and the suffering of the body form a part of the Christian understanding of Jesus' work on the cross. Instead of being inferior, the sacrifice of Jesus was superior because it took place *outside*. This *outside* character of Christianity clearly holds great importance for the writer. It must be understood in the light of verse 13, which shows that Judaism is in mind. The readers need to be assured once again that Christ's purpose was to *sanctify* (*hagiazō*) his people, an idea which has more than once been emphasized in the course of the epistle. It involved a process of separation on the part of Jesus, and it is on this basis that the readers are also exhorted to go outside the camp.

**13.** This verse may be regarded as the crux of the conclusion, a final direct appeal to the readers to identify themselves wholly with Christ. The word *therefore* (*toinyn*) draws attention to the fact that the appeal naturally follows the preceding line of argument (*cf.* a similar use in Lk. 20:25). The decisive character of this appeal is evident in the verb *let us go forth* (*exerchōmetha*), an act which involves a definite break, which is reinforced by the words *outside the camp*. Such an act involves separation from the existing society of Judaism, but this has already been endured by Jesus himself. It was part of the offence of the cross that it brought with it a rejection from official Judaism. It was a stumbling-block to the Jews. And yet these Jewish readers are being invited to leave their Jewish faith and identify with Jesus. Since he is *outside*, his followers must follow him there. But if they do, they cannot expect any better treatment. They too must be prepared to *bear abuse* for him, or more literally 'his abuse', the same kind of abuse which he suffered. It may well be that it was the certainty of meeting abuse which was deterring some of the readers from making a clean break. It is understandable. No-one welcomes abuse, and yet the writer has been at pains to prove throughout his epistle how abundantly worth while it is. The figurative use of *camp* for official Judaism is suggestive, for in the wilderness wanderings the perimeter of the camp was clearly defined. Men were either inside or outside. This is the kind of clear-cut challenge that the writer longs for his readers to face up to.

**14.** The *city* theme has been given considerable prominence in the thought of chapters 11 and 12 (*cf.* 11:10, 16; 12:22). Here the spiritual character of the community is again stressed. The lasting character of our city lies in the future, not in the present circumstances. However permanent man-made cities appear to be, the world is littered with remains of once powerfully impressive communities. Spiritual aspirations are directed towards a different concept of city, of which the heavenly Jerusalem is the perfect prototype. If at first it seems incongruous to find such a city outside the camp, it must be remembered that the writer is using the term *city* to show that withdrawal from the camp is no isolated occurrence affecting a few individuals. It is a corporate concept, for Christianity involves a new spiritual society. The city metaphor suggests that togetherness is an essential ideal of the Christian faith, which will nevertheless be fully realized only in the future: *we seek the city which is to come.*

**15.** The epistle does not close without another use of priestly imagery. Having expounded in great detail the priestly office of Christ, the writer here employs the same imagery to describe the function of believers. There is a fundamental distinction in the type of sacrifices offered, for whereas Christ offered himself, the believer is to offer *a sacrifice of praise to God.* This idea of thanksgiving is frequent in the New Testament and may in fact be regarded as the norm for Christians. Especially characteristic is the idea that such a sacrifice should be offered *continually* (*dia pantos*), in striking contrast to the once-for-all character of the sacrifice of Christ. It was clearly not considered incongruous to suggest that praise should be a constant factor in Christian living. It should be noted that the praise-sacrifice must be offered *through him* (*i.e.* Christ), through whom it is acceptable to God.

A further description is given of the nature of the sacrifice in the additional words, *the fruit of lips that acknowledge his name.* This wording owes its form to Hosea 14:3 (LXX). The idea is suggestive. What proceeds from the lips is regarded as *fruit,* which reveals the character of its source, as the fruit of a tree reveals the nature of the tree. Lips accustomed to acknowledge God will be constantly singing his praises. The same concept of confessing the name is found in Romans 10:9; Philippians 2:9ff.; Romans 14:11 (from Is. 45:23). It amounts to an open declaration of allegiance to God.

**16.** A more practical view of sacrifices is next introduced, in the nature of almsgiving. This chapter has already contained advice on social responsibility (verses 1–3), but here the requirements are more specific: *to do good and to share what you have*. No indication is given to whom such almsgiving is to be directed. Its general terms suggest that non-Christians may be included, but the idea of sharing (*koinōnia*) would be more meaningful when applied to the Christian fellowship, in view of the experience of the early Christians in Acts 4:32f. The word used for doing *good* (*eupoiïa*) occurs only here in the New Testament and is the more general idea, of which the sharing of material things is a particular expression. The exhortation *do not neglect* (*mē epilanthanesthe*) occurs also in verse 2 in connection with hospitality. In both cases it suggests that some effort is needed if the readers are to avoid neglecting their social responsibility.

*Such sacrifices*, which are declared to be *pleasing to God*, must include the sacrifice of praise in verse 15 as well as the social works of this verse. It reminds us that praise has a practical side to it. Whatever is pleasing to God is the norm for the Christian believer. Paul makes a similar point in Romans 12:1–2.

*(v) Final words (13:17–25)*

**17.** Almost as an isolated injunction, the writer introduces here the need for a responsible attitude towards *leaders*. This is the first suggestion in the epistle of any church order and even here no hint is given of what offices were held. The writer is concerned only about attitudes and mentions two which are complementary to each other – *obey* (*peithesthe*) and *submit* (*hypeikete*), the latter word occurring only here in the New Testament. The function of the leaders is described in general terms as *keeping watch over your souls*. The same verb is used in Ephesians 6:18 in an injunction to keep alert in prayer. The task of the overseers is to maintain constant watch over those committed to their care. This is reminiscent of Paul's care of all the churches (2 Cor. 11:28) and of Peter's injunction to the elders to tend God's flock (1 Pet. 5:2), which is itself reminiscent of the words of Jesus to Peter (Jn. 21:15ff.). It is noticeable that the writer here uses the word for *souls* (*psychai*) to describe people, for this is more vivid than saying 'you'. The office of leader is recognized as one of responsibility, for those who hold such office will be expected *to give account* of their work. It is important to note that those who exercise authority must also accept responsibility for their actions.

Leaders are enjoined to perform their tasks *joyfully*, which would exclude an overbearing approach. This is expressed negatively as *not sadly*, or more literally 'not with groaning' (*mē stenazontes*), a word used by Paul in 2 Corinthians 5:2 of the Christian's groaning which accompanies the desire to put on his heavenly dwelling. The idea of leadership with groaning is clearly not one to be encouraged. The writer simply says it *would be of no advantage to you*, using yet another word (*alysiteles*) which occurs nowhere else in the New Testament. There is an occurrence in the papyri where it is used of inferior crops as compared with wheat (MM). There is no more striking example of the joyful, and therefore advantageous, leadership than Paul (*cf.* his Philippian letter).

**18.** This epistle is not alone in exhorting the readers to pray for the writer and his associates (*pray for us*). Paul more than once gives similar advice. The early Christians were convinced of the importance of prayer. The basis for this request for prayer support is said to be a *clear* (*kalēn*, literally good) *conscience*. It is as if the writer felt obliged to assure his readers of the integrity of his unnamed associates. Moreover, they desired in everything *to act honourably* (*kalōs anastrephesthai*), an expression which involves the use of the cognate adverb from the adjective describing the conscience. In other words, conscience and behaviour must both be of the same fine quality. It is further to be noted that such honourable activity must stretch to *all things*. There is in fact no place for dishonourable action in the Christian life.

**19.** It is noticeable that the singular (*I urge you*) replaces the plural here, which gives a personal force to the exhortation, and is then further strengthened by a strong adverb (*perissoter-ōs, more earnestly*). This seems to show the great importance placed on prayer by the writer personally. It is implied that some circumstances are preventing a reunion between him and his readers, but there is no indication what these were. What concerns him is the certainty that events might be affected by the prayers of the readers. The author's wish to be *restored* to them shows that he must have been known to them personally.

**20–21.** This is a particularly full and expressive benediction, which packs into it much theology which repays careful attention. First God is described as *the God of peace, i.e.* one who not only himself exemplifies peace, but who promotes peace among his people. In the times of tension in which the Hebrew Christians lived, the assurance of this characteristic of God would be an encouraging factor. The apostle Paul not infrequently uses the same title for God (*cf.* Rom. 15:33; 16:20; 2 Cor. 13:11). Equally certainly our modern world needs to learn this particular aspect of God, which contrasts so vividly with the prevailing lack of peace among nations and groups within society.

It may seem strange that the writer leaves until the benediction any direct reference to the resurrection (*who brought again from the dead our Lord Jesus*), but there can be no doubt that his whole discussion assumes it. Since he reflects on the exaltation and present intercessory work of Christ, he moves one step ahead of the resurrection. But in this benediction he wants to remind the readers especially of the powerful activity of God, seen supremely in the resurrection of Christ.

Another familiar theme is the description of our Lord Jesus as *the great shepherd of the sheep*. It might have been expected that this writer would have preferred the high priest description, especially in view of the mention of *the blood of the covenant*, but his choice of the shepherd imagery contributes to the richness of his view of Jesus. There is a particular tenderness in the shepherd metaphor which has never failed to appeal strongly to people of all ages. Yet the covenant statement sums up the main gist of the epistle. This is the one occasion in this epistle where the covenant is described as *eternal*. There is no possibility of its becoming obsolete and another being needed.

The prayer is that God would *equip* (*katartisai*) the readers.

The word used means literally 'to make fit (*artios*), complete'. God alone can bring out the full potential of any believer. The words *with everything good* (*en panti agathō*) seem to refer to the instrument used for the process of bringing to completion. It could however be understood to denote sphere, in which case the process is promoted by surrounding the believer with things that are good which will be most conducive to his development. The complementary ideas *that you may do his will* and that of God *working in you that which is pleasing to his sight* show a combination of human and divine action. As Westcott here says, 'The work of God makes man's work possible'.[1] There is a similar thought in Philippians 2:12–13. The whole process of doing God's will can be achieved only *through Jesus Christ*, which completely removes any grounds for satisfaction in merely human achievement.

This extended prayer appropriately ends with a doxology. It is not absolutely clear here whether glory is ascribed to God, the main subject of the sentence, or to Christ, the immediate antecedent. A similar doxology to God the Father is found in Philippians 4:20, including the full expression *for ever and ever* (*eis tous aiōnas tōn aiōnōn*).

**22.** This closing section, which is in the form of a postscript, has been thought by some scholars to be a work of the apostle Paul which has erroneously been attached to an anonymous letter. But the theory has little to commend it. There is no indication in this section that Paul was the author. Since the only personal reference is to Timothy, the writer was clearly known to him, but any one of those who had associated with Timothy would prove a suitable candidate. The writer describes his letter as *my word of exhortation* (*tou logou tēs paraklēseōs*). Encouragement has not been a major feature, but there has been much to give confidence to those willing to stake all on faith in Christ. A similar expression is used in Acts 13:15 where it seems to mean 'homily', and that is possibly the meaning here. Certainly the treatise as a whole could well have been prepared as a homily. Filson in his discussion of this expression concludes that it is a word which throbs with encouragement,

[1] Westcott, *Comm.*, p. 449.

stern warning and earnest appeal.[1] In adding the expression *briefly* (*dia bracheōn*) the author's thought may be that the exposition given is brief compared with what he had in his mind to say (*cf.* 5:11 and 9:5b). Moreover, it has been suggested that as a homily it would have taken less than an hour to deliver, although such a sermon could hardly be called brief. Perhaps the word of exhortation refers only to what the writer says in Hebrews 13, in which case his expression would be entirely appropriate.[2]

**23.** *Timothy* has evidently been in prison, although no other information exists regarding the circumstances. It was not a detail which held much interest for the writer. Evidently the readers knew about it. The writer's only concern here is to mention his prospective visit with Timothy in the near future. Clearly he is himself not entirely sure of Timothy's movements, as the words *if he comes soon* show. This is one of those tantalizing passing allusions about which we should like to know more. Timothy is in fact the only Christian mentioned by name in the whole epistle.

**24.** The concluding greetings are the most letter-like feature of this epistle. But even these create problems, because there is ambiguity about the Italians. The very general reference to *all your leaders* ties in with verse 17. *All the saints* is equally comprehensive.

It is noticeable that here the writer addresses the group as a whole, as he does throughout the epistle, even sending greetings to the leaders through the whole body of believers. There is no trace here of any hierarchical system. The repetition of 'all' reflects the house-church situation where not all Christians would be present in any one place at any one time.[3]

*Those who come from Italy* (*hoi apo tēs Italias*) could be understood of those domiciled in Italy or of Italians who were residing elsewhere. The decision on this ambiguity will depend on what decision is made about the place of writing. The writer may be in some part of Italy writing to Rome, or he may be somewhere else and includes greetings from Italians abroad. But it makes

---

[1] *Cf.* Filson, 'Yesterday', pp. 27ff.
[2] *Cf.* L. P. Trudiger's note on this expression, *JTS* 23 (1972), pp. 128–130.
[3] *Cf.* Filson, *op. cit.*, p. 76.

little difference to an understanding of this epistle, whichever it is.

**25.** It was a general principle in Christian greetings to conclude with a prayer that God's grace should be with the readers. In most of Paul's letters grace is linked with other qualities and is specifically attributed to the Lord Jesus (but *cf*. Tit. 3:15, which has the same form as here). Whereas others than Christians could use the common greeting (*chairein*), only Christians could appreciate the deeper significance of God's grace (*charis*).